THE SUNDAY TIMES
TRAVEL BOOK

THE SUNDAY TIMES
TRAVEL BOOK

Edited by
RICHARD GIRLING
Foreword by
PAUL THEROUX

A GRAHAM TARRANT BOOK

DAVID & CHARLES
Newton Abbot   London   North Pomfret (Vt)

The Sunday Times and the Publishers would like to
thank the authors for their kind permission to
reproduce their photographs and other picture material.

British Library Cataloguing in Publication Data
The Sunday times travel book.
1. Voyages and travels
I. Girling, Richard—1951–
910.4   G465

ISBN 0-7153-8769-3

Typeset by ABM Typographics Limited, Hull
and printed in Great Britain
by Butler & Tanner Limited, Frome and London
for David & Charles (Publishers) Limited
Brunel House   Newton Abbot   Devon

Published in the United States of America
by David & Charles Inc
North Pomfret   Vermont 05053   USA

CONTENTS

EDITOR'S NOTE

All books involve a lot of people, but this one involved more than most. The fifty travel pieces collected here are a selection from an original entry in *The Sunday Times* Travel-Writing Competition of nearly 3,000. To each of these writers our thanks are due, and to some of these we owe commiserations too. Many excellent pieces of work had to be excluded from the book simply to avoid problems of duplication (we could have filled the space with entries on China, India and the Americas alone), and making the selection was made all the harder by the need to leave out several that I had come to regard as favourites. Others were luckier, for the book did enable me to turn a blind eye to the indiscretions of one or two entrants whose work had been disqualified from the competition proper because of a somewhat over-relaxed attitude to the rules. The most persuasive of these was the missionary and teacher Leila Stevenson, whose account of her visit to the Dalai Lama has waited more than twenty years to find a publisher (the competition was for journeys taken in 1984).

Particular thanks are due to the competition's co-sponsors, Speedbird Holidays; to the judges, Paul Theroux, Beryl Bainbridge and Robin Hanbury-Tenison; and to Felecia Joseph of *The Sunday Times,* who shifted several times her own weight in paperwork.

The three principal prizewinners were Caroline Dilke, for *A Visit to Dominica*; Richard Ward, for *Mani*; and Peter Mayle, for *Two Hundred Metres of Burgundy*.

Richard Girling
The Sunday Times, London

FOREWORD

A travel writer is almost invariably a person who works for a newspaper, and the rest of us are travellers who write. My immediate reaction to the pieces that are included in this collection is one of surprise at the tremendous variety of the journeys. But 'journeys' is not really the word. A bit of this is travel in the old reckless and dangerous sense, but some of it might be described as vacationing; there are outings, package tours, school trips, sojourns and overseas jobs. Some are the result of an afternoon in a place, others seem to be the concentrated accounts of years. What they have in common is that they are all personal, memorable and they take place abroad.

I think another common factor is that the trips were not contemplated with the idea of being written about. The trip was the thing – the writing came later, when *The Sunday Times* announced its Travel-Writing Competition. And only then – I feel sure – did these travellers commit themselves to paper. That is a crucial matter because it means that rather than travelling in search of a character or a subject, or pursuing a destination on behalf of a newspaper or a public relations company, these people were travelling for their own reasons – for the experience, for the fun of it, for a job or an idea, or because they had some spare time. As a result, while each includes a certain amount of practical detail about accommodation and costs and itineraries (this is a sop to the travel industry which is largely interested in selling vacations), the best of these pieces contain extraordinary details, highly personal disclosures and telling facts.

A character in Vladimir Nabokov's novel *Laughter in the Dark* says at one point, 'A writer for instance talks about India which I have never seen, and gushes about dancing girls, tiger hunts, fakirs, betel nuts, serpents: the Glamour of the mysterious East. But what does it amount to? Nothing. Instead of visualizing India I merely get a bad toothache from all these Eastern delights. Now, there's the other way as, for instance, the fellow who writes: "Before turning in I put out my wet boots to dry and in the morning I found that a thick blue forest had grown on them ('Fungi, Madam,' he explained) . . ." and at once India becomes alive for me. The rest is shop.'

Most of these pieces contain that sort of detail, and even a somewhat conventional schoolmistressy piece about a school trip to Paris, one that includes the Eiffel Tower and the Louvre, also contains mentions of voyeurism, riotous behaviour and the incursion of 'inebriated black basketball players' exhibiting themselves to schoolgirls. 'An otherwise perfect evening was marred,' writes Miss Brodie.

That is a piece about nuisances; in other pieces the risks are much worse, and in some they are a matter of life and death. Quite a lot of ground is covered here. British travel was not allowed, but nearly everywhere else is represented, from China to Peru, from the Amazon to the Costa Brava.

In many cases these are seasoned travellers and, indeed, people who travel so well that they take important aspects of the travel experience for granted. They don't remark on how they got from one place to another, they minimise their discomfort, they give the benefit of the doubt to the infuriating foreigner. But the very stuff of travel writing is the personal and particular, the nightmarish bus ride, the unconscionable wait, the totally unexpected detail. We are far more likely to read about fungus on the boots in a piece by an amateur traveller who writes than by a professional travel writer.

Travel is not everything we think it is. A trip up the Amazon is regarded by many as a vacation – there is a Holiday Inn in Manaus, and there are luxury resorts in places as wild-seeming as Kenya and Borneo. People take the most brainless holidays in desperately hungry Third World countries. We are invited to indulge ourselves and take pleasure trips to places like Bangladesh, the poorest country in the world; and it is a fact that many impoverished countries are famous for their lovely beaches.

So it is possible that travel in its old original uncomfortable sense is just as likely to be the experience of package-tour Spain than India or Africa. Good as they are, I wish the package-tour pieces in this collection were better. I have not yet read a travel piece that gets to the heart of this. Writing about a package tour to Spain, and getting inside the experience and explaining it, is a greater challenge than an account of an assault on Mount Kanchenjunga. It is a challenge that I hope will be met, because there will be another *Sunday Times* Travel-Writing Competition.

Paul Theroux

PETER MAYLE

Two Hundred Metres of Burgundy

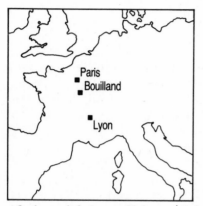

'Of course,' said the old man, 'since the telephone and mains sewage, one is as modern here as in Paris.'

He placed the last evil half inch of his yellow-papered cigarette carefully into the corner of his mouth. His hand, a freckled ham, was missing the top two joints from the index finger. A pruning accident. That and his nose, seasoned to a delicate pinky-purple by two litres of wine a day for sixty years, testified to a lifetime of labour in the vineyards.

He stood wheezing contentedly in the flat evening sun. In his brown canvas boots, faded blue trousers, checked shirt and frayed cap, one might have mistaken him for a man of no consequence instead of a senior member of local government. He was our self-appointed guide to Bouilland, population 136, sixteen kilometres from Beaune.

Our journey was to take us from one end of the village to the Bar-Tabac at the other end, a trip of some 200 metres down the straight street that led to the plump, vine-studded hills in the distance.

We started at the World War I Memorial, clearly the object of great respect and attention. The grass was clipped, and banks of flowers grew round the base, hiding some of the names cut into the stone slab. There were many names for such a small village, and the old man remembered most of them from his childhood. Fallen for the glory of France. It's a bad business, war. He shrugged and moved on.

We walked between two ancient plane trees which generations of hard pruning had reduced to bunches of arthritic grey knuckles, and arrived at Bouilland's 200-year-old launderette. It was the size of a double garage, open on one side, built of stone and roofed with tiles. In an English village it would have been converted into something quaint, selling teas and postcards. Here it was neglected.

The stone table once used by the village women to pummel their washing had patches of moss growing on it. The water trough was empty except for a layer of scum, a beer bottle and some sweet wrappers. A peeling notice warned us not to throw ordure. The old man flicked his cigarette end into the trough as we asked him when the laundry had stopped being used.

'The year electricity came,' he said, 'Madame Rivarel got a washing machine. Now the village has ten, maybe twenty machines.' He pulled the lobe of his ear reflectively. 'One must profit from progress.'

He seemed pleased to remind us of yet more evidence of Bouilland's humming modernity, and took us out into the sun again. At a slow but purposeful lurch, he led the way towards the Bar-Tabac.

The street was wide for an old village, and the houses were solid. The architecture was all of a piece; nothing recent, nothing flimsy. Wooden shutters of washed-out blue and green were folded back against the walls to show thick, beautifully patterned lace at the windows. Almost all the front doors were open, but it was impossible to see inside. Each door had its curtain – not the traditional strings of wooden beads, but bright strips of plastic or curious brown furry segments, like end-to-end caterpillars writhing in the breeze. Geraniums sat on the window ledges and oleanders grew from old Elf oil drums outside the doors.

And inside, unseen but definitely there, were the inhabitants. We felt them looking at us from behind the lace and from the shadowy hallways, peering through their caterpillar curtains at these strangers with clean shoes and light, impractical clothes. Tourists.

In a gap between two houses, an old wine barrel rested on its side doing duty as a kennel. A large mud-coloured dog was in residence, front paws crossed, the remains of a stale *baguette* within gnawing distance. He opened an owlish eye and barked unconvincingly at us before yawning and going back to sleep. We wondered if French dogs are taught in puppyhood how to cross their paws. It's not something English dogs do.

The approach to the bar's terrace was guarded by two old women taking the sun on a wooden bench. Black cotton dresses, ankle-height zippered carpet slippers, stockings like brown bandages, not quite thick enough to conceal the knots of varicose veins. We smiled and nodded. They nodded and smiled, exposing a total of not more than seven teeth between them.

'Sisters,' said the old man. 'They both lost their husbands in the war. Now they're losing their teeth. They can only eat soup.'

The bar was dim and neat, with a zinc counter and a fine rich smell of coffee and black tobacco. Taped to the mirror behind the bottles was a poster of the Lapierre of Dijon cycling team squinting into the sun, arms crossed, immense thighs bulging from long black shorts. Across the upper half of the poster, someone had scrawled, *'Un verre, c'est con. Trois verres, c'est bon'*, and drawn a crude wine glass balancing on the top of the team manager's head. Wine is more profitable than bicycles in this part of France.

At a corner table, three men and an ample woman in an apron played cards noisily, the slap of the cards punctuated by bursts of virtuoso coughing, that cavernous café cough which echoes up from the boots. The hand finished, Madame negotiated her bulk through the tables, wiping her hands on her apron. We ordered white wine. Did we want Aligoté or Chardonnay? Aligoté? *Bon.* The glasses were generous, so full that the surface of the wine trembled just above the rim. The old man dipped his nose and took a first careful sip. We followed him outside and sat at the tin table under the tree.

We were just in time to watch the evening rush hour. Led by a small boy in shorts and singlet and over-large wellingtons, a herd of cows was coming in from the fields. Buxom cows, creamy-white and clean, with proper horns that had somehow escaped the French passion for pruning. Twenty or thirty of them swayed past in dignified convoy, followed by the farmer and a matted dog of uncertain ancestry. He exchanged insults with the dog in the wine barrel and got a kick in the ribs from his master. The procession disappeared up the street as the old man sucked his glass dry and sighed hopefully.

Another? Well, since he's not pressed for time, perhaps one more. With the new round of drinks, he insisted that I try one of his yellow cigarettes. It was like smoking a bonfire rolled up in lavatory paper.

From the far end of the street came an irregular clanking sound, and a small, thin man in blue overalls appeared, carrying a handbell and a clipboard. He stopped outside the bar and rang his bell vigorously before reading the six o'clock news from his board.

'The Electricity of France wishes to announce a power stoppage due to work on the main transformer. There will be no electricity from seven until noon on the morning of Thursday, the 14th of June. Members of the commune are advised to arrange themselves accordingly.'

'*Merde!*' A deep voice from behind us. It was Madame in the doorway, loudly disputing the accuracy of the information and the need for a power cut.

The man with the bell glared at her. They were obviously familiar enemies. 'Thursday, the 14th of June. Seven till noon. *Pas de jus.*'

He flourished his bell and started back up the street before she had a chance to reply. Madame snorted and returned to her cards. The old man cackled.

'He is like the weather forecast, that one. Never correct. The noise of the bell makes an omelette of his brains. It is also my opinion that he cannot read. Not a man to rely on.'

The next day, Wednesday June 13, dawned clear and sunny, with the promise of more heat. There was, however, no electricity.

DAVID BRIERLEY

Questions in El Salvador

Where's the damn army? Why aren't they guarding the airport? At Belize, a twenty-minute hop away, there are camouflage nets and sandbags and RAF Hawks and squaddies with pink British faces. At El Salvador International Airport, not a single soldier, in a country torn by civil war.

Maybe the army aren't at the airport. They're everywhere else. So is the Guardia Nacional. Also the police. They all carry automatic weapons. The police patrol the capital in black and white gas-guzzlers, rifles poking out of every window. The army ride round in jeeps, rifles in the crooks of their arms. The Guardia Nacional wear jackboots and hook their fingers in their trigger guards.

Two blocks from the hotel is a McDonald's. It was blown up last year. Now it has two security guards. They carry rifles and check every car coming into the parking lot. This must be the end of civilisation as Americans know it.

Civil war has been eating up the country for five years. The army and the guerillas are not the greatest sufferers. Forty-five thousand (or is it fifty-five thousand – it's difficult keeping a body-count) ordinary citizens have been killed. The guerrillas shot some; most were murdered by the *escuadrones de la muerte*. These are the army and the police out of uniform. A night on the town for the boys.

The army is directing traffic at a crossroads. It's a job-creation scheme. One holds up the east-west streets. Another waves on the north-south streets. On each corner stands a pair of soldiers, rifles aimed at the lines of cars. You've never seen such careful drivers.

The National Museum has an exhibit that makes my eyes blink. A statue shows a priest dressed in the skin of a prisoner who has been flayed alive. Such sacrifices were common in these parts. Still are, when you consider the fifty-five thousand.

The victim has been scalped and the priest wears the hair. The skin is flecked with bits of flesh. It is in two pieces, like a pair of pyjamas.

It helps the crops grow, a museum guide explains to three teenage girls. They nod. Their faces show nothing. They express no horror. If I could understand why they accept such cruelty, I could understand why there is so much violence here.

The National University was closed four years ago by the army. Too many subversives, they said. The gates are barred, the grass grows long, the paint peels. It is completely deserted. Then, passing the Dental Faculty, you notice the rifles pointing at you.

I take the bus to Santa Ana, the second city of El Salvador. Its welcome sign says it has 90,000 inhabitants. It feels smaller.

The main square holds the three buildings of importance. One is the town hall, elegant with colonnades. Then there is the theatre, built in Jungle Opulent, with pillars and balconies and statues lifting off on wings. On the third side is the cathedral, which has its inspiration in Prague. It doesn't seem out of place because of the whiteness of the stonework, so brilliant in the sun it could be spun sugar. This is a facade. At the sides the cathedral is built of red brick and looks like the headquarters of some great insurance company before computers replaced clerks. Right and proper, I decide, for spiritual insurance is an urgent need here.

I'm called back by a member of the Guardia Nacional. They're the ones in jackboots. 'Where are you going?' To the square. 'Not to that building?' I realise I have been crossing the street towards an open door. A sign says it is the Governor's office. No, I insist, and bring out my passport. 'You're English?' Yes. He flips over the pages: US visa, Turkish stamps, Czechoslovak visa. He lingers over that and I wait for him to ask why I was visiting a Communist state. But he grins at me. I grin back. My cheeks ache with the grin. Okay, I can go. 'Hey,' he calls and I turn back. His hand is out to shake.

Another day, another bus. It skirts a smouldering rubbish tip outside Santa Ana. A man and a woman pick through the filth while cattle forage. The bus passes nameless villages. Posters hold the shacks together: *Coca-Cola es asi, Doberman Jeans – New York, Paris, London, San Salvador.*

The bus halts. It is an army roadblock and everyone gets out. The men stand with arms raised while soldiers search for weapons. A young conscript feels my back, my crotch, my legs. Nobody speaks. My passport causes excitement and a soldier thumbs through the pages. When he reaches the photo, he realises he's been holding it upside down. If they cannot read, why check papers? It's a ritual, showing who has power.

He goes off to report to the sergeant. We stand like cattle in the sun for a quarter of an hour while the sergeant clears me on his radio. Finally we climb back and the bus continues. Nobody comments on this check. Happens all the time. And so pointless: the soldiers never searched the luggage.

The land is dry and poor. The hills are tiny. They look violent, as if just made. Crows circle, looking for carrion.

Metapan is squalid beyond imagining. A two-storey building would be a skyscraper. The town centre is a huge jumble sale: combs, mirrors, ballpens, lipsticks, exercise books, clothespegs, Chiclets, knickers, buttons, baseball caps, sweetcorn, dried fish, the Encyclopedia of Sex (in eight Roneo-ed pages), belts, scissors, batteries, plates, machetes, crucifixes, razor blades, padlocks, strips of mango in plastic bags, everything well-fingered.

'Senor.' I turn back. There are three of them, Guardia Nacional. 'Your papers.' They inspect my passport and I do not find favour in their eyes. 'Why are you here?' To see the church and have a meal. 'Where are you from?' England. 'Where is your car?' I came by bus.

Behind them in a doorway is a man wearing plain clothes and dark glasses. Anger runs in furrows across his forehead. 'Why Metapan? Where are your companions?' I am alone. He wants very much to take me inside for further 'questioning'. It shows in his face. Reluctantly I am let go.

That pain in the back of my neck is four pairs of eyes watching every step I take to the church.

I have an introduction to L, an army conscript. He picks me up in his mother's car and we drive through Colonia Escalon to a roundabout where cars park beside snack stalls.

How long have you been in the army? 'Two years.' How much longer must you serve? He shrugs. 'Until this is finished.' Or until he is finished. He pushes back his sleeve to show scars where I have vaccination marks. A bomb blew up near his truck. Shrapnel wounds never look healed. The skin is purple and puckered.

How is the war going? 'It is getting worse.' The guerrillas are highly motivated. The conscripts have little stomach for a fight. If they surrender they expect to be stripped of uniforms and weapons and sent back naked. An officer would be tortured for information. Corruption is widespread. Wherever American aid goes, dollars stick. An officer becomes a colonel, moves into a mansion, buys a bulletproof Mercedes. He never goes on patrol. Instead he visits army corps with a photographer.

L drops me near my hotel. Perhaps he should have dropped me further away.

A man comes on to the terrace while I'm eating breakfast. When I finish, he walks over and sits down. 'Are you American?' British. 'I could have sworn you were American. What are you doing here?' Looking and listening. I ask what he does. 'I'm a businessman from Indiana.' Here on business? 'On vacation.' You must be the first tourist in years. 'Right.' Been here long? 'A couple of days.'

His tone is friendly but the questions are direct: where I've been, who I've talked to, what I'm doing that day. He calls for our bills in Spanish. I sign mine. He pays cash. When he leaves he doesn't deposit a key at reception. And his face is very tanned for a man two days away from an Indiana winter.

The coast is a different world, humid and lethargic. There's a shanty town built of flattened oil barrels and packing cases. People camp inside their shacks: a hammock, a bed made of driftwood, a Madonna, a machete, a doll, a dangling lightbulb. Outside children play among fermenting puddles. Why don't they run on the beach? Afraid of its freedom?

The beach stretches to the horizon. Coconut palms, bananas and papayas shade the edge. The sand is soft, the colour of old pewter. The beach is all mine but I cannot stay long for I lack a senorita to oil my back.

I walk into the village and choose a restaurant. A *mariachi* band approaches and launches into a lively lament on what it is to be alone and without love. I order a second beer. We are very macho about it here, drinking straight from the bottle. Pacific breakers curl in, the sun blazes, the prawns are amazing.

I leave and there he is, the man from breakfast, walking along the back of the row of restaurants. He carries no bag, such as might hold a towel and swimsuit.

'Hi,' he says, 'I see you made it.'

That night I ask the opinion of an American reporter. 'Paid cash for his breakfast?' Yes. 'Didn't leave a key?' No. 'Followed you down to La Libertad?' Yes. 'When are you leaving?' In the morning, I say, and order more drinks, doubles.

The taxi goes down Paseo Escalon. We pass the statue of Jesus standing on top of the globe. El Salvador del Mundo, the Salvadorans call it. Christ on the ball, the Americans say. We turn right and left and I check the route, just in case.

'American?' the driver asks. No, English. 'What is your profession?'

Questions, always these damn questions.

DENNIS McDONNELL

HEAD TRANSPLANT AND THE HANGING TREE

On a bend of the Colorado river we made camp for a month.

Well, to be strictly truthful, camp had already been made for us by some hi-tech realtors. And the mighty Red River, having been dammed six times for hydro-power, was actually the motionless mud-coloured Town Lake in the middle of Austin, the State Capital of Texas.

The University of Texas at Austin is very rich – it had the good sense to find oil on its own land. Some of the money has been spent on a great collection of literary manuscripts. We had come to study some of them.

It's hard to be humble if you're from Texas
– car sticker

Not all Texans are true Texans
. . . send $18.95 for your Authentic Texan Heritage
certificate (suitable for framing)
– ad for The Association of Certified Texans

To describe the 150 miles from Houston airport to Austin as un-dramatic would be to over-dramatise unforgivably. For the first sixty miles, State Highway 290 offered hardly a bend, hardly a hill: just dry pastures and an almost empty road. Once clear of Houston there weren't even many billboards, apart from those offering acreages for sale – some as 'farmettes', others as 'ranchettes'.

Every now and then a straggling two-dimensional township, with its sign: BLOGGSVILLE CITY LIMIT. Pop 912. Groggy with heat, Jackie wondered feebly if they changed the sign with every birth and death.

LITTERING IS unlAWFUL
– highway sign

Our rental car was called a Ford Escort, but you could have fooled me; somebody had smoothed off all the corners. Still, it went, and the air-conditioning worked.

After a long flight your perceptions are dulled, and everything is synthetic. But on Highway 290 unreality ruled. In the unchanging landscape we drove but we didn't get anywhere. In the October heat haze we sat in stately convoy among huge 5-litre cars – all floating like ships becalmed at a docile 54mph. I will never understand how a country that savagely defends the right of every citizen to carry a gun (and that won't enforce seat-belt laws because they interfere with the rights of the individual) meekly accepts the 55mph speed limit.

CHILD RAISED AS CAT
– newspaper headline

Austin is a good deal smaller than Edinburgh, but has about as much motorway as the UK. We rolled recklessly down concrete channels, bombarded now by meaningless names and unfamiliar imperatives: E. NACOGDOCHES; R LANE MUST EXIT R.

'Look – Hyde Park!' shouted Jackie. 'Stella said that's near the campus – very posh.' But next to the Hyde Park Drug Store is the Hyde Park Tattoo Parlor, and The Texas Plasma Center ('Earn $$ in your spare time!') and the Wild Snail Pawn Shoppe.

But clinging to the numbered street grid system we found, and flopped into, our riverside home.

All the frogs legs you can eat – Monday nite $7.95
– sign at Cactus Joe's Watering Hole

The apartment was new, and cool, and decently furnished, and we liked it. We were appalled, though, at its appetite for electricity, even apart from the air-conditioning: the tiny kitchen had the water heater, the mighty cooker (with its spotlights and extractor hood), the fridge, the dishwasher, the waste disposer – and, already plugged in, the coffee-maker, the toaster and the electrical can-opener. A terrific place to have breakfast in, but hopeless to cook in: no strainer, no grater, and not a knife sharp enough to cut a lemon.

Little more than a century ago, when the river ran free, the Comanche would have taken our scalps for being here. Now the Indians are in their reservation, which you can visit like any zoo ('a special part of Texas' say the billboards tactfully). And our air-conditioned box is a stunning assertion of man's victory over heat and danger and wild country. It differs from a moon-shot only in degree. A power-cut, though, would leave us like stranded fish, unable to live.

If you don't like the way I drive,
stay off the sidewalk
– car sticker

'Hi, yo'll! I want you folks to have a nice day, now!' said an official in what was surely a parody of a Texas accent.

But *everybody* talked like that. And everywhere, even in restaurants, enormous men strode around in cowboy boots and 10-gallon hats. We weren't prepared for Texas to be quite so – er, Texan. It was as if all Scots wore the kilt, or all Cockneys dressed as Pearlies.

Passer-by weds jilted bride
– newspaper headline

The official was helping us get a parking pass from the Campus Police. The university has 50,000 students and 20,000 staff, and parking is a serious business. There are Campus Police roadblocks as you go in, and parking in the wrong place gets you a $12 fine. We heard that some rich kids just ignored their fines; theirs will have been the Porsche 928s we saw about the place. The university's smart answer has been to withold their degrees, but a law student is currently taking them to court, claiming violation of his rights.

Theatre tour of London
If you love the theatre, here's a tour you must act on.
You'll be treated to four of the hottest plays in London:
CATS   SINGIN' IN THE RAIN
THE MOUSETRAP   NO SEX PLEASE WE'RE BRITISH!
– British Caledonian ad in Texas paper

At first we thought we had no neighbours down by the river: nearly all the picture windows were blank. In fact people kept their drapes drawn as insulation. Practical, but eerie. Most of them looked to be students, but in a month we never managed a longer conversation than 'Hi! How are *you* today?' Then they vanished into their square caves.

'V–P Bush utilised his sense of humor by laughing'
– University of Texas speech coach, adjudicating on V-P TV debate

I noticed a job ad which ended 'an equal opportunity employer: m/f/h'. But on Channel 21 (of our 42!) when a Baptist minister was asked about homosexuality he almost frothed at the mouth: '. . . an abomination . . . Leviticus . . . a nation shall vomit them forth . . . We get 1,500 homosexuals a week who come to us, glad to give it up and turn to Jesus!'

In this land of big boots and Stetson hats, it's probably hard to be (m). Or (f). Or, particularly, (h).

'I'm a firm believer in the old hanging tree'
– Stuart Huffman, Sheriff of Johnson County

Austin didn't exist until 1846, when some prominent Texans decided it would be a good place for the new state's capital. Antiquity is in short supply, and over-valued. We felt almost guilty that our unremarkable house in Edinburgh would have been one of the dozen oldest buildings in Austin.

And we didn't know what to make of The Butler Window, a landmark in Zilker Park. Mr Butler, it seems, was a prosperous merchant who supplied the bricks for some of Austin's main buildings earlier this century. He died, and when the time came for his house to be demolished, a window from it was preserved and rebuilt in the park on a pedestal. Through it you can look out on some trees.

HUMAN HEAD TRANSPLANT
– newspaper headline

Though nobody knew we were there, our phone rang quite often. Usually it was someone congratulating us on having won a free dancing lesson or test drive; but there were quite a few grumpy wrong numbers, which made us feel at home. (Scots get very querulous if you're not the person they thought they were ringing.)

I read in a paper that in some states more than 50 per cent of subscribers are now ex-directory. This must make it hard for the agencies who undertake to deliver telephone sales messages. If the trend goes on, their teams of congratulators will be calling fewer and fewer people, more and more often – until the remaining subscribers are always engaged, because they are always being congratulated.

> **'This is a dry county, very dry . . . the beer drinkers here carry posthole diggers in the backs of their cars. They don't throw the beer cans out; they bury them'**
> *– Dan Saunders, Sheriff of Martin County. (Quoted, like Sheriff Huffman, in* **Texas Monthly***)*

Some of the campus buildings have unnervingly jocular names, like the Sid Robertson Building, or the Harry Ransom Center. We make condescending jokes about Johnny Balliol College and the Bert Sheldon Theatre. We're wrong, of course. Paying public respect to eminent people is a good thing; and using the names by which they were known is direct and refreshing. (All the same, we mumble, we didn't call it Winnie Churchill College.)

We work in the Harry Ransom Humanities Center, where the

facilities for study are magnificent and the people very helpful – though we had to get used to being greeted each morning with loud cries of 'Hi, you guys!' from the librarian. Not at all like the National Library of Scotland.

The building itself, though, worried us. It's new, a massive seven-storey cube, with only a few, irrelevant, windows. Inside there are spacious archives and art galleries, but you have no sense of the form of the building, or of which part you are in. The lifts are scattered about, and each one serves only selected floors. Ours went, I think, to 2, 5 and 7; the other floors might have been in another building, or another town.

One morning we went in out of blazing sunshine. Four hours later we came out to find that three inches of rain had fallen, creeks had burst their banks, cars had been swept away, and people were injured and homeless. Up in the vast cool reading room, none of this had happened.

A few days later we heard a reading room receptionist telephoning the ground floor police desk to ask if she needed her umbrella to go to lunch.

> *(film of ambulance; male voice over)*
> **'. . . it's nice transport – even sleeps two . . . but it's never saved a life on its own! Our trained people do that! We don't only get you to the hospital – we get you there *alive!*'**
> *– commercial for private medical firm*

Dept of Coy Euphemisms: Austin is, of course, a very proper city. But less-than-proper advertisers offer real dollar notes to Yellow Pages, so an accommodation has to be reached. This must be why Abracadabra Nude Modeling and Midnite Cowboy Exotic Massage both solemnly undertake Outside Calls to Residences and Nursing Homes. ('Nurse . . . nurse . . . Aargh!')

If guns are outlawed, only outlaws will have guns
– car sticker (Is this the silliest piece of circular logic ever?)

During our stay there was a two-day symposium about 'The Texas Myth'. Much high-powered theorising and introspection. We smiled our superior Old World smiles, of course. But we couldn't think of many states with a strong enough identity to have a symposium about. 'The Idaho Myth'? 'The New Hampshire Myth'? No. We were, after all, visitors to the most interesting state in the union.

JONATHAN CROZIER

THE VALLEY OF SIN

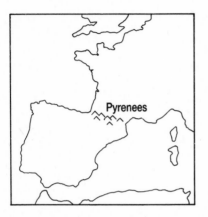

Beyond the pass the terraces fell away with unexpected steepness and the valley lay framed between pine and birch. The farmer working below showed no sign of taking a siesta. The old mule dragging the hay-sledge took exception to this and stopped dead halfway up a difficult slope in protest. The man yelled gee-up until he was hoarse; he even took a stick to the animal, but the mule remained glued to the spot, head hung low in stubborn opposition. In desperation the farmer tried pushing the sledge from behind and the mule, feeling a lessening of the load, finally agreed to move.

Returning downhill from the upper meadow with the laden sledge hard on his heels, the unhappy animal broke into a smart trot. *Whoa,* cried the man in alarm. Not anatomically capable of raising two derisive fingers, the mule did the next best thing and broke into a gallop. Over went the sledge; the upright staves were smashed all down one side and the hayload spread itself down the hillside. Slowly the old mule turned his head and looked his master straight in the eye.

So the farmer worked right through the midday heat to repair the sledge, while the mule rested in the shade of the ash tree with wisps of sweetening hay within easy reach. In the Valley of Sin even the animals are opposed to change.

At the turn of the century Hilaire Belloc said that the vast area of the mountains, allied to the conservative attitude of its people, made it certain that the Pyrenees would never be overcome or changed by man. In the last two decades the Spaniards have been doing their best to prove him wrong. Entire valleys have erupted in a rash of hotels and apartment blocks. Sadly, many others are almost depopulated, casualties of civil war and industrialisation.

The Gistain valley, with its seven small villages, falls somewhere between the two extremes. Sin and Serveto, locked in their own high valley by the limestone cliffs of Arties and Sin, are the least modernised and life is lived at a gentler pace.

The wealth of these small communities is based on good arable land well-watered, and extensive mountain pasturage communally owned. In earlier times they tanned their own hides, spun and wove their own cloth, had their own blacksmith and miller; even grew their own hemp. They needed little from outside, olive oil, wine and salt being the main exceptions. The climate is bracing, and nineteenth-century gravestones show a population that reached its three-score years and ten and often much more.

The cluster of houses that make up Serveto lie in a patchwork of fields with long avenues of poplars laying black fingers of shade on the bright green of alfalfa and gold of mown hay. In summer the scars of erosion on the far hillside are splashed bright yellow with the dense pads of Spanish gorse, and the air is laden with a subtle fragrance compounded of elderflower and pine resin, honeysuckle and flowers of the meadow.

The first person to discover my tent in the poplar grove was the village bore, who settled himself comfortably on the stone wall. His first complaint was the weather (the year was the wettest in living memory), the second rising prices. In no time at all I learnt the cost of everything from a working man's suit to a kilo of onions. 'I ask you,' he wheezed, 'eighty pesetas for a kilo of onions. Whatever is the world coming to!'

For a repeat performance he picked the subject of the Civil War, unabridged but clearly adulterated. 'That it should have happened was a crime; that Franco won was a tragedy.' Fame and fortune are such fragile things and in the mountains of Aragon they pass quicker from the mind than a year's drought.

Finally he came to the subject of my presence. 'I can't remember a foreigner stopping in Serveto before. Mind you, a Dutch girl once stayed in Sin and a lot of Dutch people go to San Juan. There were six of them there once!' In Serveto 'a lot of' is measured by a shorter yardstick.

The deserted village of Señes nearby is unusually spacious and with no untidy jumble of houses cluttering up the hillside. In the yard of one of the ruined houses a block of six rabbit hutches had been carefully roofed with red tiles, the side walls rendered, the owner's initials and the date 1960 written boldly in the rendering. Just as his ancestors had dated the house 1743 to stand through the centuries, so the man had dated his own contribution to his heritage. For in the hills the social unit has always been the house, and as such it assumed greater importance than the family or individual. For generations may come and go but the house, as the physical embodiment of estate and lineage, endures for all time.

But men had left their heritage in the days of no running water, no electricity and access by foot only. A time when men found it hard to support their families and impossible to educate their sons. It was the lure of an easier life with good money in an industrial town that emptied Señes and other villages like it.

In Señes the apple trees still bloom in spring, but the grizzled plum that leans to the greening lane scatters no blossom in its dying years. The inevitable iris, found on every village wall, its roots interwoven with the stone and dead leaves from many years cascading free like golden tresses, now has the freedom of the vegetable garden. At dusk the shuttered windows look out unseeing across the green valley, blind to the twinkling lights of distant Saravillo and the last faint flush on the snow-capped peaks.

The death of a village is always depressing but doubly so here. The megalithic culture that flourished in southern Iberia and then spread northwards reached the Pyrenees almost 4,000 years ago. Though few dolmens are left standing, the eye of the earth goddess worshipped by these early people appears in many places where stone has been appropriated from defunct shrines. An eye stares unblinking from a lintel in Señes, and the head of the goddess appears on a quorn.

Next day in Serveto one of the women stopped me as I photographed the street. 'You like our houses?'

'Yes, they're beautiful. I wish I could live here.'

She was middle-aged with the strong handsome features common in the hills, and she surveyed me with ironic amusement, as an alien from another time and place. 'They're old and dilapidated,' was her acid comment. 'And they've no proper drains,' she added, scornful of my stupidity, and marched off without another word, her plastic basketful of washing clasped firmly beneath her arm and patterning the dust with its dripping.

Sin is a more populous version of Serveto. The two old men sunning themselves in the street were startled to find a foreigner in their midst. 'We did have a Dutch girl here once.' Clearly it was the event of the century. I say century but time scales are difficult to evaluate in the Pyrenees. I've often been asked whether I'm the English professor studying the Aragonese language, yet his travels date back to the Thirties.

Wandering down the street, I saw the doorknob, big bold and brass, set centrally on the door. It was clearly hand-made and beautifully embossed with entwining scrolls.

'He's photographing my front door,' one of the old men squeaked excitedly, and hobbled over. 'Hand-made? I don't think so. It came off the old church door when they made a new one.' He opened the door and proudly showed me a two-foot latch, elegantly wrought by the hand of some fifteenth-century blacksmith. Pyrenean villages are full of unique artefacts, fashioned by craftsmen who knew how to combine beauty and usefulness.

The builders were busy butchering a house at the back of the village, hacking out a channel for a six-inch sewage pipe and trusting to luck that the entire wall didn't collapse. 'We're gradually restoring Sin,' one of them remarked to me with great pride. Visions came to me of other villages with rendered houses painted in hideous colours, and red Mediterranean tiles that fell with the first snow, and I shuddered inwardly. I prayed that restoration didn't include hacking away the unruly mass of lilac that filled unwanted corners. The essence of spring in mountain Aragon is the perfume of lilac and song of the nightingale at every turn.

But though I may be saddened to see the mellow golden stone disappearing under a characterless coat of cement, I don't begrudge the villagers the affluence brought by high farm prices. It will take more than a few superficial cosmetic changes to keep me away from Sin and the beautiful Gistain valley.

GILLIAN CRAIG

AGAINST ALL THE ODDS

'Over a million of our people were slaughtered by the Turks in one year alone.' Passion in this student's voice belies the cold statistics. A sorrow like a shoreless sea permeates the history of Armenia, according to one of its poets. And if words say too much, or too little, you can see the evidence for yourself in the bloodstained, fire-scorched pages of ancient manuscripts in the Institute at Yerevan.

He had asked if he might join us as we sat drinking coffee: strong, dark and thick, brewed upon burning sand. 'What I want to know is . . .' his fist shook the table, 'what is life really like in the West?' No jeans or cigarettes, but a thirst for information: his favourite words 'Punk' and 'Pop Music' and an admiring incredulity in his cry, 'Why do you allow people to go around looking like that?'

What is difficult for us to believe is that we are in the Soviet Union. This pavement café under bright umbrellas, couples strolling past hand in hand, music leaping and falling from an underground source like the Singing Fountains in Lenin Square. And beyond, the massed bands of jets that lead down to the Eternal Flame: 2,750 in all.

Water, one of the four elements that have played a key role in forging the history of this ancient land. 'People used to kill each other for water,' he tells us. 'In country graveyards there are inscriptions testifying to this.' A simple statue of a boy holding a pitcher stands at the entrance to the Park of Communards.

Why had we come to Armenia? he wants to know. Curiosity, we say. And a desire to break down some of the barriers – barriers made not out of distances or languages (and here we compliment him on his excellent English) but out of ideologies.

'*How* had we come to Yerevan?' By Lake Sevan. 'Ah, the only way.' He sighs. The lake that lies at the mysterious heart of Armenia, its clear turquoise waters defying all attempts to discover how it was formed. 'A piece of sky come down to earth among the mountains,' according to Maxim Gorky. One of the highest and largest in the world. You could fit all the Swiss Lakes into Sevan and still have water to spare.

Twin symbol, with Mount Ararat, for the Armenians.

'Look at it!' It is almost impossible not to, for wherever you are in
the rose-red city of Yerevan, the twin peaks of this biblical giant dominate the skyline. 'Just think where it is! In Turkey!' His face wrinkles
with disgust. Ararat, its snow-covered cap catching the last rays of the
sun, its lower slopes obscured by mist, so that it seems to belong entirely to the sky. 'The best time to see it. At dusk or at dawn.'

And the best time to gaze out over the city, when the fifteen different shades of pink volcanic tufa that form the blocks of the modern
buildings turn an even deeper hue. Harmony and unity in stone: stone
that was formed in the belly of the earth by the element of fire. The
landscape of this geologically ancient land is punctuated with extinct
volcanoes, a landscape where history throughout is written in stone.

'Armenia has over 4,000 protected monuments.' Statistics again,
but considering the size of the country it *is* impressive. 'The first
Christian church, the only Pagan Temple.' On Soviet soil, of course.
The only thing that's small about the smallest of the Soviet Republics
is its size. You can reach Yerevan in less than a day by bus from
neighbouring Tbilisi in Georgia.

'As you won't sit down to eat with anyone who comes along,' he
grins, flourishing his coffee cup, 'so you won't build a house with any
stone you find. Armenian proverb.' Master craftsmen: the carvers in
stone. The intertwined bunches of grapes and pomegranates, sheaves
of wheat and heads of birds and animals that enrich so many buildings
seem to be moulded out of rather than carved into the stone. And an
unexpected pleasure, as you travel through the austere beauty of this
land of mountain peaks, plunging ravines and fertile valleys is the sight
of the *khachkars*, or standing stones, carved with a cross: the symbol of
the Tree of Life.

'You know what were the first words ever written in Armenian?
"To know wisdom and instruction, to understand reason expressed".'
He leans forward, spreading his hands towards us on the table, a ges-
ture of intimacy not encountered in the impassive coldness of the
North. 'Our alphabet is far older than Cyrillic.' Contempt shows on
his face.

But haven't the Armenians, like the Georgians, been allowed a con-
siderable measure of freedom? The hands are withdrawn, suggesting
that we may have probed too far. 'It is important to know how to beat
the system.' The entrepreneurs: famous throughout the world for
their wheeler-dealing. No sooner had we arrived in Yerevan than a
bus driver offered to turn his empty bus into a taxi. He would take us
anywhere, he assured us, but at a price that would have kept his family
for a week.

And corruption? He laughs, tossing back the wine that has inevitably succeeded the coffee. 'Here we don't call it corruption. We call it

operating round the edges of bureaucracy.' A determination to succeed against all the odds? A phrase which keeps surfacing in the mind in Armenia. As far back as 782 BC the Urartu King Argishti built the fortress of Erebuni 'to increase the might of his kingdom and deter hostile countries'. So much of the energy of these courageous, quick-witted people expended in an attempt to keep out invaders. Romans, Persians, Mongols and Turks who set their greedy sights upon the strip of land that separates the Black Sea from the Caspian, and the historic trade routes linking Europe to Asia.

There is a spurious romanticism about a struggle, we say, but there is nothing romantic about the possibility of extinction.

'To survival!' He raises his glass. 'See how it glows with the sun's clear light!' This wine, he tells us, gives people the strength of the mountain eagle. It infuses the spirit with the warmth of the sun. We tell him about the exuberant wedding party that was in full tilt when we arrived at the hotel: tables overflowing with food, band at its most boisterous. Armenians, he says, are great lovers of children and the family. They have the lowest divorce rate in the USSR.

And some of the highest land. Is it something to do with another element, the purity of the air? The creativity, the wealth of imagination. Being so near to the heavens . . . 'Perhaps it is because it was here that Christ was supposed to have come down to earth,' he replies sardonically. Echmiadzin: the seat of the Armenian Gregorian church, the holy site that attracts Christians from all over the world for the ceremony of the preparation of the myrrh.

Is he a believer? we wonder. It would be impertinent to ask. But as our plane flies over the majestic peaks of the Caucasus en route to Leningrad, we ponder his final question. What would we take home to remember Armenia? Brandy from the vineyards of the Ararat Valley, dried apricots from the home of Prunus Armeniaca, a lump of basalt from the high triangular plateau where Mitridat built his splendid Temple of the Sun, the delicious flavour of Ishkhan 'prince of fish' which swims in the sparkling waters of Sevan, postcards of the masterpieces in the State Gallery . . .

But, most of all, the sound of singing in the remote peace of the chapel in the cave monastery at Gegard, whose cells are scoured right out of the rock: the defiant and triumphant song of the spirit, surviving against all the odds. And the look of longing on your young face as you said: 'It must be wonderful to travel. To go exactly where you please.'

FRANCES CRAIG

HOT WATER AND THE FIVE YEAR PLAN

CZECHOSLOVAKIA

'All services connected with your stay in the Czechoslovak Socialist Republic will be secured for you by the ČEDOK travel agency,' informed the brochure. I was in ČEDOK's London office, trying to buy a phrasebook. 'We don't have any phrasebooks,' said the girl, 'all the ČEDOK guides can speak English.'

But I am stubborn; and I don't like being escorted around historical monuments by English-speaking guides. Besides, we couldn't afford the ČEDOK hotel prices; our holiday was to be a camping holiday, and when camping you need a phrasebook.

We tracked one down in Bayreuth. It was German/Czech, not English-Czech, but it would have to do. I sat in the car and studied it while Phil drove on over the border.

The border town of Cheb was grey, silent and peeling; like Wigan without the night-life. We began to feel we shouldn't have come: within a few hours of arriving in Czechoslovakia we were fined fifty Korunas for driving in the wrong place without a permit on a Wednesday. Worse, it looked like rain.

We pitched our tent in Carlsbad, now re-named Karlovy Vary. The campsite was full of East Germans, so I exercised my German on borrowing a mallet to knock in the tent pegs and a foot-pump to blow up the airbed. As the only Westerners on the site, we attracted a lot of interest; or to be more honest, it was our car, a red Citroën, that attracted the interest.

We ate that evening in a restaurant on Karlovy Vary's main street. There was a large cassette player on the bar to provide the background music. They were playing Frankie Goes To Hollywood; and, despite the crowd of soldiers at the next table, we relaxed. Several glasses of *Becherovka* later we took the bus back to the campsite in a far more cheerful mood.

We spent the next few days driving in Bohemia and admiring the countryside. We saw a bi-plane spraying crops in southern Bohemia;

we saw fields of hops which go into the Plzeň, or Pilsener, beer. Once when we were lost we stopped to ask the way at a farmhouse. I could still barely understand any Czech, but the whole family came out and argued among themselves as to which was the best way to go. In the end I was confused but grateful that they had taken so much trouble to help a stranger.

Since we are tourists with cultural pretensions, we also saw the sights. The sights in Czechoslovakia are mainly medieval, baroque or revolutionary. In the official tourist publications one is encouraged to visit the modern meat-processing plant or the orthopedic and trau-matologic clinic; I'm ashamed to say we missed these and settled for the more historic sights.

One of these is Karlštejn castle. It is set on a hill surrounded by woods, and is supposed to be one of the most important monuments of medieval Bohemian art. We were told on no account to miss the golden chapel of the Holy Rood, with its gilded ceiling inlaid with jewels; but unfortunately the chapel is closed for repairs until 1989. Never mind: there are plenty of other buildings.

For baroque magnificence one goes to Prague – to the church of St Nicholas, for example. Imagine praying inside the crown jewels, with a backdrop of cherubs and seraphs, and you have some idea of its opulence.

The campsites, in contrast, occasionally reminded one of 1984. Not because there were thought police listening outside the tent, but because of the descriptions of the site facilities. 'Hot water is available from 7am. to 11am.'

'No, it isn't,' we complained the next morning, 'the showers are stone cold.'

'Yes,' said the lady at the desk, 'but there is hot water.'

'We don't understand.'

'It says here,' the lady pointed to the notice, 'that there is hot water between 7am. and 11am.'

'But there isn't any.'

'It also says this in the five-year plan.'

We apologised and left. After all, the Czech government could not help it if we were unable to feel the hot water it had so thoughtfully provided.

The above exchange was spoken in English. Outside the campsites, however, few people speak English; and my Czech, though by now sufficient for asking the way to the bus-stop, was not quite up to con-versational level.

We found it best to speak German. Many Czechs are fluent in it, especially the older people who remember when this area was called the Sudetenland and German was the official language. But it is not a good idea to give the impression that you really are German: we once overheard a lady mutter *'Scheißdeutsche'* as we passed, and from then on established the following ritual.

'Mluvite anglicky?' (wearing hopeful expression).

'Ne.'

(Crestfallen look, immediately followed by new hope:) *'Mluvite ňemecky?'*

Yes, they usually did speak German. But it was worth making the detour, in order to establish that we were English; we were then served more quickly in restaurants, and received a more friendly reception when we spoke to anyone.

Most of those we met had not been to the West, and they asked an assortment of questions. What did we make of Reagan's jokes about bombing Russia? Did Mondale have any chance in the presidential election? Did Kohl really want Honeeker to visit Bonn, or was it all a publicity stunt? Everyone from factory workers to geography teachers asked politically searching questions. But their ideas about ordinary life in the West seemed to be based on old Sherlock Holmes films: London, we heard, was permanently foggy, and if you lived in the East End you were unable to breathe because the smoke from the factory chimneys drifts into your house. Which is why the rich live in the West.

But if they know little about life in modern Britain, what do we know of life in Czechoslovakia? Here are some of the questions we were asked on our return:

Did you have to queue for bread?

Was your itinerary subject to the authorities' approval?

Did people come up to you in the street and offer to buy your jeans?

The answers were no, no and no.

With regard to your itinerary, we were restricted only by an event totally out of the authorities' control. Our car broke down. The mechanics at the garage spoke no German, English or French. I didn't like to try Russian. 'Tell them it just about goes if you pull the choke right out,' said Phil. But it was unnecessary: they had already gone into the standard mechanic routine, the same in any language, which consists of a slow intake of air sucked over the teeth accompanied by a worried frown and a despondent shake of the head. 'It'll be a long job, guv,' was evidently their meaning.

They couldn't have seen many Citroëns before. One man took out the carburettor, spat on it, showed it to a few curious bystanders and tried to work out how to replace it. Then the two of them fiddled around for a while, and eventually, to our amazement, the car started. 'Tell them the idling speed's too high,' hissed Phil. 'No,' I said firmly. Getting the thing back on the road was achievement enough.

A pump attendant brought us some lemonade. 'Buy a Skoda next time,' he advised. I said we would.

So: we couldn't drive to the Polish border and admire the beautiful scenery; we couldn't visit the sights of Moravia or Slovakia. Instead we stayed in Bohemia, eating and drinking in bars and restaurants, meeting people, exchanging addresses and drinking toasts to peace. And that, rather than the historic sights or beautiful scenery, was what provided the memories.

(Opposite) The village of Sin in the Pyrenees

Temple of the Sun at Garni

ARMENIA

(*left*) The bell tower at Echmiadzin Cathedral
(*right*) Rock and stone carving at the cave monastery at Gegard

ANN REEVES

Chinese Tea and Sympathy

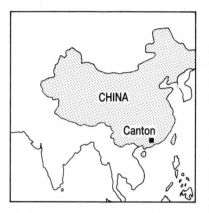

We woke to the sound of 298 tooth-brushes clashing furiously with 298 sets of Chinese teeth. Then out came the ever-present floral-printed facecloths, and 298 wiry torsos received a scrupulous going-over.

It was morning in China, and the old dilapidated ferry was still chugging up the Pearl River from Canton – destination Wuzhou, some 130 miles to the west. Three hundred passengers, and us the only foreigners. Our fellow travellers on this odd Noah's Ark, all awake before dawn, were crowded round the ship's six taps, going through their morning ritual. The taps were furiously pumping in river water – chocolate in colour but not in flavour – to meet the demand.

It was chaotic and noisy. But a cheerfulness prevailed over the hubbub and the scramble for water. And this sharing, this absence of ill-temper amid the incredible lack of privacy – anathema to Westerners – was to be typical of our two-month journey through China.

To us the boat seemed ridiculously overcrowded and ill-equipped to cope with so many passengers. But to the Chinese it was almost a picnic. As we were to learn, all forms of public transport fairly burst at the seams – passengers, luggage, live ducks and hens tied together and stowed beneath the seats, live fish in water-filled plastic bags, long fish fillets hanging from luggage racks, and the occasional armadillo curled into a tight ball of terror, obviously aware of its fate as a medicine of some kind.

For the duration of the boat journey we had 298 pairs of curious eyes upon us. We must have looked hopelessly out of our depth, for we were ill-prepared for the ways of Chinese travel. Our £1.70 fare provided a bunk 18in wide, a straw mat and a brick cunningly disguised as a pillow. Each bunk was separated from its neighbour by a 3in partition. And that was home for twenty-two hours. There was little room to walk and stretch our legs. More's the pity. Of all the bunks, six were shorter than the rest. And out of 298 passengers well under 5ft 3in, it was just our luck to be allocated one of them.

From the boat there was a frenzied and totally chaotic leap for the bus which was to take us to Yangshou, a remote village over the mountains. It was a twelve-hour bone-shattering, horn-blasting, cyclist-avoiding, hair-raising cacophony, during which we tasted hot bean curd with caramel syrup, cane juice, steamed buns and sour plums from roadside stalls.

The toilets were getting gradually worse. But a group of women did their best to help. They gathered round and issued unintelligible hints to me as I squatted – one of them obligingly held the legs of my jeans up off the floor.

Concussed, confused and constipated, we arrived in Yangshou. We lodged ourselves firmly in a dormitory-style hotel (the only type available in most of rural China), scrubbed ourselves squeaky clean and slept for twenty hours.

Yangshou nestles between tall limestone peaks and verdant rice fields. Every morning the incoming roads were filled with local far-mers walking to the town market with baskets of fruit and vegetables on bamboo poles slung across the shoulders, or wobbling in on bicycles laden with live pigs or chickens.

The market was at once fascinating and horrific. Cane baskets of fruit were beautifully and intricately decorated. When I paused to examine one more closely, a frantic movement on the handle made me recoil – a dozen live green and yellow frogs, which I had taken to be floral decoration, were hanging in a bundle tied by their hind legs. They were desperately trying to hop away – reluctant fresh meat.

We backed off into a medicine tent, where a young woman patient was apparently suffering from knee pain. A stooped old crone applied wooden suction cups to and around the offending spot, and plunged a none-too-clean skewer (evidently straight from kitchen duty) three inches into the knee.

Ruth and I almost passed out, but the patient was doing fine. After a casual pull or two on a cigarette, the doctor removed the skewer and applied another suction cap. That was lifted, and a dubious-looking fluid dribbled out. We bid a hasty retreat from the tent. For my own ills, I think I'll stick to a cup of tea, a Bex and a nice lie down.

Half an hour of this and even the fresh fruit and vegetables seemed to be writhing and pulsating. But it seemed that we, too, were cause for excitement. Sitting in the local café, over many a mountainous dish of rice, vegetables and pork washed down with warm local beer, we were often confronted by Chinese excitedly pointing us out to their children – who sometimes burst into tears at the very sight of us. And more than once we were the cause of bicycles colliding and a basket of eggs crashing to the road as cyclists craned their necks for a second look.

After several weeks I became convinced that God first created the teacup, then attached a Chinaman to it. Each and every Chinese car-ried his own lidded mug or screw-top jar with a small smattering of tea-leaves inside. Whether on a boat, train, bus or in a café, it was an essential piece of equipment. And everywhere there was a monstrous vacuum flask or samovar. No sooner had a sip been taken than the flask came round to top it up. One serving of tea-leaves thus lasts for a two-day journey. All over China is the sound of hot tea being slurped through teeth clenched to avoid the leaves and jasmine flowerets.

The village that evokes my happiest memories of China is Dali, tucked away in the south-west corner. And there lives – indeed thrives – the best eating house of all. The only family-run café in town, it goes out of its way to attract custom.

This tiny courtyard affair was pure bedlam, morning to night. An Alsatian guarded the door; a bicycle was parked between tables. Mum ran round in sole charge of the thermos operation while Dad dozed in a corner. Live eels slithered round in a bucket and pork fat hung from the roof. The staff washed offal in bowls at our feet, while two rats pranced about. The chef always held our rapt attention as he plucked last-minute goodness-knows-whats from our dishes before serving them.

But the food was great – tofu with tomatoes and shallots, lightly sautéed vegetables, crispy-skinned fish, spiced pork and chicken. freshly-made noodles, an unpolished nutty rice, and hot peanuts. And hot beer.

At the Dali bath-house, the luxury of a marble tub (made from local stone) could be had for 15p. And there lived the town masseur, a deaf mute with the most expressive, joyous eyes I have seen. He performed acu-pressure massages (all good ladies must remain fully attired), and displayed a wondrous collection of home-made potions and lotions.

But the poor fellow almost gave up his profession after an encounter with a young American. Unbeknown to the mute, his new client wore contact lenses. (I doubt he had ever laid eyes on such things.) One part of the treatment is a rather vigorous but stimulating massage around the eyes. Unfortunately this caused one lens to pop out and roll on to the dusty floor. When the American began groping for it, eyes closed in pain, the poor mute thought he had overdone the vigour and knocked the young man's eye out. It was some time before he included the eye treatment in his repertoire again.

Then there was the local bakery – a tiny shopfront packed with fresh, aromatic sweetmeats. At the rear of the shop, covered from head to toe in rice flour, sat the fat, beaming baker, kneading wonderful rice cakes stuffed with a sweet blackbean mixture. Our only deadline during those two idyllic weeks in Dali was to hit the bakery at 2pm daily in time to meet these delicacies on their way out of the oven. The aroma would waft halfway down the street, enticing us on.

And that, exactly, epitomises China for me: fragrant, evocative, enticing, and always, always beckoning us on.

STUART ROCK

OMAN: ANCIENT AND MODERN

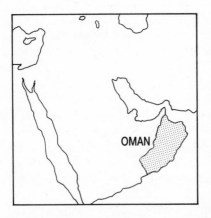

If your pilot is honest, he will tell you that there isn't much to see as you fly over Saudi Arabia. The brown, grey and gold piles crumpled at the end of the Arabian peninsula, which comprise much of Oman, take on added interest. So too does the notion of entering a country with no official tourism.

We are just in time for Oman's national day. Fourteen years ago Sultan Qaboos ousted his father, filial reaction to years of suppression, violence, and a resolute blindness to 'development'. Now that process has come to Oman, but running parallel with sweeping freeways, international hotels with air-conditioned bars, is an enhanced and determined nurturing of Oman's inheritance and culture. There is an impressive museum, fastidious restoration projects, reintroduction of wildlife such as the oryx – the fabled unicorn – and a firm control on architecture. All buildings must be in sympathy with the traditional vernacular. Even the Pepsi stands are arched and crenellated.

It's at the very heart of Oman's development where national day celebrations are centred. Over the new harbour of Mina Qaboos the air is studded with fireworks, raining over container ships, neon signs and the harbour forts. Muttrah, squeezed into a strip between water and mountain, glistens as each building is thick with swags of red, green and white bulbs. Western, Arab and Indian music thumps out of cars, and the warmth is permeated with the throb of talk and the smell of curry.

In the sober blue light of early next morning, we reach the camel races, another fixture in the diary of celebrations.

Out of a dusty, swarming mêlée, camels are dragged out in batches of six and seven. The head and neck of the animal are twisted down to the ground, a submission of grunting and wheezing and snarling. Once down, the rider has to be quick, vaulting on to an impromptu saddle of wool and cushion as the beast's legs jerk explosively upwards. A few smacks to the side of the neck with a stick, and the pair lope, splay-legged, to the start two kilometres away.

The crowd's faces are a sea of honey, sand and rosewood. Some are thin and etched, sprouting wiry grey strands of beard. Others are pockmarked, or brushed with adolescent growth. Most men and boys are crisp and white from the neck down, wearing their *dishdasha* robe, and slung around their waist the *khunjar,* Omani symbol of virility, a short hooked silver knife tied to a silver filigree belt. The family groups are more vivid: women and children swathed in lime, turquoise, red, silver, gold, green and orange.

It's a microcosm of the Omani melting pot, created through centuries of seafaring and the recent years of oil and construction. Traditional Arab, garish Indian, ubiquitous and anonymous European. Skins which range from deep, profound black to pale, freckled cream.

A muffled voice heralds the first race. It starts chaotically. Four camels career off at forty-five degrees from the track and into the few cars parked on the far side. On the second race a camel breaks loose, ripping up posts and fence in its entangled wake. A rodeo of police, riders and a truck weave through the thorn bushes in pursuit.

After the races most will return to the mountains, the dominating feature of Oman's landscape and its irresistible pull.

The chief town in the interior is Nizwa, the former capital. Until six years ago the journey took three days over stone and sand. Now it takes three hours over smooth tarmac, cutting through the Hajar range. All is arid, thousand feet slabs of blue-grey, tinged with black and ochre. At intervals we reach villages, clutched around *wadis* (dried river beds), where simple round towers break out of a sway of green spiky date groves.

Nizwa fort has the appearance of an opened tin can; a large circle with spare battlements around the rim. It, and the shining deep mauve of the mosque, are the centre of the town. In its shadow is the covered *soukh*; swarthy, round, gentle faces, white robes crouched in the dusky gloom, surrounded by frying pans, cheap scents, matchboxes, sacks of cloves, dusty coffee pots and metal trunks painted with crude Taj Mahals. Arab perfumes meet Indian Brylcreem. Another store holds piles of dusty redundant rifles, another symbol of virility.

The next day Nizwa is frenetic with auctions. Between two rings of bidders, goats and bullocks are pulled. Negotiations are literally freewheeling. Once a bargain has been struck, the animal is pushed through the outer ring into the dusty square where garlic and limes are sold, and men furtively roll wads of notes into their lace caps.

No undisturbed, unspoilt town; as one conversation with a small boy reveals:

'Salaam aleikum.'
'Hello.'
'I smi Stuart. I smuk ay?'
'My name's Mustafa.'

There is a Nizwa Motel. Seasoned expatriates bemoan the absence of bargains: 'You could buy a *khunjar* for a few rials. Now it's three hundred rials.'

From Nizwa there are two musts – Misfa and Jabrin. All the expatriates go there, but this does not tarnish their charm.

Jabrin is the showpiece of Oman's heritage – the seventeenth-century seat of Sultan bin Saif. Curiously, it was from here, 140km inland, that bin Saif presided over Oman's period of greatest naval power.

Jabrin lies off the main road, a quiet village where the tarmac runs out. Once the generator has been switched on we are guided by the swift-talking Amer. The atmosphere is cool and shadowy, thick white geometric blocks in harmony with teak and rosewood shelves, windows and benches. The library has an ornate wooden ceiling of red, blue and green, depicting stars, sun and moon. Contrasting with this elegance, at the base of the fort are the date cellars with blackened walls and channels down which rivulets of date honey can flow.

Jabrin took a team of Italian restorers three years. Misfa, on the slopes of the Jebel Akhdar (green mountain), has centuries of continuity behind it.

The village steeples down the spine of a rocky slope, disappearing into date and lime trees so that only the flat roofs, circles of clay, are visible. The first impression is smell, pungent and aromatic, wafting from sacks of dried limes.

The village is reached by a black-stoned slippery path, shining from use. It is a compact honeycomb of uneven alleys, thick with smells of goat and donkey and cooking. On the walls are posters exhorting vigilance against the rat.

A thrumming, splashing sound grows louder, an alien sound in this dry land. It is the *falaj,* or irrigation channel. Neatly cemented sides, about eighteen inches apart, guide a steady flow of inch-deep water through glades of banana, lime and date trees. Each person has his allotment of land and his sluice from the *falaj*. The manure is dried donkey droppings. The *falaj* is also shared by divisions of time, based on the movement of the sun and stars. A share of the water supply is put aside for auction or for crop development, the profits from which go to the maintenance of the *falaj*.

The day is spent walking the donkey tracks and lunching in the shade. Towards the end Misfa's magic is revealed; from above, a thin sheen of coppery light smears the flat terraces, which are dappled by yellow smudges of limes. The village sinks into shadow and haze, and the ravine fills with the cry of children and the bleat of goats. In the foreground an old honeystone cylinder of a tower stands empty and pockmarked.

We have only glimpsed. Oman is a land of discipline, history and beauty. Buy pomegranates, silver, and frankincense. Do not leave your car dirty for too long as the police can fine you . . . severely. Join with the fishermen as they haul in their catch of sardine, tuna and kingfish. But until such time that the Straits of Hormuz are safe and political stability is guaranteed in the area, we will not see true tourists in Oman.

ROBERT TASHER

A DAY IN NARNIA,
A NIGHT IN PHANG NGA

On the village green in front of the Chinese Bhuddist temple a fairground was being erected. The skeleton of a Ferris wheel loomed; shooting galleries and hoopla stalls were being knocked together.

The purpose of the structure immediately outside the temple was not so obvious. The men hammering it together had beckoned us, beaming, inviting inspection. A raised wooden runway, carpeted with the pin-sharp points of six-inch nails hammered through from the bottom, ran out 50ft and ended in a bed of nails laid on the grass. At the foot of the bed, guyed by wire ropes, a forty-rung ladder rose vertically. The rungs were steel knives, blades up.

The message was clear – 'Come back at nine this evening' – though they spoke no English, we no Chinese and no help was to be had from the Thai phrasebook.

We had come to Phang Nga to visit the limestone islands that rear in their hundreds from the bay. These natural wonders occur only here and in the gulf of Tonkin: connoisseurs rate Phang Nga. A day-trip from Phuket had only whetted our appetite and we had left that tourist ghetto by local bus and moved into a hot and grubby Chinese hotel in Phang Nga town.

The boy who had carried our bags up to our room so eagerly was of course a boatman. Would we like to sail out into the bay? As a matter of fact we would, tomorrow. He would take us all day for 1,000 bhat. We threw up our hands and bargained, and agreed that he would find two more travellers and we would each pay 200 bhat. That settled, we wandered down to the river looking for food and natural wonders.

The limestone scarps that rushed down to the sea and broke up into islands hung over the town, dripping green and yellow trees. Women sat under carved wooden verandahs preparing vegetables, fish and chicken. Children abandoned their play and pointed at the Farangs.

We had travelled only forty-five miles and had moved into a culture completely different from that of Bangkok, Chiang Mai and Pattaya. Everything was in Chinese. The banners of yellow paper hanging between the bright silk banners and red lacquered columns in the temple by the village green were covered in lists of Chinese characters. The advertisements for Coca Cola were in Chinese. The three dozen life-size turtles, made of dough and coloured red, standing on racks in the temple forecourt, had their names, perhaps, painted in gold Chinese ideograms on their crusty shells.

After dark we followed the smell of sizzling meat down to the fairground. Families eating candyfloss under strings of coloured lights, crowds of bikers guzzling frogburgers, country music wailing from loudspeakers; we could have been on Hampstead Heath on Bank Holiday night. Except for the drumming and chanting coming from the temple, and the photo display of the horrors of VD which had attracted a huge audience of twelve-year-olds.

We found a tent where they were cooking omelettes filled with clams. Two huge frying pans were being wielded on charcoal fires by a pair of vividly made up girls in blue jeans and flowered blouses. But a few sidelong glances revealed them to be He-Shes. The Thais are very keen on transvestism; way off any tourist route we would find them, making up and giggling, modelling clothes for each other and generally being girlish. Nobody seems to mind; as an aberration it rates low, on a level with Christianity or driving carefully. We sat down and gorged.

Sharp at nine a conch shell sounded and the temple courtyard filled up with Thais, dressed in white trousers with embroidered aprons, chanting and shaking in time to gongs. The first one mounted the runway and briskly walked its length, barefoot on the nail points. Stepping down at the end, he lay on the bed of nails and rolled across it to the foot of the ladder, which he climbed, pausing on each blade to detach a yellow paper prayer flag and send it fluttering to the ground.

For those unmoved, the Ferris wheel spun its neon lights and the shooting galleries popped. But as more young men, then older men, then women, came forward to walk the nails and climb the knives, so the general air of fun increased. Spectators eating ice cream crowded round the performers thirty deep, and cheered and clapped. As the only Farangs there, we were drawn by friendly hands to the best viewing spot, and beamed at and invited to climb the ladder. But still we could not discover the why of this ordeal by steel.

Next morning in the market, shopping for a picnic, our struggles with the phrasebook brought an English-speaking Thai to our rescue, explaining that the quail eggs we had bought were raw, but could be cooked for us in the soup cauldron wherever we took breakfast. And the performance with the nails and the knives? A thanksgiving. All those who went through the ordeal had at some time survived an accident or illness when their lives had been despaired of. In gratitude they undertook to walk the nails and climb the knives every year until they died. They spent the day chanting and dancing, and when they came to walk and climb they could be heard speaking Chinese, a language none of them could speak during the rest of the year.

Sapan, the boatman, had found two other tourists to share the fishtail boat and the cost. Peter was from Germany, and Helga was from California: they were solo travellers looking for entertainment, travelling together for her convenience. Sapan had brought along a couple of passengers too. Mike was from Phang Nga town, back from studying economics in Bangkok; Strawberry was from Panyi Island, like Sapan himself. We had a momentary chill when they climbed aboard . . . piracy? Would we ever be seen again? But when Strawberry reached under the seat and produced the first bottle of an apparently endless supply of Star Tiger rice spirit we realised it was not going to be that kind of adventure.

The islands rose sheer out of a millpond sea, pillars of white limestone with ochre splotches capped in crinkly green. Rank on rank they stretched to the horizon, their reflections shimmering towards us on a blue mirror. The coast dropped away into mist and we nosed into a world of fantasy. It bore no resemblance to our map.

Getting closer we saw that the islands rose more than sheer, their bases eaten away by the sea. Sapan sailed in beneath the overhang of limestone. He leapt up on to the ledge of rock which ran around the whole island under the overhang like some inside-out cloister, and tied us up. From the cool of this cloister the island-dotted sea shimmered in the sunlight. We found our torches and entered the caves beneath the island.

Later we drifted and found: a beach, 20ft of yellow shingle under a dozen palm trees; a grotto more lurid than Lourdes, every glittering bowl crying out for a plaster Madonna; a lagoon in an island's heart reached through a rock tunnel. In a gallery of stalactites, baobab roots seeking water winding down from the roof, we asked Sapan what the island was called.

'It has no name,' Sapan said, 'but when I told some other people I brought here that it had no name, they said to me that it was called Narnia.' He looked puzzled.

We ate quails' eggs, drank Star Tiger, swam in the warm sea floating from sun into shade and back again under trailing vines. The sun tumbled the islands' shadows on the sea.

Panyi island, where Sapan and Strawberry lived, had only enough room on it for the mosque. The rest of the village was on stilts, a Southend pier of teak, and we stopped there for petrol and beer. Oily water glittered through gaps in the teak boards as we climbed the gangplank. A plump old man sitting in a wooden scaffold on a marine building site sawed the top off an immense teak column to make it flush with the decking. The village was expanding. Seen through the lacy walls of the village pool hall the polystyrene floats of the fish farm bobbed busily.

While Sapan found the petrol we strolled the boardwalk where ladies sold shells and coral jewellery. One in jeans and blouse laid a hand on Ann's arm. Despite the nail varnish, it was a man's hand.

'What's your name?' He-She asked huskily.

'Ann. What's yours?'

He-She simpered prettily. 'My name is Linda.'

Sitting in a bus next morning, eating pineapple and waiting for the driver, we heard that the survivors were going to walk on fiery coals that night down on the fairground. But we were bound for Tekua Pa, and rumours in our guidebook of an ancient city.

ALISON SMITH

HOLDING UP THE EIFFEL TOWER

Linda Phillips was in my class in the wee school. She had a snub nose and long black hair in a ponytail, sharp, and she wore a red anorak and she was a little madam; my mother said so. She stole my best friend and my boyfriend and she won the class election and she came to the Hallowe'en party dressed as a witch, and she said Bloody and For God's Sake and played with all the boys, and ran round the playground yelling nee naw nee naw.

Linda Phillips was the first one to go to Paris. She brought her photographs to school. There was one of her taken so that it looked as if she was holding up the Eiffel Tower. There was one of her little sister like that, and one of her brother whose name was Mark Phillips (really). Sister Vincent said that the photographs were very good and put the one of Linda on the wall.

There weren't any photographs of dead cats in Linda Phillips's collection. She didn't see the dead Parisienne cat with its legs in the air, stiff and cold, like dead cats look in cartoons. That was why I got such a fright when I saw it, ten years later, ten years late. I saw it when we got off the overnight bus. I pointed it out to Julie. 'Jings,' I said. 'I thought they only looked like that in cartoons.'

We were on holiday at the top of map number three in the paperback book. My rucksack made me feel sick in the back of my neck and head and throat. We were there for three nights and we stayed in a Youth Hostel. First we visited Notre Dame. There was a smell of urine. It was lovely inside. Lots of people were taking photographs. Someone was taking one of someone else praying and a lady was explaining in German about the rose window to a group of Germans. That was the first day. We did lots of things. We went on the Metro, and we went to see the Eiffel Tower. A coloured man tried to sell us plastic Eiffel Towers but we told him our mothers already had some, though I don't think he spoke English. At the Arc de Triomphe at the top of the Champs Elysées I opened the back of my camera by mistake and ruined my film and went into a bad mood; then Julie went into one because I was in one, and we didn't come out of them until we reached the Youth Hostel and ate supper.

We were really tired because of the overnight bus. I was in a top bunk. There were two other girls in with us. A boy with a foreign accent knocked on our door and asked did anyone have a cigarette but nobody had any. I zipped myself into my sleeping bag and looked across. The other two girls had nothing on. I pushed down further into my sleeping bag.

'Jings,' I thought.

The next day we went to the Louvre and got in for nothing because we told the lady we were only sixteen. We went on a guided tour and saw the Mona Lisa and lots of other things. I thought some of it was good and some of it was boring, like the portraits, but Julie's doing art next year so we stayed until dinner-time. Then we went to a restaurant and ordered snails. The man said he'd run out of snails so we just had steaks. The steaks were full of blood vessels and strong so we reckoned they must be *cheval*. There was a French lady sitting near us and she started talking to us because she'd never seen people put vinegar on chips before. We asked her was it *cheval* and she looked offended and said no, *boeuf,* and told the waiter when he came back what we'd said, so we got out quick and went to a big garden for the afternoon because it was so hot. Then that evening we found Sacré Coeur on a map and went there. It smelt of urine outside too. I think they must just not use their toilets. I suppose you can't blame them. Some of their toilets are just holes in the ground (for ladies too).

There were different girls in our room that night, and they wore things in bed.

On Thursday we went to Versailles. It was really hot. We hired a boat on the lake and then we hired a tandem, then we sat on some grass and a policeman on a motorbike told us to get off. It wasn't just us. There were lots of people. That night we went to the Champs Elysées and ate hamburgers from McDonald's. I had one called a Big Mac. That's two hamburgers in one sesame bun with salad and cheese and sauce and a gherkin and *pommes frites* and Coke. Julie just had a cheeseburger. That's just one hamburger, no sesame seeds and no salad. We sat in a doorway to eat it until a man came out of the shop with a bucket of water. A lady asked us to take her photograph with her friends. The Champs Elysées has cars parked up the middle, queues of cars going towards the Arc de Triomphe and queues of cars coming away from it. One of the cars in the middle had been bashed into by another. All its windows had been smashed and one of the doors was jammed open with a big dent in the middle of the car.

There were two American girls in our room that night. They weren't in it until about 2am. When we arrived back their clothes were everywhere and there was a bottle of Bailey's Irish Cream with not much in it and a book open, pages down on the floor. The book was called *Europe on Fifteen Dollars a Day*. I fell asleep really quickly but Julie says they tried to smuggle in an Italian at half past two and that she had to pretend she was asleep.

The next day was our last one and it was hot again. We had to carry our rucksacks so I felt sick all day. First we went to the Jeu de Paume to see the Impressionist paintings, and Julie took lots of photographs, especially of Van Gogh ones because she's doing art soon. Then we went and sat on the Champs Elysées and I fell asleep and Julie woke me and told me there was a man flashing at us and there was; he was sitting on a motorbike and wiggling, and I felt sicker and said look for a policeman and he must have known the word because he went away.

When we were on our bus leaving Paris that night we saw an accident. A car had burned right out on the main road into the city and it was all black shell and smoke and white ambulances and red fire engines, and the cars on the accident side of the road were queued for miles and all the people who couldn't see the smoke were standing outside their cars with their hands on their hips, and some were buying ice cream from a van.

When we got home, Julie lost her spool. I got mine, though, and even though I'd opened the back of my camera most of them still came out. My one of the Eiffel Tower came out all overexposed and this makes it look quite good. The sky in it is all red and orange and on fire, and, sure enough, if you look at the bottom you can just see Linda Phillips in her red anorak, holding up the Eiffel Tower in burning Paris.

ROBERT CHEVALIER

The Monastery at Roukouniotis

At six I walked down to the harbour. The air was sharp, particularly in the shadows of the narrow descending lanes. The sun was rising and all of the houses facing the approaching light began to glow, but the bay – still in darkness – kept a chill ink-blue. High over the town the crests of the encircling hills flared orange and bit into the sky. In the silence of an island's summer dawn I reached the path by the water's edge and came into the town.

There were few people about at that hour. The old chap with his hook and line of gut had already found his spot along the quayside. I went into the *kafenion* belonging to Vasili to buy water. The main room, rather like a cave with its crumbling walls and rough floor, smelled very strongly of damp. Vasili was preparing food behind the glass counter. He asked where I was going. To the monastery, I said, to Roukouniotis.

I paid for the bottle of water. Vasili followed me out and we stood for a moment watching the sun rise and the colours changing. A hot day, Vasili said, as a warning to me.

I walked to the back of the town. A flight of steps led from there into the hills. The way was steep and I did not look up as I began to climb.

At the summit I paused to get breath. All of Symi Town was presented to me from this height, a small neat capitol now. I could see beyond the town to the deserted peninsulas and wide open sea, and to Turkey, a finger of land trembling in the haze of distance, watchful. A Greek warship floated in the sea and returned the gaze. I started on the path inland.

The north of the island was humped like a bull across its shoulders, and the path rode it. I climbed higher until the ground fell away on each side and the mass of the sky grew greater and nearer. I felt as if I travelled without earthly contact. Far below the sea lay calm and vari-hued and faded into the horizon. Islands and islets and mere rocks jutted from the sea, waterless, abandoned, life only for sheep and goats.

Then I descended into a region of scrub and friable earth. Ahead the path cleaved, parting around a squat white house. A woman stood at the door and I asked her which path I must take to the monastery. She signed to the right and then, with that singular Hellenic gesture of a downward flapping hand, invited me into her home.

The room in which I sat had a stove and shelves in one corner and a bed in another. The rest of the space was filled with an assortment of furniture, and on the walls hung a collage of pictures, photographs, mementoes, redundant calendars and printed icons. What illumination there was issued from the doorway. The floor was set with slabs of stone, cold to the touch.

The woman did not speak but worked over her stove, preparing coffee. Presently a man came in, her husband. His clothes were old and dust-smeared, and at his neck appeared a thick woollen vest, such that many of the older Greeks favoured. He had a scratchy bronchitic voice and twice a great racking seized him. In those moments he arched forward, putting a flat hand on his chest and coughed frightfully. Tears rose in his eyes.

He wanted to know where I lived and what work I did and how much I earned. He was fascinated by the differences in our lives, and each answer he passed on to his wife who understood well enough but held back in the shadows of the kitchen.

I saw behind her a shelf on which curds of cheese sweated, and when it was time to leave I went over to examine them. They were conical in shape and exuded a thin milk. Suddenly the woman grabbed up one of the cheeses and, wrapping it in paper, presented it to me. I did not want the gift, nor did I want to refuse her; I took the parcel and thanked her. She inclined her head, smiling. I said goodbye to both of them and stepped out.

The sunlight was brilliant, scouring. It reflected off the yellow earth and burned into my eyes.

At midday I arrived at the gates of the monastery. A vast low-spreading cypress tree concealed the front of the monastery and in its half-light I sank down to cool. The heat was very great, more an impression of sound than touch – a dynamic hum. Another sound persisted in counterpoint, the whistle of the cicadas. All about me the heat vibrated and the cicadas pulsed; I lay dazed.

The gates opened on to a courtyard paved in black and white cobblestones. I called and a man appeared on a landing above the courtyard. He was the keeper and he led me to his dwelling beside the domes and crosses of the monastery roof. He brought me water obtained from a hole in the landing. The water was ice-cold and shocked my teeth. I drank and looked from a narrow window on to hills and sky and barrenness. *Kyrios,* I said, addressing the man, how quiet it is

(*Opposite*) Camel racing in Oman

Thailand: Climbing the ladder
of knives in Phang Nga

Limestone islands in Phang Nga
Bay

here. He came to the window and also looked out, as if he had not been aware of any quietness before.

When I had finished the water the man took me along a corridor and down to a deeper level. We halted at a door which he unlocked and pushed open.

After the simplicity of the external buildings I was unprepared for the dazzle of the *katholikon*. Save for a floor of cool bare stone, the rest of the chamber was exclamatory with a mix of gold leaf, carved wood and frescoes all squeezed together under a blue and silver ceiling hung with chandeliers and censers.

This extraordinary interior had further, in a niche, a shield of silver reaching six feet high and worked into the form of a warrior. This was the Archangel Michael. Sections had been cut out of the silver to reveal his face and hands, and he wore a rather astonished expression as he trounced the dragon squirming at his feet. Thick wads of votive tablets had accumulated about the sculpture over the years and along the way collected dust and cobwebs; now they suggested woven occult images.

I stood at the rear of the room, watched by the keeper. He distracted me but still I wondered why a building had been built precisely here, in this area of aridity; and furthermore, why this island, indistinct from any other (they were all lovely). Perhaps it was that men could look all around them in this situation and feel contained and safe, and perhaps too that the clouds and stars came closest to the earth at this point: the heavens seemed within reach.

Now the monks had gone and the place was silent. Pilgrims called but no-one stayed. In November hundreds of people gathered to celebrate the feast day, eating and drinking and carolling beneath the cypress tree, and celebrating within the church. With the dusk they packed to go home, bringing together their bags and blankets and cradling up their sleeping children.

The song gone, the prayers said. And the monastery at Roukouniotis once more still and dark and concealing a diamond at its centre.

SARAH COOPER

THE GRINGO TRAIL

It was under our seats they had wedged the plastic covered boxes: the obvious place to hide cocaine on a bus to Bogota is with four gringos admiring the view. Not so stupid, though, and we soon dragged them out and returned them, not without some difficulty, to their rightful owners, two baseball-hatted characters sitting a few seats behind us. Coffee is the second biggest export from Colombia; cocaine is the first, a commodity becoming increasingly popular in the developed world. Attempts are made now and again to quell this growing industry, but assassinations of those who speak up against it are common and corruption is rife. Nevertheless, our bus from Cucuta to Bogota was boarded at several checkpoints; each time torches were flashed around, money changed hands and we all passed on undisturbed.

Travelling became much lighter after the Colombian border, where we were relieved of much of our camera equipment by a thoughtful hotelier, and we eventually arrived in Ecuador (where we stayed a few weeks). Quito was welcoming its new President into office with a series of strikes, one of which was a bus strike. This vastly improved travelling around town, necessitating hopping on to the back of a truck or *camionetta* as it momentarily halted at lights, and hopping off as it neared one's destination.

On my first excursion across the city on my own I landed a *camionetta* all to myself, only to find myself crushed as a crowd jumped on at the next stop and being sicked all over by a baby next to my ear.

Otavalo is a dusty, sleepy little town high in the Andes. In the main, the Indians live in small villages surrounding the town, which clusters around the base of Mount Imbabura. They are a relatively prosperous group, making a living out of the tourists from their Saturday market. Market day begins before dawn when crowds of Otavalans descend on the town bearing great bundles of woven rugs and jumpers. The Plaza de los Ponchos on weekdays is a purpose-built collection of concrete monstrosities, but on Saturdays it is submerged in gaudy textiles brought especially for the gringos, who love them.

We preferred the food market, a colourful mêlée of gold-beaded ladies with cooking pots, guinea pigs and chickens; a veritable feast! In the evening the Golden Eagle Coffee Shop was full of Europeans in chunky hand-knitted pink and purple sweaters. The Otavalans, meanwhile, were returning home, on packed buses and on foot. A man stumbled to the ground in a drunken stupor and his wife crouched by him; they stayed there until the following morning.

We had not come to Otavalo to acquire purple sweaters, but to collect several hundred saliva samples from the Indians for a medical research project. When we asked them to spit, the request provoked much guffawing and eager salivating; spitting is something Otavalans do readily and often. It is not, however, a pleasant experience, collecting spit, although I know of a group that went to collect faeces . . .

With these maize- and mucus-drenched bits of cloth well dried and packaged, and looking dangerously suspicious and therefore hidden at the bottom of my rucksack, we set off for Lima to dump our grisly parcel.

The scenic route was recommended and we booked ourselves on a bus to take us all the way to the border. The journey started well; by this stage we were almost oblivious to the inevitable taped South American chanting turned up to distortion level and played all night – and, anyway, we were experts at de-wiring the speakers.

Squashed in the back of the coach with us were a crowd of lecherous young men, with whom, once we had established that we were not gringos but 'Ingleses', we sang loud songs and decided that Las Malvinas should be donated to Bolivia. But by 2am smoke was rising from the floor, and by 2.30 the driver was attacking the axle with a sledgehammer. We abandoned ship, as everyone else had done, to promises of refunds (the driver had run out of money) back at the town we'd come from, and went to sit in the mud on the roadside to wait for a lift, wishing we'd never heard of the scenic route.

As dawn broke, a lone truck appeared on the horizon and everyone jumped to attention, preparing to leap on. It approached and slowed; there was a mad scramble as a lot of bodies hurled themselves at it, and it shot off in panic at great speed. I was relieved to find Sonia also inside once I had oriented myself, and fifty miles further on, when it stopped, we discovered the others clutching the roof and their luggage for dear lives.

We hitched the remaining 200 miles to the border – no joke in the blazing equatorial sun. We were carried there in great style by a dirty old oil tanker belching out thick black smog behind it. Wedged in the ten inches of space between the tank and the guard-rail, we became progressively blacker, and chugged through many peaceful Andean villages like a carnival float, to jeers of laughter and cries of *'gringo!'*

The Peruvian immigration office is a large brand new building staffed by a worrying number of officials. When I entered, David's rucksack was already on a table being emptied. I approached, with my suspicious package burning a hole in my rucksack and memories of *Midnight Express* looming large. But Dave made a joke, the officials laughed; and we were waved through. As soon as we reached Lima we dumped our parcel on a doctor friend there, greatly relieved to be rid of it, and now free to travel where we pleased.

Bolivia having been recommended by everyone we met, we took a ten-hour journey by train from Cuzco to Puno, on the Peruvian shores of Lake Titicaca. We travelled second class, on seats that provided no comfort whatsover after half an hour, and it became more comfortable to stand. The journey was made bearable by the Indians continually wandering up and down the train selling food. At every stop a new crowd with different food would get on and, since no-one got off, the aisle soon became a solid mass of Indians squeezing past each other. Each had her own cry – annoying nasal whines of *'Chicha! Chicha blanca!'* or *'Mandarinas!'* – with which they punctuated their journey through each carriage.

The journey began with coffee, served by huge women in voluminous skirts and little bowler hats, with enormous kettles and only one mug which was wiped out on a fold of skirt after use. The standard breakfast followed: plates of meat and potatoes cooked up at one end of the carriage and handed out on request. Lunch was roast pork – half pigs carried in pots by even larger women who squatted in the aisle to rip chunks off. With it we drank *chicha,* a vile-tasting brew. We ate continuously, trying everything and stopping every new face for more.

Later in the afternoon we took turns at sitting outside on the footplate of the train watching the barren altiplano whizz by, mellowing in the evening sun to a golden glow, until prodded back to our seats by the guard with a large gun.

Two weeks later we were back in Peru on our way to Lima to fly home. We stopped at Nazca in the desert of the same name, and over breakfast an opportunist guide offered to take us on a day's tour. He drove us miles out into the desert in a red Volkswagen, and led us to the middle of a huge burial ground. Eight hundred bodies, buried one thousand years ago, had been uncovered by the wind to reveal piles of bones, and corpses still with patches of flesh and hair clinging to them. They were sitting in depressions in the sand, all that remained of their tombs, in crouched, contorted positions, the ropes and cloth that bound them still undecayed.

Our guide sat in his red car and left us to wander among the people of a past civilisation. Their descendants survive and eke out their existence despite successive invasions and attacks which have swept away much of what went before.

The Incas came as the super-power of their day and established their rule and control on a wide scale. The Spaniards had superior fire-power and swept away all but the indestructible stone cities of Macchu Picchu, Winay Wayna and others like them. The third invasion has already begun. The big white tourist coaches roll daily along the Hiram Gingham Highway. This army needs no weapons; it has all the dollars it needs to buy control. The new *conquistadores* are moving in.

CHRIS DAVIES

A MIXMINGLE BEHIND THE SNOW CURTAIN

The tourist officer for Finnish Lappland had advised me well: 'You for sure must try the air-dried reindeer meat when coming yuip in the dark blackness.' His letter was similarly clear about behaviour in the fell wilderness: 'No more Chivas Regals or other tea-mixtures are allowed above one galloon – we have strict spiritus restrictions, ie alco monopoly belongs to the state. Learn theose regilations!'

Enthusiastically describing a metre of snow and minus 35°C as a 'jolly good winter', he concluded with a jubilant 'Sii you in Muonio headquarters half-past March on the Trafalgar'.

Arriving in Finland a week early, I skied out daily on the ice-sealed Gulf of Bothnia, and inland through the deep powder snow of the woods. I had joined up with a group of five Finns from Suomen-Latu, the Finnish Ramblers, planning to spend seven days in the wilderness of the Pallas-Ounas National Park, moving from shelter to shelter with one night in a snow-hole. The leader of the expedition was a man called Reijo, nicknamed the wolverine (*'Ahma'*), and evidently one of the last great *pulkka* – pullers of the North. His sledge was laden with the equipment too bulky to fit into our already outsize rucksacks.

But, on the second day, with fever coming on, I stopped. Removing my heavy rucksack I pushed it into an orange survival bag to slide rather than carry it down the hillside, thus saving me from further exhaustion. Only then did my comrades understand the weakness of my condition; however, in jettisoning my rucksack I had unwittingly shattered the Suomen-Latu code of conduct.

It is important to do things right in Finland. On previous visits I had seen over-casually clad Germans squirted with teargas in a hotel night-club. I had once been asked to leave a dance-floor because my shirt-tail was untucked, and a fierce 'Whose friend are you?' had quickly moved me on when innocently perusing the Finnish Parliament. Thus I put up no struggle when my frowning comrades removed my rucksack from the orange bag and started ferrying it downhill in a series of long stretching zig-zags. An operation, however, that took over twice as long as the ferryer repeatedly had to retrace his steps to recover his own load.

The nearest wilderness hut was hard to find, and with my fever worsening it was clear that I would be taking no further part in the expedition. Eventually we located the warm Hannukurun hut, its special telephone crackling out our call for help to the local policemaster. The next day two soldiers arrived trailing a heavy metal sleigh from their snow-mobile – the reindeer-drawn wooden *pulkka* long since outmoded. Cocooned in a black snow-mobile suit and looking out from under two balaclavas, I watched the co-driver being pulled along like a water-skier, occasionally flinging out one arm, rodeo-style, for balance. Narrowly missing low branches and bouncing over undulating forest and lake terrain, our arrival was something of an event in the hamlet of Keräs-Sieppi. The onlookers seemed amused, and some checking of watches even suggested it had been a timed run.

An ambulance was waiting to take me to hospital in Muonio, ten miles away. And lying there, in the stillness of my hospital bed, one hundred miles north of the Arctic Circle, I reflected upon the once so strangely irrelevant advice of the tourist officer: 'Always try a phone in the wilderness. You see you must mixmingle with the operator when calling from behind the snow curtain.'

The Siberian jay or *kükkeli* is the good-luck bird of the Finnish forest, so five days later I regarded its sighting as a good omen, having fully recovered and made a successful rendezvous with an English friend further north in the village of Hetta.

Skiing from Hetta took Alan and me to a bleak viewpoint on one of the higher peaks in the National Park. A vastness of pine and lake extended in all directions, and the fells conjured up visions of the ancientness of natural forces, over millenia preying upon the jagged quartzite to grind it to its present rounded form. Lower down grew pines and Lappland spruces, but on the higher slopes only the dwarfish mountain birch withstood the harsh environment. Above these neither tree nor shrub survives; the snow is icy, refrigerated into wind-sculptures and rutted furrows.

Leaving the marked trails, forest skiing from Hetta was not easy. Alan, with shorter and narrower skis, floundered thigh-deep in the light powdery snow of the woods. There, we discovered the peculiar *kelo* tree, a pine found only in the coldest climates. Bark-stripped, it suffers and dies standing: a brown beard-like fungal hair clings to its trunk and branches which turn smooth, grey and twisted. But then, above the tree-line, out on the icy crust of the fells, it was me who was struggling, extra ski-length only making turning difficult and dull edges making little impression.

We happened to be in Hetta on the weekend of the Festival of the Annunciation. Red-felted flocks of Lapps from neighbouring regions descend to enjoy this annual orgy of dancing, drinking and meeting old friends. Outside the church a troll-like Lapp did a great black spit into the snow. An old woman told me of a bear in a hole at Akaslompolo. Mangy splay-footed reindeer dragged skiers at full pelt around a track on the frozen lake. And Alan bought a racoon-fur hat thinking it might be wolf.

Leaving Alan, content with his new headgear, I hitched northwards up the 'arm' of Finland to reach the Arctic Highway in Norway. Waiting on this windswept route, I opened out the greaseproof paper containing my closely-packed reindeer-meat slices and tried hard to imagine how such scraggy creatures could be rendered so tasty. The meat is dried in huge lumps – hung out on rooftops around the chimney-stacks and protected from predators by a wire cage. Some houses had ground-level cages, the hanging meat a gruesome substitute for the expected Alsatian guard-dog or mynah bird.

Turning south-west through an area scarred by Nato war-games, I arrived in Narvik, where the Germans had suffered their first defeat of World War Two. In the oil town of Harstad I boarded the coastal 'steamer' heading for the Lofoten Islands, which form a jagged metatarsal-like cluster pointing down towards Bergen in the south. My felt-insulated Finnish army boots sank deep into the freshly fallen snow on the quay. I was now in Svolvaer, the main town of the Lofoten. Standing beside me, amidst a mixture of display stands, Turkish pictures, and cardboard boxes was Cüneyt Cizer, the world's northernmost street trader.

In the months around Easter, cod-fishing is the main activity on the Lofoten. Fish-drying stands, like estates of half-built A-frame houses, cover the available flat spaces between village, mountain and sea. The main fishing village is Hennigsvaer, where long jetties raised up on rickety wooden stilts flank a sheltered inlet. Breaking off from the close-in armada of little fishing smacks, single boats constantly arrive to deposit their catch. In front of low warehouses, men in oilskins quietly gralloch and decapitate the flabby cod, in preparation for drying.

Behind the village rise up some tempting mountains. Still frustrated by my stay in the Finnish hospital, and tired of tourist guides, neat maps and Scandinavian caution, I found myself exploring. A boulder-strewn slope led upwards, and crossing a snowfield I trudged up a steep gully to finally claw my way on to the mountain's Arctic cornice, a giant reminder of the ice-sculptures of the Lapp fells. At the lonely summit my only companion was an eerie marker post held firm by wire guy ropes, its almost annihilated red paint a testament to the severity of the Norwegian winter.

1000-year-old human remains in the desert near Nazca, Peru

Market day in Oravalo, Ecuador

(*left*) Alison's haircut (*q.v.*)
(*right*) Resting between mountains (*Alpine Cliffhanger*)

Festive occasion in Lappland

Hong Kong: an exotic mixture of East and West

NOTICE TO PASSENGERS

TO AVOID LONG WAITING OF PASSENGERS AT ROUTE 2 BUS TERMINUS AT MUI WO, AND THAT THEY MAY ARRIVE EARLIER AT PO LIN MONASTERY IN NGONG PING, OUR COMPANY PUT IN SERVICE BIGGER BUSES TO CARRY PASSENGERS FROM MUI WO TO SHUM WAT ROAD TURNING CIRCLE, AT WHICH STATION, THEY HAVE TO TAKE OUR SMALL BUSES GOING UP TO NGONG PING.

FARES FROM MUI WO TO SHUM WAT ROAD IS AT $3.50 PER ADULT PASSENGER IN WEEKDAYS AND AT $5.50 IN SUNDAYS AND PUBLIC HOLIDAYS. FROM SHUM WAT ROAD, PASSENGERS MAY GO TO NGONG PING ON FOOT WHICH WILL TAKE ABOUT 30 MINUTES WALKING, OR THEY MAY TAKE SMALL BUSES FROM SHUM WAT ROAD TURNING CIRCLE TO NGONG PING, AND THE FARES IS AT $1.70 PER ADULT PASSENGER IN WEEKDAYS AND AT $2.00 IN SUNDAYS AND PUBLIC HOLIDAYS. FROM NGONG PING, PASSENGERS CAN EITHER WALK DOWN OR TAKE SMALL BUSES TO THE TURNING CIRCLE WHERE THEY CAN TAKE BIGGER BUSES FOR THE RETURN TRIP TO MUI WO.

N.L.B.

(*left*) Senior citizen (*right*) Do not pass GO!

HONG KONG

Police shopping for fish in Tai O village, Lantau

That same day I left Svolvaer, the cold night air lit up by the Aurora Borealis, and I reflected on my island experiences before dozing off to the throb of the ship's engines. Two days later I was talking to a Norwegian sentry outside a remote army camp in the Skibotn valley, whilst trying to hitch back to Finland on the E78. The sentry's job was to blow up roads and bridges should there be a Soviet invasion. This seeming an unlikely event on April 4, 1984, I suggested he might be better employed helping me stop a vehicle. Fingering his machine-gun, he accompanied me out into the path of an oncoming truck. The manoeuvre worked, and I was soon back in Finland.

Trucks carry the heads and guts of Norwegian codfish to large mink farms further south in Finland. I hitched my second lift in such a truck, bound for Kokkola four hundred miles distant. En route the driver stopped off at a garage in Muonio, the home of the tourist officer, and there the ambulance which had taken me to hospital was itself being repaired. I drank coffee with its driver, nodding, 'Yes, I am the person you picked up at Keräs-Sieppi.' We smiled, I really had taken part in 'overrunlonged ski-tours', in the words of Juoko, the tourist officer. And his final words of wisdom: 'Try it, and you will find the real Naturre in Yourselff!'

ALISON'S HAIRCUT

Albir
Alicante■

Three weeks before the holiday Alison had her hair cut. A shaved back and sides and a 'flat top' of six inches or so of hair standing erect was the creation of David from the 'Nuthouze'. Although she was the only person she knew who bothered to ask, Alison asked her shell-shocked dad for permission to dye the top strip of hair blue.

The already-purchased blue dye was given to her boyfriend who does things without asking, or perhaps has much more understanding, modern and liberal parents. Surreptitious bleaching and colouring made a gradual change which fooled no-one, but Alison was happier.

We were going to Spain for the first time, but the morning of our departure differed little from every other holiday morning. Ron became tight-lipped but only his eyes betrayed his disbelief in the amount of luggage I planned to take. It was Alison's dress which Ron objected to, but a resigned sigh and a shake of the head was all he allowed himself. A brief memory of a little girl in a white dress and pretty sandals flashed before both our eyes as Alison breezed downstairs ready for the off, in her 10p jumble sale and ripped pumps.

Her appearance caused heads to turn, and actually stopped people in their tracks. Everywhere we went, eyes followed us. On our way to the airport little children tugged at their mothers' skirts and asked them in loud voices to 'Look at the lady's funny hair'. Throughout, Alison remained cool and talked just as loudly about such mundane plans as having her nose pierced or aired her views on the older generation's dull and unimaginative ways of dress and life.

The flight to Spain was uneventful. We arrived at Alicante after only an hour's delay. The reception party, however, was unexpected and a trifle disconcerting. Beyond the arrival lounge awaited a crowd of Spaniards holding large cards bearing the names of their expected visitors. To reach the hired car and eventually our apartment we had to run the gauntlet of an excitable, voluble crowd who let off a cheer and roared with laughter, quite spontaneously, at the sight of our daughter's crowning glory.

Our friend's apartment in Albir was everything we wanted. We had seen photographs, and they hadn't lied about the wonderful view from the patio. It was a short distance to the bars and restaurants and we were soon sitting uncomfortably with a bottle of red wine and a bowl of strawberries and cream, and once again trying to ignore the nudges, stares and comments.

Although she would not admit it, even Alison got fed up with the interest in her hair. She was stopped and asked to be photographed by French, German and Dutch citizens and she was just snapped without permission by unknown nationalities. She was commented upon, laughed at and stared at by the Spanish, and more than once she nearly caused an accident when motorists forgot their road sense at the sight of the girl in her third, fourth, fifth jumble sale dress with 'the hair'.

Disaster struck after a few days of sun, good food, and an occasional beer for Alison. She developed a 'Spanish tummy', accompanied by pains in the head, throat, legs and elsewhere, which brought her down. She could not raise the energy to use a can of hairspray to ensure her hair stood up correctly, and she took to her bed.

But Ron and I felt fine, and after making rather smug use of my well-stocked first-aid box and making sure that Alison was well dosed and comfortable, we went out.

It was pleasant to be able to move around incognito. No-one took any notice of us and we relaxed. As we had, up to now, felt it necessary to stare into the middle distance and pretend unconcern, we had actually missed out on the sights. Now we looked and listened for the holiday anecdote which we would collect, repeat and savour along with our photographs. One year in France we had met and made friends with a family whose young son rushed out to the sea each morning uttering in a controlled upper class accent, 'Oh decent fun'! in true Enid Blyton Famous Five fashion. Rarely do we enter the waves without these words on our lips.

On a very crowded Channel ferry, when the cafeteria had run out of food and the toilets were awash with an unspeakable mess, we once overheard two portly young men complete with deerstalker hats, binoculars and sweaters with the *Times'* motif, discussing the merits of sitting by the 'bulkhead' to watch the captain 'casting orf'.

In Spain we did not have long to wait. 'You don't know a good man when you see one. You need a good . . .' sounded promising but unfortunately I had positioned myself wrongly and the words had to be relayed to me. I could see the speaker but Ron fed the words to me whilst I gazed fixedly, but discreetly, at the couple at the next table.

A middle-aged man, heavily built, with a florid, perspiring face sat opposite a blonde, smooth woman wearing a full-length towelling kaftan. The next words, ' . . . an upper class scrubber', prompted Ron to fantasise and the man became a pimp or a white slaver; but the anguish on his face made me dismiss this completely and Ron's whispered commentary was translated into a scene from a Harold Robbins or Joan Collins novel. The female lead in the drama sat unconcernedly ploughing her way through a huge meal whilst the distraught male complained about the meals she had ruined for him, and his 'Sole Picasso' remained untouched.

'I can't eat because you annoy me,' he spat.

'You want it all . . .'

'I used to care a lot . . .'

'You do that to me after fifteen years . . .' The recriminations continued until I could hear them clearly and I was able to hear the one and only response. In a cool, detached voice the woman said distinctly, 'It was only a little sex talk.'

From the other side of the table came an incredulous expletive and he accused her of being 'a spoilt petulant child'. The evening wore on with accusation heaped upon accusation until at last there was nothing more to say. The four of us sat satiated with the raw emotion.

A few drinks later, he, sullen and broken, and she, hard and cold, left the table to reveal our heroine's crippled leg encased in a monstrous caliper, a leg iron which gave her a curiously heartbreaking gait which almost made one switch sympathies.

When Alison recovered, though still feeling a little weak, she wore a trendy black cap to cover her limp 'flat top'. She looked stunning in a black mini-skirt, a black teeshirt and the black cap, but she went unnoticed, which was actually a strange sensation and by now an unfamiliar experience. But as her recovery became complete, up came the spirits and up came the hair.

Our evenings once again became punctuated with comments and our table at the restaurant became a point of interest.

One evening we drove to a tiny town built on a hilltop. To get to the church at the very top we wound our way through what seemed like communal back yards. It was fascinating, both for Ron and me, but more so for the inhabitants. Old ladies dressed in black stopped chatting and crocheting. In fact the whole population ceased their ordinary lives and, with sharp intakes of breath, stared. Young children let their mouths drop and their ball and skipping games stopped in mid stream. Avoiding the amazed stares, I fixed my sights on the church and the overwhelming splendour of the surrounding view of almond groves. Winding our way up the steps, we were aware of footsteps and to our dismay we found a steady, clamorous procession of Spanish children, babies included, crawling unsteadily but eagerly, and their dogs of uncertain breeds, all following in our direction. One bold, handsome fourteen-year-old reached to the front of the queue, threw out a hand and touched the golden ridge carefully arranged on the top of Alison's head. He received a clout, delivered furiously across his own head for his cheek, and amid guffaws and hilarious shrieks we, like the children following the Pied Piper, proceeded in unruly order.

Descending was even more noisy as we collected a few children who seemed to have been missed out on the way up. Looking rather like an insulted Egyptian Queen, Alison haughtily climbed into the car ignoring her waving fans.

Ron and I needed a drink after the excitement. We found a restaurant which was Spanish in ethos and soon, soothed by a gin and tonic or two, we sat entranced by a beautiful, young, extremely slim girl singing Spanish love songs. The atmosphere was seductive, flowers trailed around bowers and arbors and the air was warm and sweetly scented. After the meal, discreet waiters brought brandy and the girl accompanied by an electric organ seemed to appreciate Ron moving tables until he was sitting close enough to 'hear the words'.

What do you do when your daughter, in horrified tones, begs you not to get up and dance as she will be 'shown up'?

What do you do when she becomes bored and fidgets distractedly and resorts to cutting remarks about her dad being too old to make eyes at the Spanish girl, implying that he was making a fool of himself?

Nothing actually, but just silently plan next year's holiday which does not include one member of our family.

ALPINE CLIFFHANGER

Austrian Alps

The thin, sun-bronzed fingers deliberately and surely looped and fastened the bright blue rope across my chest. I trembled with nervous excitement, afraid of the vast expanse of glacier stretching ahead, yet unable to admit my terror and ask to go back. My husband had told me it was a chance not to be missed. He was back at the Studl Hut (2,802 metres) with the rest of the group, waiting for their local guides to bring them up to the foot of the glacier which led to the highest Alpine hut in Austria before attempting the summit of the Grossglockner the following day.

We were on a walking holiday based at an Hotel in Kals, and for the past twelve days had slogged up through pine forests, plodded across snowfields, scrambled over scree slopes and clung to cables on rocky outcrops. My head for heights had not improved, but my blisters were healing and the exhilaration of my minor peaks such as the Böses Weibl, at 3,127 metres, had kept me going.

There were twelve in the group, ages ranging from twenty to forty-plus, all reasonably fit with the stronger lads helping the slightly slower oldies across snow gullies and the occasional cornice. Hugh, the little Scotsman, preferred to make his own descents in the snow unaided – on his behind, wearing waterproof trousers and controlling speed and direction with his ice-axe. He told us afterwards that his 'wee heart' missed a beat when he skimmed past a vast hole in a snow gully which had opened up to reveal the rushing river beneath. On some days when the temperature soared up in to the nineties Hugh would remove his walking breeches and don a pair of pale blue pyjama trousers. His fair skin prevented his wearing shorts like the rest of us, and he was quite unperturbed at the ribald remarks passed on the first occasion of his change of dress.

During our two weeks in Austria the weather varied from a snowstorm when we wore balaclavas, gloves and all the spare clothes we had carried in our rucksacks, to intense heat when the sweat made our sunglasses slip off our noses into the snow unless they were tied round the backs of our heads with a spare bootlace.

The time came at the beginning of the second week when we had to decide whether we wanted to go on the two-day trip to the top of the Grossglockner – at 3,798 metres the highest mountain in Austria. I had made up my mind days ago – not me! Nine of the group made the booking, including my more adventurous husband.

The group leader knew I was the most nervous member of the party – why ask *me* if I'd like to go up to the top hut and wait there for the rest of the group? Just the two of us could make it there before the rest of them met their guides at the lower hut. 'Chance of a lifetime,' my husband said. So here I was, perched like a paralised budgerigar on a slither of rock while the leader roped me up. The psychological security of being attached to the strong, slim figure in front of me worked wonders. I stomped across the glacier like Scott of the Antarctic. The sky was postcard blue with the Grossglockner a mere cardboard cut-out. After an hour-and-a-half we arrived at the ridge. I looked up – bloody hell! 'Only a few hundred feet of rock climb and we're there,' said my guide. We made it, of course, and I felt that pure, heady feeling of having pushed myself far beyond what I thought I could achieve; and from the platform of the Adlersruhe, at 3,454 metres, I looked *down* over the mountaintops of Austria.

I stayed out there on my pinnacle for three hours. The wind started to blow, but the sun shone down and the sky stayed blue. I watched as a tiny line of ants emerged from the far side of the glacier. The long, matchstick shadows enabled me to count a group of five, a gap, and then a group of six. How slowly they moved. It was not until they paused at the foot of the rocks that I was able to make out individuals. Later, one by one, attached to the Austrian guides and to each other they hauled themselves over the final rock on to the Eagle's Rest.

'Which way did you get here then Jean?' they asked. I didn't blame them for not believing I had made it the same way they did.

Young single women, take up mountain-climbing! The hut was crammed with suntanned, strong, confident, laughing mountaineers. We wolfed down steaming hot pea soup, fried eggs, spam and mashed potatoes, followed by cold tinned plums – at that height a feast indeed. By 9.30 everyone was ready for bed – two beds for all eleven of us. Six in the top bunk and five underneath. I slept very little, although the others must have done so as there were snores, heavy breathing and grunts throughout the night. It didn't matter; it was fun just being there. At 5.30am everyone was on the move; most had slept in their clothes anyway. The group were going to the summit while I awaited their return. The party leader and myself would then make the descent while the Austrian guides had breakfast before bringing the group down.

Coming down the rocks was even more frightening than going up. My personal guide was sure-footed, and laughed when I denied my ability to do it. 'Of course you can.' And of course I could, even though my legs trembled uncontrollably.

Only the glacier now.

'Mind the next bit – step over.'

'Step over what?' I thought. 'It looks the same to me.' And I was up to my armpits in the snow, one leg dangling in thin air and goodness knows where the other one was. 'I'm in a hole,' I yelled.

Again the laughter from my guide. 'Roll out and I'll pull.' I felt the tug of the rope on my chest and followed my instructions. I was beyond fear now. I'd fallen in a crevasse and there were no terrors left, just a strange elation. I could take it all in my stride. I was happy. Just the two of us, roped together in the middle of an enormous white snow bowl, the sky an unclouded blue.

My heart is still there, in that virgin white snow, the blue sky and my undying gratitude to Mary, the group leader, who taught me to conquer fear and have fun achieving what I thought was impossible.

LIZ VERCOE

MADE IN HONG KONG

The little Chinese boy wearily shrugged the five-foot snake into a more comfortable position around his shoulders. The snake readjusted its balance by adding another kink somewhere between its head and its middle and continued to stare into the warm Hong Kong night. It looked as if it were thinking of dinner, which struck European eyes as unfortunate since it was, in fact, an advertisement for the steaming pan of take-away snake soup just to its left.

Fortunately demand wasn't great. The local reptiles, much sought after for their winter blood-warming properties, had been given a stay of execution by the balmy October weather. Only a few elderly men, their faces tiger-lined and golden in the oil-lamp light, dallied to discuss the merits of the snake.

In fact more people were staring at us, staring at them, staring at . . . which was why I nearly tripped over the man making false teeth in the gutter. Somehow in between the shadowy shuffling of a million and more legs, in this street billed as Hong Kong's Poorman's Nightclub, he was managing to work gleaming steel wire and not-so-gleaming second-hand human teeth into dentures. But all you could see of him was the sheen on the back of his sinewy neck as he crouched over his work.

What I'd been elbowing my way towards in this thronging night market was a bird telling fortunes. This was equally popular with the local population, but one good thing about being averagely western height is that in this part of the world you can see over most people's heads . . .

The bird, a sort of sparrow with red trim, was selecting a card from a deck dealt on to the ground by its master. The reward, for the bird, was a beakful of seed; for the tensely crouching subject of the fortune, a nasal Cantonese prophecy. The seeker after good fortune began to look happier; the crowd more disappointed – the news must have been good.

Where now?

Palmists, herbalists and scribes clustered side by side along Temple

Street in a sepia-toned vision of an Eastern evening out. But suddenly I was brought up short by a bright red, ER-inscribed pillarbox indicating that the next collection was No 1 at 8.30am. It was like finding Dr Who's police box on Mars.

But even after only two jet-lagged days that's what I was learning to love about Hong Kong. Just as you're beginning to reel, saturated by the sights, smells and sounds, you're spun into the western familiar. And then you just start again. It's like enjoying the thrill of arriving in the East for the very first time, twenty times a day.

We'd already made that space/time journey that evening. Earlier we'd fled the more famous of Hong Kong's night markets. Spread out on the ground in the car park at the Macau Ferry terminal on Hong Kong island, it had brought back every childhood disappointment associated with 'Made In Hong Kong' labels – all those gaudy toys in too-bendy plastic and Christmas cracker puzzles with bits missing. I was finally driven away from the rows of cheap and cheerful by a flower-decked plastic toilet that squirted me in the eye when its seller lifted the lid.

It was ho-ho humour for happy tourists in an area of the colony where the department stores and glittering glass towers – even if they are scaffolded with bamboo – would make you feel at home whether you came from Manhattan, Melbourne or Manchester.

But when you want a little safe adventure the metro can whisk you 7,000 miles back into the Far East in just seven minutes. And even though the station you get off at is called Waterloo, incense burns at shop doorways to keep out evil spirits and offerings of rice, fruit and fragrant sandalwood are placed at street corners to help the souls of road-accident victims make the difficult path to heaven. Here the crowds are closer, friendlier, more at ease to stare back.

Temple Street gets its name from the shrines at its heart. The vast golden statue of Tin Hau, Queen of Heaven and Goddess of the Sea, sits cross-legged and serene. She presides over the bowing, bobbing, heads of supplicants who clutch their hands together and rattle boxes and offerings and fortune sticks as vigorously as WI charity collectors.

'Tin Hau is a very kind buddha,' a bowing matron volunteered. 'You can come to her with your problem.' She took a cool, slant-eyed look. 'But I don't think you have any problem.' And I suppose she was right, though I felt a sneaky disappointment that she wasn't having any problems getting her tongue round the word problem. 'I think tourists to *your* churches leave gifts for the poor,' she suggested. I was only too grateful to oblige and only regretted too late giving silent paper money instead of good, rattling, goddess-attracting coins. But I needn't have been fearful that my Western ways would be unfamiliar to Tin Hau. When I next came across one of her temples – on the edge of a white-sanded tropical cove – its entrance was guarded by the golden arches of a McDonald's.

Hong Kong is also home to the biggest Buddhist monastery in South East Asia. It crowns a high, wild, sunswept plateau on Lantau, the largest of the colony's 235 islands. And after even a few days rubbing shoulders with a six million population that's crammed into tower blocks at 78,000 people to the square mile – on open ground that's only six square yards per person – escaping to near-deserted Lantau is close to heaven whatever your beliefs.

That morning, at the end of a forty-minute, and 40p, ferry trip past serene convoys of pointed-peak islands we'd climbed aboard the unsprung, speedometer-less bus that had rattled us up the mountainside to the marble-and-gold shrines of Po Lin, the Precious Lotus. The bus was packed and completely orderly. Moon-faced Chinese women in baggy trousers and black flat sandals clutched at their basketloads of fruit on the bends and beamed bewilderedly at the uninterrupted sky. At the back of the bus, Madge and Jean from Stockport shrieked with laughter and confided they always left their men 'at 'ome once a year and 'ave a 'oot of a time'.

'I speak a bit of Cantonese, me,' Madge admitted coyly, all gums and teeth. 'I work with some Chinese. Ooh, I 'aven't 'alf given 'em a shock 'ere when I've 'aggled in Chinese!'

They grimaced at the vegetarian lunch being served by shaven-headed monks and nuns and agreed Hong Kong had something for everyone. They recommended I go and see the whales perform at Ocean Park; that was the best thing they'd seen. Then they took photos of each other among the lotus ponds and headed back. It was their last day, and that night they'd promised themselves a slap up meal at an Australian restaurant they'd found: 'They do really good pies'.

Hong Kong eats twenty-four hours a day: from street vendors selling baked free-range eggs to battery housed customers, at takeaways of every nationality and in Chinese restaurants where the round tabletops are bowled between heads-down eaters like some new circus act.

The street restaurants are the key to Temple Street's 'nightclub' fame. Under hissing gas lamps, boiling vats of water steam bamboo baskets of shellfish. And finned fish, still flapping when you order, arrives in moist, bite-sized morsels with mountains of white fluffy rice. The live entertainment is a caterwauling competition of Chinese street opera, each of two dueting girls and bamboo-playing musicians. More entertaining still are the faces of the virtually all-male audience in which you can read every twist of the Barbara Cartlandish plot – fear, fight, tears, flight, and finally love and cheers.

It would be easy to picture such wholehearted participation in the back of some unsophisticated beyond. And yet just behind their backs the market traders have set up altars to high-tech and the very latest, very smallest and very cheapest Far Eastern electronic wizardry. Even half-hearted haggling here brings prices tumbling to levels that would cause three-day queues at the summer sales.

And so at midnight, refreshed by an internal clock that insists it's mid-afternoon, we carry our stereo treasure trove back on the metro to Tsim Sha Tsui and a hotel that boasts it's Western the world over. Anywhere else in the world I would have blushed a bit to admit staying there, but in Hong Kong it's exactly right. East and West, ying and yang, tomorrow Ocean Park, the day after that . . . China. That's what it's all about.

AMY LAUREL

TICKET TO RIDE

Seattle, Washington. An August afternoon. If you can't afford to fly you go by bus, telling yourself it's an experience, the stuff of life. That in bus stations at 3am, that's when you see the real America. My friends look tearful as they wave me off; I smile, the embarrassed, concealed smile of one who expects to enjoy herself. I'm going somewhere, after all.

I have expended enormous energy on looking mean and unwelcoming so that no-one will sit next to me. Now I am faintly disconcerted by my success. The bus is full of conversation. Behind me sits a black woman in a white hat labelled 'spring meadows', which looks like something you might put over a cake to keep off the flies. Across from me are two elderly white men to whom I take an instant dislike. Nastier has beer-gut, greased blond hair, protuberant lower lip. The other is your all-American pensioner, baseball-capped and polyester-clothed, and wearing that sprightly smile that tells you he knows how lucky he is to be here, in this best of all possible worlds.

We are driving between lakes and sharp mountains. Everywhere the firs are being felled, every hillside half-logged, giving the ugly naked look of partially shaved skin. Slowly the landscape becomes strange lumpy hills covered with yellow grass. Wooded once, perhaps; in the distance the rising ground has the look of creased, corpulent flesh.

Ellensberg, Washington. The first billboards, hunky men crouched in the left-hand corner, eyes focused on the southern distance. Already my legs do not feel part of me: I jog round the filling station, remembering those stories of thrombosis brought on by long plane journeys.

More doughy hills and a grey sky, spruce-blue bushes. There are now only two of us – 'spring meadow' and I – who have retained our splendid isolation of seating. I decide to believe that she, too, is choosing the position of bus outcast.

George, Washington, early evening. Running back down the road (still thinking the legs might be saved) I realise that all the roads look the same in this high, featureless place; a terrible fear strikes at the thought I might be stranded here. The bus has become my only point of connection with the world. Meanwhile, lingering near the safety of its door, a blonde woman in blue does yoga, ogled by the rest. I buy my first postcard, of the local dam, a vast expanse of concrete and still water. In the diner, truck drivers talk about hitting something repeatedly in a parking lot: vehicles or people, who can say?

The endless evening of late summer stretches on into a smoothed-out landscape of scrub-layered sand, flat and an eerie yellow under a rain sky. A sign on the back of a truck says, 'If Dolly were a trucker, she'd be flat-busted'. The night crawls by. Others sleep, while in the seat in front of me a Seventh Day Adventist tells the story of his conversion. Later he reads aloud from a volume of fundamentalist moral tales. The middle-aged woman to whom he speaks says he gives her new hope for the youth of today.

Butte, Montana, 6am. Thick sweet cocoa and pallid coffee. Women in hairnets cooking up a storm, singsonging out hot cakes, ham and cheese. I am instantly in love, want to stay here and eat breakfasts all day in this warm place, stretch out on the orange plastic banquettes to sleep. Outside, the dawn is clear and cold. The Seventh Day Adventist lurks by the bus door to capture a new audience. The all-American pensioner has become demanding and querulous, an aged child who feels himself every woman's responsibility. Ceaselessly, indeed, women rise to plump his cushion and read his timetable reassuringly.

Through the last of the Rockies, with the light an early morning slant. From a distance the mountains are like a dragon's tail, sharply ridged. Humped and shadowed foothills acquire an extreme, painful clarity.

Whitewall, Montana. A woman gets off in this silent, god-forsaken town: heat, emptiness, men in plaid shirts and ten-gallon hats. I can imagine no life worth the living in this place. It is a still dead morning hour.

Columbus, Montana. Now the bus is packed tight, the first blast of real depression hits. We have acquired a relief bus that has gone ahead – it will get there (wherever that is) soon, and suddenly this matters extremely. Resentment is palpable all around me. I grind my teeth quietly.

Montana, still. Noon. We are into the badlands, have been travelling into them for hours; the aridity begins to penetrate. All roads between these stark yellow cliffs of sand go to places called Preservation Creek. A desolation greater than the ocean.

Miles City, Montana. The solid, extraordinary heat of it. Fly-screens on the windows, the natives all with dead-white faces under huge hats. The shops full of old saddles and battered bison horns. I walk with effort through the drained humid silence of the streets. Life flickers briefly in the park, a mirage of green, where a great herd of starlings shriek under the sprinklers.

Dickenson, North Dakota, evening. The hot dark. I feel likely to perish from an overdose of calorie-free drinks and from the message on the can that explains in careful detail the incidence of cancer among rats fed a saccharin diet. The freedom to knowingly sweeten yourself to death seems at the moment appropriately American. The café where we stop has a bowling alley in the back, loud with men in patterned shirts. I stare at them through a vast plate-glass window, as at the ritual antics of another species.

Minnesota passed in a sleep haze, just when I thought I would be staying awake for ever . . . but now in Wisconsin it has departed, leaving me to stare out indefinitely at a charmless, night-wrapped landscape. I pin down another necessary condition of bus travel, along with the person who talks loudly and tirelessly through the night: the alien feel of a stranger's warm arse pressing into your thigh as he snuggles down to the sleep you yourself are unable to achieve.

Illinois. Dawn breaks on definitive corn belt. The boredom of the Mid-West grips me, too. Like a faintly industrialised Norfolk, but without churches or sea coast or the sound of waders. And yet these views – of a red wooden farmhouse and its silo across a solid field of maize, brooding – are somehow emblematic, moving. The sky is still high and clear, and the width of the horizon immense.

We have been waiting so long for Chicago; here at last is to be my bus station experience. We drive into an underground cavern – a timeless, brightly-lit, echoing place of neither day nor night. I am tense with expectation. But we have time only to leave our bus and catch someone else's, half-empty and unfamiliar. The new driver repeats soothing words into his microphone while we worry at him, frayed by this sudden removal from our accustomed place of safety. We crowd feverishly at the window, unable to believe that anyone has remembered our luggage.

We are far enough east now for British tourists. Not having seen one in a while I have forgotten that they exist, and that I am one too. I try not to feel associated with the two across the aisle who take pictures through the window and wear Mickey Mouse teeshirts. Instead I stare intently at the man in front of me who is balding under his crewcut. The exposed flesh is lined and grey, faintly crumpled. Not like a head at all; more like a dirty neck, perhaps, or a disused thigh.

Buffalo, New York. I eat yet another breakfast. The same menu spreads from state to state as if a whole nation believes you can always start the day over again. Have another coffee, never say die.

The pace of travel seems to have increased radically – rest stops curtailed, always late, in perpetual fear that we will take off in the wrong direction, that we have lost something . . . is this the east taking over, this new frenzy? I remember the bus picking its way leisurely across the western plain, imperceptibly for nothing and no-one.

Syracuse, New York, afternoon. We have acquired a ninety-eight-year-old man – a frail, other-worldly person in the white cotton suit of an Edwardian summer. He stays on the bus, sleeping, when we get off; I am afraid that he may die while we drink saccharin in some plastic diner.

New York City. Another humid, subterranean place. When I emerge from the toilets free of layers of grime-laden clothing, I notice that I am still clutching my timetable as if it will tell me what to do next. It takes a moment to realise that my bus has gone, that I am alone again. I seem to want to linger, to wallow a little in what has after all been an enveloping experience. But there is no escape from having arrived. I force myself to turn away toward the subway.

D. A. CALLARD

THE DRUMS OF NEFTA

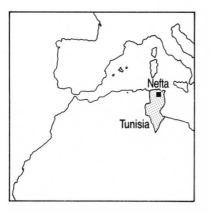

It is late evening and Marianne, Walter and I have just finished a large *couscous* washed down by several bottles of heady local wine. My companions start talking in Arabic again and I have the depressing sense of being a hick tourist fallen among real travellers. Wine-numbed and bloated, I lapse into silent recapitulation of what has brought us here.

I met Marianne on Jerba, an island claiming mythic status as the place where the Sirens held Ulysses. I too was becalmed, though the Sirens were inaudible. I would take bus trips from the island to towns in southern Tunisia but they never lasted longer than a day. Their chaos and squalor did not compare well with the pristine beauty of Jerba and, as a lone male out of season, I was prey to a horde of street hustlers. On Jerba I had made it clear that I was not in the market for anything and they left me alone.

Returning on the bus from Medenine I noticed a solitary blonde whom I assumed was a stray package tourist from one of the hotels on the west of the island. I asked if she was lost. She was not. She had just arrived and was looking for a cheap hotel. I suggested mine which was cheap, central and practically empty. So our friendship began, and the Siren spell was broken.

Her story is barely credible. She is Dutch, in her late twenties, and she has been in North Africa for one-and-a-half years. During this time her sole contact with a European has been a fortnight with a German woman in Algeria. She has almost always travelled alone and has lived with very poor and very rich families, participating in the most private aspects of Arab family life. At times she has dressed as an Arab woman, worn the *ha'ik,* looked at the ground as she walked, among women only. At other times she cut her hair short, wore a *djellaba* and travelled as a man. In relatively Europeanised Tunisia she has shed these disguises. She is fluent in the Moroccan dialect of Arabic, to the amazement and amusement of the Tunisians.

She has penetrated other exclusive worlds before this. In spite of the slimmest Jewish credentials, a surname inherited from a non-practising father, she spent six months at a *yeshiva* in the ultra-orthodox Mea Shearim quarter of Jerusalem. By virtue of her fluent Hebrew she once led prayers at a Passover feast of wealthy Moroccan Jews – the only one present who could read them in the absence of a rabbi. She had no ideas of conversion since she previously spent six months in an ecumenical Christian community in the South of France. Why had she done these things?

'How else do you find out?'

I have no answer to that.

A trail through several Saharan oases brought us to Nefta, close to the Algerian border. If Jerba was picturesque, Nefta is magical and I regret that I must fly home in a week. Our hotel in the medina is run by an amiable eccentric whose vagueness probably results from constant imbibing of palm wine and smoking *harar,* a local herb similar in effect to mild hash. Last night he claimed that President Bourguiba used his hotel before he came to power and that Brigitte Bardot, accompanied by a canine entourage, stayed there in the early Seventies. He produced newspaper cuttings proving that BB came to Nefta but I am not convinced that she stayed in the Hotel de la Liberté, whose plumbing leaves everything to be desired.

But little would be surprising in Nefta. It is on the edge of the Chott el-Jerid, a saline depression in the Sahara once part of the Mediterranean. From late morning onward the combination of sunlight, heat and the reflective properties of its salt surface throws up a host of mirages. Seen from the hills above the town the Chott becomes not an arid wasteland but a phantom sea, piercingly blue.

Dominating Nefta is another extraordinary feature, so incongruous that at first sight it might well be a mirage. It is the Sahara Palace Hotel, the most luxurious in Tunisia, a cavernous, currently near-deserted edifice with all the charm and intimacy of an international airport lounge. Below it is the old palmerie, the Corbeille, nourished by channels of water running from a hot spring poetically named The Source. In the heart of the palms is a pool credited with miraculous curative powers where the Neftis come to bathe: women in the morning, men in the afternoon. Looking toward the town from here, the sky is dominated by the seat of a religious brotherhood from whose minaret a human muezzin, instead of the usual loudspeaker, calls the faithful to prayer. Nefta has more than sixty places of worship and is a centre of Sufism, but there is no fanatical edge to its people. Once, being led by a boy through the maze of the medina, Marianne asked our guide if the people were religious. He laughed loudly. 'No, we are not religious. Nefta is a town of drunks and revolutionaries.' I was heartened by this news though Marianne, who has experienced the unpredictable effects of alcohol on the North African male to her cost, was less amused.

We both met Walter a few days ago. He is a German working at a doctorate on the post-colonial development of the region. He has lived here for eight months and knows more about the town than the Neftis, who are infuriatingly vague when it comes to giving directions. He knows nothing of Brigitte Bardot's visit but confirms that President Bourguiba used to stay at our hotel, though he now spends two months every year at the Sahara Palace.

Mercifully Walter and Marianne soon exhaust their mutual stock of Arabic and, in the silence that follows, we all become aware of a faint constant drumbeat in the medina. Walter says that it is probably a wedding but suggests that we investigate. We leave, and Marianne stays behind picking at a fruit salad.

The drums lead us through the warren of narrow alleys to a courtyard whose entrance is blocked by a knot of people. Walter sees a friend among them and asks if this is a private wedding party. He is told that it is a ceremony connected with Sidi Bou Ali, a long dead Sufi mystic whose precepts many Neftis follow. The friend is an invited guest and asks us to join him.

The courtyard is illuminated by a single light and against the far wall five drummers keep a constant rhythm, breaking into occasional chanting. Beside them a group of older men sit impassively, eyes closed, listening intently to the music. To the fore of the courtyard about twenty male, mostly young, dancers shake their bodies rhythmically but independently as a man carrying a pot of burning incense weaves among them. A larger group of people stand on the outskirts surveying the spectacle and we join them. In two rooms off the courtyard are women, children and a few greybeard patriarchs.

Walter's young black friend serves us tea. Drinking it, I wonder what to do about Marianne since this is an all-male affair and I am reluctant to leave. Walter solves the problem by volunteering to report back to her and I am left alone, highly conspicuous but undisturbed and ignored by the crowd.

There is a sudden scuffle as one of the dancers collapses, delirious on to the stone floor. Two spectators jump in, seize his trembling body and carry it away from the dancers. I watch as the convulsions subside, the delirium leaves his eyes and he returns, slightly dazed, to normality. Then it happens to another dancer and, as I am watching the same pattern of recovery, the man next to me throws his arms into the air, totters forward and begins to experience apparently involuntary spasms. Two other watchers take hold of him, lift him up to remove his shoes and thrust him into the dance.

The drums and the chant continue. Others join the dance in the same way and others collapse. To dance, it seems, is not by choice: you dance when the drums call you and you stop when whatever moves you to dance ceases. For a supposedly religious ceremony there is a very secular feel about the whole affair. The spectators smoke and laugh among themselves: near the doorway a youth records the drumming on a cassette recorder emblazoned with a Rolling Stones decal. Many of the men are black or half-caste descendants of freed Saharan slaves and I feel that what I am watching is not Islamic at root but a practice brought by their ancestors and grafted on to the religion.

From the corner of my eye I see Walter return and realise with a start that the person accompanying him enswathed in a black *bournous* is Marianne. Fortunately all eyes are elsewhere and no-one seems to notice. However, Walter's friend is not fooled and, drawing a seat and offering tea, whispers pointedly, *'Bonjour Mademoiselle'*. He seems very amused by the subterfuge.

The drumming and dancing continue for another hour, reaching no climax and no greater or lesser degree of intensity. Suddenly it stops and, it seems within seconds, drummers, dancers and audience disperse. As we leave someone tells Walter that there is a later, private part to the ceremony.

Back at the hotel we hear the drums begin again and continue long into the night, past the time when exhaustion overcomes the excitement which keeps us from sleep for many hours.

MODERN HISTORY

Mohan Lal was waiting for us when we came out to breakfast on 31 October. We decided to hire him for the day, and negotiated a price. Before we set out, he showed us his letters of recommendation from delighted tourists. But with Mohan Lal this went a bit further. We were to ride in a rickshaw which was itself a gift from a delighted tourist. The name and occupation of the donor were painted on the back: Professor x, Institute of Theoretical Physics, Stuttgart.

He dropped us in a short street which led to the entrance to the Taj. We bought our tickets and went through into the grounds, sitting down just inside to admire. The building was so perfect that it became fantastic, and we imagined a huge finger coming from the sky and pressing on the dome. The minarets would start to revolve, and organ music would strike up ('Oh, kiss me my sweet, it's the loveliest night of the year'). We explored, we gazed a bit more, and I discovered the pleasures of walking barefoot on marble. The world's greatest monument to the exploitation of women had its appeal, I had to admit.

On the way back to Mohan Lal, we stopped for soft drinks. The pips of a time-check echoed across the street. 'Funny,' I said, 'that's the first time I've heard the pips this trip.' A boy rushed up with a transistor radio. '. . . attempt on the Prime Minister's life. Leaders of all opposition parties have condemned the act. The President is flying home from his visit to the Gulf . . .' and on, with statements from every leading politician but no hard information till right at the end. 'A bulletin on the Prime Minister's condition is expected shortly.'

There were seven of us round the radio, English, Hindu and Sikh. One of the Hindus asked, smiling, 'Prime Minister gone out?'

'Not yet, I don't think,' said Ruth. We all laughed.

We walked back to the rickshaw, saying 'well' to one another, not knowing what else to say.

We spent the middle of the day at the red fort, returning in the late afternoon to catch sunset at the Taj. We arrived again at the street where we had heard the news of the assassination attempt. Men were pulling down the shutters of the gift shops. It was five o'clock.

At the Taj, Indian families were grouping themselves for the professional photographers who swarmed over the central platform.
Tourists of all kinds wandered by. A plaque beside the empty reflecting pool and its silent fountains explained that the water system which
filled it had become 'obsolete' in the nineteenth century. The sun set'
behind us, reflecting gold on the building. The Taj turned silver, and
then a late pink. The light went. It was getting cold. The dogs were
appearing.

Back at the Agra Hotel we ordered coffee to warm up and started a
game of Scrabble. Some Indian guests arrived and sat under the
portico. The manager joined them. 'Mrs Gandhi died today.' We
froze.

'She's actually dead,' said Ruth. 'There'll be riots everywhere.'

November 1. We sat down to breakfast in the garden, and listened to
the World Service news. There was mention of trouble in 'some
areas'. The next programme started – an analysis of political and social
life in Cedar Rapids, Iowa. As we heard a description of a day in the life
of the mayor, a Sikh in a green turban wandered out into the garden,
brushing his teeth.

The car which we had ordered to take us to the station never appeared, and we travelled instead in a dilapidated tonga. We arrived at
9.30, went through the usual contortions to buy a ticket, and were told
to expect a train at 10.30. We sat down to read. Ruth constantly complained about the fidgeting child next to her. Ten-thirty came but the
train did not. We wandered up and down to the inadequate refresh-
ment kiosk, drinking soda and eating buns. Up the track came an engine pushing a blazing box-car. It seemed odd, but not remarkable. I
looked at our fellow passengers. There were two men in identical
fawn clothes. One was short-haired, dark and fat. The other was a
Sikh, very small and slim. They looked like a comic turn. There was a
tall Englishman, dressed in white, with silver and turquoise earrings
and a beard down to his waist. There was a young Sikh in a red turban,
wearing a blue quilted jacket despite the heat.

At one there was an announcement. The train from Bangalore
would soon arrive. We leapt into a carriage at the end of the train. We
were followed by a family – mother, father and daughter. The
mother, large and jewelled and forceful, was determined to let us
know she spoke English. 'So this is a second class carriage. It is not
bad.' They ate an elaborate snack. 'You might as well get as much
pleasure as possible out of every situation,' she said, packing the dishes
away.

Ruth and I played a spiritless game of Scrabble. We dozed. When we
woke, the light was low and yellow. We passed a sign saying 'District
of Delhi'. Ruth was by the window. She turned to me as the train

slowed, her hand over her mouth and her eyes wide. 'There's a dead body out there.'

We are on a train, I thought. This is what they did in 1947. They stopped trains.

'A body? What do you think's happening?'

'I don't know,' she said. 'It's just someone's body.'

Through the window I could see a group of men walking away. One was carrying a crash helmet. They cast long shadows. They started to run. The train moved forward a few yards and stopped.

'What the hell's happening?' asked Ruth.

I knew what was happening, and my voice expressed the knowledge. 'Shut the windows!' I shouted.

On the other side of the train, the mother protested. 'They will think we have something to hide.'

'But you have already got your windows down,' we shouted back, as we pulled at ours.

Young men walked through the train, looking under seats, looking hard at faces.

'They are looking for someone who is hiding,' said the mother.

'Who?'

She leant towards us and whispered, in dramatic tones. 'A Sikh.'

A large group of men passed through the carriage. They were carrying bamboo poles. They were intent on murder. The mother told her daughter to get on a top bunk. I said to Ruth that we should do the same. I did. She did not. She sat with the mother on the station side of the train. She took her earrings off.

'What the hell's happening?'

I had read about 1947. Now the same thing was happening only yards away. More groups of young men pushed through the train. Just out of sight, someone started to shout. The mother shushed them.

Scuffling outside. Another train passed, going the other way. The mother said something to Ruth, which the daughter repeated to me. 'You know the young man on the platform in the red turban and the blue jacket? They are burning him now.' 'But why?' 'Because he is a Sikh, and they have killed Mrs Gandhi.'

I wanted to express my fear and my horror. I wanted to drum my heels and wail and be comforted. But how could I seek comfort? I was not central to this drama. I lay peripheral, uncomforted, afraid. Time passed.

'Here are the police.'

'A bit late,' said Ruth.

There was running and shouting outside, then a long wait in silence. There was nothing more to comment on, and no comment to be made.

The train started to move. Everyone was climbing on to the top bunks. 'What's happening?' I asked Ruth as she joined me.

'The train which was coming the other way had all its windows broken.'

'Protect your face,' cried the mother to the daughter.

From where I lay I could see the repeated pattern of the sleepers slowly passing beneath the train. Again and again we slowed, almost stopped. We drew into the suburban station where the train terminated.

We were advised to catch the local into New Delhi. As we tried to calm ourselves with sweet coffee, a Swiss traveller appeared. 'There are a group of us just down the platform, come and join us.' Twenty tourists of all kinds had huddled together. Among them was the young man I had seen earlier. 'Look,' said Ruth, 'his beard's gone.'

A few minutes later we were in Delhi. We crossed the footbridge and went out into a silent forecourt. To our left were rows of deserted taxis. Straight ahead, the motto of the Indian Railways was written, seven feet high, in English, on the wall. PUNCTUALITY, SAFETY, SECURITY.

Poland: Cloth Hall, Krakow – the city has a more Central European atmosphere
than the grey towns of the North

Polish peasants selling smoked goats' milk cheese

R. H. SOPER

A Glimpse Behind the Curtain

At 4.30 in the cool greyness of the in-between time before sunrise Tom waved from the window of the Chopin Express to the armed Czech border guards who stood along each side of the track every few yards for the last half-mile before the Austrian border. Most of the guards looked fixedly at the train, betraying no emotion, but one young soldier grinned and waved back. I hope he didn't get into trouble.

At the last stop before the border we heard footsteps along the carriage roof – border guards checking. A soldier opened our door and stood wordless, looking round at our sleepy faces and our luggage. He seemed to be tethered by the wrist to a thin leather thong which disappeared under our seats. Then the little grey terrier emerged, attached to his very long lead – just checking. He was our fourteenth visitor since we had left the Polish mining town of Katowice the previous evening. We had had money checks, passport checks and only one little problem with a lady passport checker. This formidable official with her face of carved slate could not seem to work out why five of us had only three passports. When she was finally satisfied she hardened her features into steel, shot a piercing glance at each of us in turn and left – just checking.

It was two weeks since we had left Harwich for Esbjerg to start a three-week summer holiday incorporating a visit to friends in Poznan. Sue and I had visited Poland the previous year for the first time and now we thought that Rebecca (15), Lucy (13) and Tom (10) should have the experience as well. Our plan was to go by boat and train to Poland via Denmark and Sweden. Then return through Czechoslovakia and Austria, spend a week by Lake Garda and fly home from Milan.

With our ten large suitcases we arrived at our Copenhagen hotel. It was the children's room that overlooked a street full of sex shops.

(*Opposite*) Cobweb Cave on the main river passage Guning Mulu National Park, Sarawak

Thank goodness there was the unsophisticated, noisy, glorious fun-fare of the Tivoli Gardens to provide a diversion. No visit to Copenhagen would be complete without beating the tourist track to the Little Mermaid. Isn't it strange how one can build up an illusion about famous sights that one has never seen? I thought she was way out in the middle of a large harbour, quietly basking on a remote rock. No, she is actually close to the water's edge. Scramble over a few rocks and you can stroke the scales on her tail. I suppose it is not surprising that she has been violated. Some years ago she lost her head. It has been replaced, of course, but there is still a reward on offer for her original one. What hadn't been replaced was her arm. It had been lopped off the night before our visit by some Copenhagen students.

A stay of only a day in Stockholm left us with the feeling that it is a stone-grey, cool, clean, efficient city with little of the colour of Copenhagen. The Swedish railways too are efficient; that is until you want to catch a boat to Poland. The railway at the Port of Nynäshamn stops about a mile short of the quay and there are no luggage trolleys or direction signs; but there is a large ship in the distance and so we fol-low the general flow of humanity, all of them carrying, pulling and dropping their baggage. Everyone has parcels or bulging cardboard boxes. Of course, they are all Poles returning home with their shopping. We didn't realise it at the time but the Iron Curtain begins at the ship and we are all caught up in its magnetic field. We trudge into the departure hall with our baggage and there encounter the hallmark of the eastern bloc, our first long queue.

Everybody is being carefully checked before being afforded the privilege of boarding the Polish Baltic Ferry *Rogalin*. Supposing the boat goes before we get to the head of the queue? We could be here in this soulless hall for another week. The time for the ferry's departure comes . . . and goes, and still we queue. We are not the last and even-tually make our way to the gangway, our cases feeling heavier with every step. The plump old lady ahead of us has no fewer than six large cardboard boxes tied with string. She has been moving them along in stages, two at a time, then trotting heavily back for another pair. From her little depot of cartons at the foot of the steep gangway she clambers up to the ship with the first pair, but there is not enough room for two cartons plus the rotund lady and one carton bursts open, scattering toilet rolls down the steps towards us. We all help her to repack them, wondering why she went to such lengths for loo rolls. We hadn't been in Poland long before we discovered the answer. Lavatory paper is at a premium and shops rumoured to be having a consignment develop queues of hundreds. The ration is five rolls. In the streets of Poznan we saw a really happy man. He had a string of rolls on a loop of cord round his shoulder. We counted fifteen so he must have been to the start of the queue three times.

Lavatories in Poland, like many on the Continent, are guarded by a lady with an apron. She has the privilege (Party members only) of dispensing, for a few zlotys, the paper. However, Polish loo rolls have no perforations and it is a matter of luck whether you get enough for your needs.

From the port of Gdansk we took the train to Poznan. Polish railways resound to the nostalgic noise of steam engines and Tom was agog. So much so that he got an eye full of smuts. The lady sharing our compartment saw the problem and produced some eye ointment from her handbag. Before she got round to administering it she pointed excitedly to a dull block of flats we were passing. 'Lech Walesa live there.' Two fellow travellers in the carriage nodded approvingly and one said, 'He is a good man for us.' None of the passengers knew each other and they certainly did not know us. It was heartening to hear the Solidarity leader praised openly. The middle-aged man went on to tell us in faltering English that at least ninety per cent of people in Poland wanted a change in the regime.

Krakow (pronounced Crack-oof), Poland's second city, is in the south near Czechoslovakia. Onion-shaped domes on churches and pavement sellers of carved wood and peasant dolls give it a much more central European atmosphere than the grey towns of the north. We arrived on the overnight train from Poznan now carrying only seven suitcases (the coffee, chocolate, soap, clothing etc having been distributed to our friends in Poznan) and we wanted to deposit them at the Left Luggage Office. Despite there being only twelve travellers in front of us it was forty minutes before we reached the head of the queue. Each case needed a label handwritten in blunt pencil and pasted from a grimy pot with a tousled brush. Hence the queue. The leaders of another queue outside a shop sat on folding stools and had blankets and flasks. The shop was expecting a delivery of wallpaper on Wednesday; it was Monday. In the centre of Krakow beside the large covered craft market in the main square a vigorous little gypsy band added to the atmosphere. The leader was a deformed, blind, child-sized Romany. He held his violin like a cello and his colourful fiddling was far more animated than he could ever have been and his cap was overflowing with zlotys. A child thrust a piece of neatly-written script at us. It said 'I am a poor boy with six brothers and sisters, give me fifty zlotys.' Rebecca was moved by this little waif and produced some coins. I watched him hurry away across the square to a cheese seller sitting by a fountain. He gave her the money, as did several other gypsy children, in a steady stream.

At Katowice we boarded the Warsaw/Vienna Chopin Express to carry us back into the West. As we exchanged farewells with our friends there was a sudden commotion in the next compartment. A French woman who had just boarded the train had mislaid her passport. We all joined in the search, torches were shone on to the track, seats were pulled out, and somebody searched the platform. How could she get through to Vienna without a passport? Weeping, she heaved her cases out of the train as it began to move off on its journey to the West.

As the train gathered speed on entering Austria the watchtowers above the Iron Curtain barbed-wire barricades could be seen stretching away into the distance beside the Dyje River. This awesome reminder of the world's great division was soon submerged by the bustling colour of Vienna and the warm clear waters of Lake Garda.

R. G. WILLIS

THE CAVES AT MULU

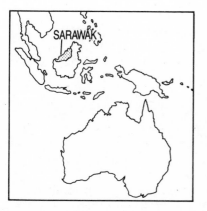

The dawn chill creeps through my sleeping bag, nudging me to consciousness. Stretching, I strike the poles from which my hammock hangs and feel the blow transmitted through the wooden structure of our camp, disturbing the others. Lagang, the eldest of our labourers, is already up; squatting by the fire he blows gently into yesterday's embers until flames begin to heat the kettle and the pot of breakfast rice.

Sandflies cluster on the outside of my mosquito net and I curse inwardly, always astounded that a tiny insect can cause such vast discomfort with its bite. I huddle into the sleeping-bag, postponing their inevitable success, and scratch the evidence of yesterday's insect feasts.

This is Mulu. To be exact, it's a sub-camp of the MAS Expedition to the World's Largest Caves ('Sarawak '84' for short) on the bank of the Melinau-Paku river in the Gunung Mulu National Park, Sarawak, Borneo. Since 1978 this place has become a legend among cavers throughout the world, a closed speleological utopia from which the public has, so far, been excluded. In 1978 a huge scientific expedition, organised by the Royal Geographical Society, had settled in this park, working for over a year with the Sarawak Forestry and National Parks Departments to produce a comprehensive management plan. That team had contained, for a brief while, a group of six British cavers. In only a few weeks they explored and mapped over thirty miles of the largest caves ever discovered. Two subsequent years of planning brought a larger group back to Mulu in 1980, and together with the local people we found a further thirty miles of caves. In one of these we had discovered a single chamber large enough to accommodate Wembley Stadium twice. Now, in the spring of England's 1984, we are back again; a smaller group this time and for a more limited period but working closely, as always, with the local people.

Heavy drips fall on to the camp-sheet overhead, disturbing the pattern of huge dead leaves which have fallen and settled in the week since we made this camp. There are no walls to this 'tent', only a roof; the rain here falls vertically. Through the veil of the netting I can see dimly through trees to the base of the slope up Gunung Api. This 3,000ft limestone mountain is the object of our attentions; its interior is honeycombed with huge passages, a three-dimensional maze of tubes and trenches, chambers and ramps, fast clear rivers and treacherous, muddy boulders. Two million years of the heaviest rainfall on earth have conspired with the thick forest above to produce the faintly acid water which, even now, remorselessly eats out the rock.

Already we have completed one of our objectives. On this expedition we intended to produce a good photographic record of Sarawak Chamber, the largest piece of nothing in the world, which had been found at the end of the last trip. Jerry, our photographer, had amassed a huge number of bulky, fragile and expensive flashbulbs, each the size of a normal lightbulb. He and a team of dedicated friends had assembled numerous 'slaves', compact photo-electric cells which would trigger one flash gun from the light of another at a distance of up to half a mile. All these had been transported with care from England, packed delicately into heavy-duty cardboard boxes and carried to our camp. We had unpacked them, stuffed them into rucksacks, towed them in a wet rubber dinghy up an underground river, hauled them up waterfalls and over boulders and finally dumped them unceremoniously at our campsite, deep in the cave, still hoping that they would work. They did. In a three-day epic we had photographed the chamber from every possible angle. The flashlights from six pairs of cavers faintly illuminated the arch of the cave and the house-sized boulders over which we had had to manoeuvre. Occasional rumblings proved that the boulder slopes were still unstable, and we would wait for the distant curse which told us that our colleagues were OK. Directed by walkie-talkies we spent hours arranging strings of flashes, firing them, waiting while the Polaroid print was checked, moving to a new position and repeating the process. At the end of the day we trudged back to the campsite, a broad ledge of boulders levelled with the efforts of a lump hammer and smoothed with hand-gathered gravels. Water was collected as drips falling from an unseen roof far above, then boiled into gallons of tea, made up into milk for muesli, stirred as porridge or left for hours to soak the dehydrated meals into a digestible form. A waterfall was a shower. Crevices between boulders were toilets. Cave crickets, up to a foot long from feeler tip to tail, watched impudently from the rocks, waiting for the opportunity to sneak up and eat through cardboard and plastic wrapping into our food. Red pinprick glows in the beam of a light showed up the eyes of spiders waiting to eat into the crickets. Overhead, the swish of wings and a gentle stream of barely audible clicks was a constant reminder of the passage of the thousands of swiftlets which flew in and out of the cave, from their nests deep in the pitch darkness underground to the endless supply of insect food in the forest outside. Their droppings rained thinly down, a dry brown inconvenience to us but food for our thousands of unseen insect neighbours.

Out here, in the cocoon of my mosquito net, the memory of that underground camp seems almost attractive. In Mulu, unlike most caving areas of the world, the underground camps are usually far more pleasant than those above ground. In the cave you can often stay dry; out here on the surface it is almost an impossibility. The rain gets everywhere, slowly seeping through the seams of the camp-sheet and forming small pools on the hammocks. The labourers have made tracks around the camp, formed by saplings and sections of tree trunk laid on the ground and stabilised by pegs. But the rain erodes around these, and the pegs loosen in the mud until eventually the saplings move and your foot slips through. Underground there are no leeches and no biting flies, although each caver has an attendant swarm of fungus gnats destroying themselves in the flame of his carbide light. But the surface camp has the fire, and varied meals – fresh bracken tips and the edible pith from a certain tree, tinned foods and chocolate, fresh pig – not the endless dehydrated foods of a lightweight camp underground. The surface camp has the radio and the chance to exchange news and jokes with our colleagues in Gunung Benerat, the next mountain to the north, or with our contacts down on the coast. The underground camps also lack the colour of the forest, an infinity of shades of green, the occasional flash of colour from a flower high up in the canopy and the brilliance of a cloud of butterflies settling on a patch of yesterday's urine which the rain has not yet washed away.

Around me now the others are beginning to stir. Nilong is brewing the tea and Berang is beginning the never-ending process of chopping wood for the fire. They, and most of our other labourers, come from the agricultural people who live around the park. Their home is at Long Terewan, a few hours' boat ride down the river from the park and a place which gives me fond memories. In 1980 we had spent Christmas with these people. Badly hung-over from a Christmas Eve celebration we had travelled down to Long Terawan and been re-soundingly thrashed at a game of football played on a pitch which closely resembled a marsh. Afterwards we had been shown the most superb hospitality, entertained, fed and given lots to drink. It was one of the best Christmases I have known. On the following morning we had been invited to make social calls to a series of families. At each stop we were presented with a selection of small snacks and glasses of *borak,* the local rice wine, which I can most charitably describe as an 'acquired taste', although I have never acquired it. On leaving we were am-bushed by most of the villagers, some armed with bowls of soot and oil which they smeared on our faces while the onlookers shrieked with delight. Eventually we escaped, their laughter and ours drowned by the roar of the outboard motors as we set off back up-river.

In the hammock next to mine Dave Checkley climbs out of his sleeping bag and into his damp clothes. Our task for today is to continue the exploration of a cave we found yesterday. Lagang's Cave, as we had called it, was like a six-lane motorway tunnelling straight through the south end of the mountain, and we had high hopes that it would have an exit on to the opposite side of Gunung Api. Its entrance was a series of arches under a cliff which we had first seen from the river below. Lagang had cut his way up the vegetated boulder slope to the cliff, leaving us plodding in his wake, and had shouted with delight and pride on finding the cave. He had refused to come in with us, however, and we had left him to check the rest of the area while we explored. A hall of boulders led us down to a low wide passage and a choice of routes. We took the easy one, following on the floor a clearly marked snake track, a line on the rock made brown and smooth by the passage of snakes which come into the caves to feed on bats. This led us into an echoing space; the roof was only a few feet above our heads, and roosting bats flew off in alarm, but the walls were nowhere in sight. After an hour of walking and skipping over boulders we realised that this was a passage about 300ft across. We were ecstatic but, because of lack of time, we left the exploration for a later date and began the laborious task of surveying out, mapping the cave as we went. At the entrance Lagang was waiting and by signs we described the cave to him. Dave wanted to take some photographs in the entrance and eventually we persuaded Lagang to come with us. He made his way carefully over the rocks and stood as a model beside a massive stalagmite pillar; his first ever caving trip. Later, safely back at the entrance, in the familiar world of the forest, his delight showed through and his face cracked into a huge smile.

I smile now at the memory and begin to pull on my clothes. I brush the netting and the sandflies rise up in an expectant cloud. It's breakfast time, for all of us.

CATHERINE CHARLEY

A RIVER JOURNEY
IN THE AMAZON BASIN

The port of Pucallpa was bustling with activity at 7am and the *collectivo* waiting to leave for Masisea was already packed. Passengers sat along the long, hard, wooden planks at the sides with their possessions piled up in the middle. I had my belongings in a large corn sack so they looked little different from anyone else's and were less likely to be stolen. After negotiating a good price for my journey to Santa Rosita – 3,500 soles (about 70p), 1,000 soles less than the normal price – I settled down to wait for our departure, watching the vendors walking along and on to the boat, bartering furiously with the passengers over bread and other foods.

Eventually we squeezed our way out of the throng of boats and set off upriver away from the noise of the port. The *collectivo* resembled a barge but was much narrower and lighter with a wooden roof to shield the passengers from the sun. It seemed very flimsy and this one, like all the others, had obviously seen better days. It creaked ominously as we chugged up-river.

The Rio Ucayali is wide and grubby. We motored along the edge away from the main thrust of the current. Dry cracked mud led up to the green vegetation on top of the bank. There were many banana trees with little wooden huts scattered in groups at intervals along it. The girl beside me, dressed in Western clothes with a neat modern haircut, pointed out places she thought might interest me and named birds. I nodded and smiled, understanding little. She got out after about two hours at a small village. It seemed that she worked in the large jungle town of Pucallpa and was spending a few days' holiday with her family in her old home.

Opposite me sat a young Indian woman dressed in the traditional short blouse and wrap-around embroidered skirt. Her black, black hair fell beyond her shoulders but was cut in a severe fringe across her forehead in the typical Shipibo style. She held a young child in her arms, far too old by Western standards for breast feeding, but whom she fed from time to time without embarrassment. She sat slightly apart from the rest of the passengers, glancing at them nervously and warily – the town dwellers wearing their Western clothes and Western watches.

Three young boys in jeans and cowboy boots were merrily drinking their way through a crate of beer and smoking quantities of cheap cigarettes. They became louder and more boisterous, at times nearly drowning the irregular noise of the ancient engine. Passengers chatted together and children cried.

Being the only white person aboard, I was surveyed with looks ranging from mild interest to deep suspicion. Again I regretted my limited Spanish which prevented me from really communicating with the local people.

The boat zig-zagged across the wide Amazon tributary, putting down and picking up passengers, the captain always noticing the tiny figure waving from the opposite bank. After about four hours we had a lengthy stop at a large village. Children rushed out on to the boat selling fruit, vegetables and rice dishes, carrying the bowls and baskets on their heads. I bought some *camilo* – a sweet green fruit about the size of an orange, tasty but with an extremely sticky pith. It was rather like coating one's lips with glue.

The halt gave me an opportunity to have a closer view of the women squatting at the muddy water's edge, washing clothes and pots as they had been at villages along the route. Many used thick bars of soap to aid their clothes-washing, but for pot-scrubbing they still used the riverside sand. When they had finished their tasks they climbed the steps back up to the village with their pots and bowls on their heads. The husbands were no doubt out on the river fishing in the dug-out canoes and long boats with puttering engines we had occasionally passed.

One of the wooden huts in the village on the bank had a large but faded Yamaha sign outside it. It seemed rather incongruous but perhaps this was the central spot in this area for repairing the outboard motors – fifth-hand they might be, but they were the pride and joy of their owners.

New passengers embarked with more cargo. Chickens were hoisted roughly aloft by their clipped wings and dropped among the others on the floor of the boat, their legs tied so that they could not even scramble away. A girl put down a small square cardboard box. Only half-an-hour or so later did I realise what was in it as a little yellow chick tried to squeeze its way through the flaps at the top and was shoved roughly back down again.

A young boy had brought an enormous bunch of bananas, probably to sell at Masisea, the larger town further upriver. They were the greener, tougher cooking bananas, eaten as part of the staple diet of people in this area – much as we eat potatoes.

The *collectivo* resumed its journey. The man who now sat opposite stared at me in an unpleasant way. I shifted my feet on to my luggage and watched it closely in case he should try to slit it with a penknife while my attention was elsewhere.

The beer-drinking youths got out and others climbed aboard. Often it was difficult to guess where the passengers who disembarked were going. It just seemed to be empty riverside land, the houses no doubt hidden by the banana trees and other vegetation.

Eventually, towards three o'clock, the boatman pointed to the place where I was to be left – a mud-bank on the junction of three rivers, and not a house or human being in sight. I jumped out, said *ciao* to my fellow passengers and prepared for a long wait in the hot sun. Me, my sack, the mud and the river – nothing more except a few birds. I heard afterwards that a man had been murdered there two months earlier. No boat had chanced by to take him further on his journey up one of the smaller rivers and he had resigned himself to spending the night there. Several hours later two escaped prisoners had come past the lonely spot, stolen his possessions and knifed him to death.

I was somewhat luckier. Within an hour of my arrival a dug-out canoe came in sight. I waved and it approached. Was it passing the little village of Santa Rosita on the Rio Tipishca? 'Si,' said the man; he could take me there.

He sat at the back; I was directed to the plank in the middle and my sack of belongings was balanced precariously in front of me. His two young sons, aged about eleven and seven, sat in the front side by side. All three had short broad wooden paddles. As the boat made little noise and this river was much narrower, the wildlife was more obvious. There were birds of numerous varieties – beautiful gliders and divers, small ones, large ones, many brightly coloured. Others with long legs and small bodies ran across the mud at the water's edge.

A beautiful green parrot sat perched on a branch overhanging the river, framed by the jungle on either side – the whole picture vivid and bright in the hot sun. Suddenly it flew from the tree squawking in protest as a crocodile dived into the water beyond it – I saw only the reptile's back and tail, and a splash. The wobbly wooden canoe suddenly seemed very insecure.

The river widened as it flowed over sandbanks. We tried to weave a way, but because the water was low we became stuck fast in the mud. No amount of pushing and shoving with the paddles could relieve the situation and the man and his sons got out. My offer of help was politely refused. However, as it still remained firmly wedged, I rolled up my jeans and clambered gingerly over the side. Now the canoe was lighter and we could push our transport out of the shallows and re-embark.

The boys at the front amused themselves by pointing out birds, monkeys and other wildlife on the banks, and giggled together when I could seldom pinpoint what their sharp eyes had spotted. One got so excited about the antics of a monkey that he dropped his paddle, but fortunately father snatched it out of the water as it floated past.

Although it was long past midday the sun was still beating down and I longed for some shade. It was with relief that, turning a bend in the river, I had my first sight of the wooden stilted huts of the village of Santa Rosita.

JACQUEE STOROZYNSKI

PACKAGED ORDEAL

I should have realised that a coach trip to Lloret de Mar on the Costa Brava was not the right holiday for me when I found that the no-smoking part of the coach was in the middle of the smoker's section. I travelled with various other non-smokers in a smoke haze. They included a young baby with what sounded like whooping cough, and we all suffocated and wheezed all the way to Spain.

The advertised air-conditioned luxury coaches with all mod cons turned out to be microwave ovens equipped with television sets to watch videos.

One Scottish gentleman, who had decided to start the holiday early by drinking himself legless before we left King's Cross, wept all the way to Dover because there was no loo on board. He had foolishly believed that mod cons meant loos. Apart from the mini-revolution over the lack of a toilet the journey was uneventful. When the heat finally sent you into a coma you could recline the seat just far enough to kneecap the person behind whilst someone in front gave you the same treatment.

At last, Dover: we were refreshed with tins of warm orange and informed that the returning point would be Gloucester Road. Hard luck on anyone who had made arrangements to be collected at King's Cross.

We enjoyed the benefits of fresh air on the crossing and then returned to the smoke-filled sweat-box and journeyed across France, nodding gently and coughing violently. After twenty-four hours we arrived in sunny Spain. Well, overcast, cold and windy Spain; it was the coldest May for years.

Now Lloret is a beautiful resort, something like Canning Town. A wonderful Spanish aroma assails the nostrils as beefburgers and chips pervade the air from every other building. There is music to the ears with an authentic Spanish flair as a constant drilling and banging signifies that yet another hotel is being built. The beaches are pleasant, but a fortune is spent on plaster to repair the damage to the lacerated soles of the feet – and if you should venture into the sea you would no doubt catch double pneumonia. The water was freezing. The sun was hidden by an enormous dustcloud hovering over the building sites, but as compensation the men could feast their eyes on the bevy of top-less sun-worshippers displaying their goosepimpled wares on the beach. Even this display did not raise the temperature. There was a de-finite look of boredom on the faces of the sunbathers and even the sight of one nude male did not achieve the raising of an eyebrow, let alone anything else.

As you reclined in the dustbowl your ears were assailed by the jeers and abuse of the resident beach bum who arrived every day clutching a bottle of cheap booze and invited people to do unmentionable things to his anatomy.

The hotel where we stayed was a delightfully olde worlde concrete block, catering for thousands and with an atmosphere somewhat like Butlins by the sea. The double room with cot that we had booked for myself, husband and baby turned out to be a dark sunless room over-looking the dustbin yard. Well, in the day it was dark and sunless. At night it was just dark, as the lights did not work. There was no cot, but six beds and a mattress on the floor. If there had been any overspill, no doubt we would have been invited to accommodate it. There was already a cockroach in residence in case we were lonely.

Now what really makes a holiday of this kind is the food. The cuisine provided by this hotel was beyond compare. Every day we were treated to Spanish delicacies such as boiled bones and spam balls, together with a plate of vegetable oil and a few sodden chips. Various lumps of unknown animal origin but of an unusually hirsute variety were frequently served, and what looked on one occasion suspiciously like an eyeball floating in gravy. There were rolls galore, but butter – what's butter?

In case of bad weather, the hotel provided a solarium to improve your suntan. This was the indoor pool with yellow cellophaned windows.

If you had young children a kiddies' club was on offer. All sorts of wonders could occur for two hours a day to relieve the parents of the burden. As two young women were in charge at any one time of ap-proximately sixty-four children, no doubt all sorts of wonders could occur and frequently did. There was a play area available all day, which consisted of a climbing frame set in concrete by the swimming pool. One could laze around watching the children sustain varying de-grees of injury, and listen to the wails as they hurtled past you from the top of the frame.

If you were brave you swam in the pool which was littered with dirt and rubbish and used as a toilet by toddlers held in position by doting mums.

If after trying all the facilities on offer you still had free time, there were of course the optional excursions. The main object of these appeared to be to make you as drunk as possible and have you carried home paralytic, minus purse, wallet, passport or handbag. The trips to Tossa and Barcelona involved assembling at the crack of dawn in a car park to watch coaches being moved on by the police. Having at last boarded, you were found hours later still circumnavigating the same area picking up people who were left behind; and you spent the rest of the journey sitting on each other's laps because they'd overbooked. Apart from a demented boat trip where numerous pleasure boats raced against each other in an attempt to see who could smash themselves on the rocks first, the Tossa excursion involved a tour round a town during siesta time when everything was shut – everything, that is, except an expensive restaurant which had stayed open especially for us. As most people were still recovering from the boat trip, a loo was the only thing required. This was demonstrated by the queue which took up most of the stopover time.

There were daily pony trips on offer. You were trekked across rugged terrain, plied with cheap booze and returned minus an eye thanks to low hanging branches.

The evening excursions were far superior. You returned from a trip to a night club in the early hours of the morning. After queuing in a drunken state of *bonhomie* you squeezed into one of the two lifts (each held only four people) and, on reaching your room somewhat the worse for wear, you fell asleep. Being in a stupor you managed to sleep through the night for the first time, being unaware of the crashing and banging as the garbage men removed the dustbins at 4am and other drunken residents tried to shift the furniture or break down, for whatever purpose, someone's door.

At last the final day arrived and we gratefully climbed on to the coach to go home. No such luck. The coach was overbooked and there were no seats. One family was left behind and was retrieved only after an argument with the courier. We got on coaches, off coaches, put our baggage in the baggage compartment and took it out again; and this was to travel only half a mile outside Lloret. By the time we were actually on our way we were exhausted. Still, at least we could watch a video. No chance! They had forgotten to fit the video recorders.

STAN GEORGE

One More Burmese Day

At five in the morning Rangoon shakes off sleep. Paraffin lamps cast pools of sputtering light on the wet streets. After a night of drizzle, the city murmurs as though sound, like the dust, has been cleared from the air by the rain. The lamps wheeze. In a café doorway a man slaps chapati dough on to a board, and stacks the rolled balls into ranks. A boy yawns and adjusts his *lunghi*. He oversees a water tank parked in the road. Water splashes from a faucet into a jerrican, and when it fills the boy sluggishly replaces it from a line of empty ones. A truck, far off, grinds gears and whines, coming slowly closer.

At dawn the city has a somnambulant purpose. Gaunt men emerge from doorways, and proceed, swinging rolled umbrellas down the street. The city is empty. Traffic lights blink impotently at the odd cyclist who now, as later, ignores them. And in the soft light which permeates below the cloud cover, the city is familiar. Awash in greys and blues, the Victorian tenements melt into the dawn mist, reminiscent of Glasgow or Liverpool, once grand, now in decline. Except that here the foliage is more determined.

Rhizoids of jungle creep between the paving stones. The buildings weep ironwork. Gutters, overhung with herbaceous toupees, wave dangerously from the rooftops. Balconies cling to walls like frightened climbers. Stucco lies in drifts of powdered plaster. Street lighting is spasmodic and piped water comes in sluggish fits and starts. Blocked storm drains flood the streets. It seems as though a slammed door would level the city.

Writing in 1934, George Orwell feared that modernisation would sweep aside Burmese culture. He needn't have worried. The Burmese are truly living in the past.

The country goes its own way. Even in the capital, life ticks by with the rhythm of the rice-growing cycle. There are no slums, and no discernible wealth, just an equal distribution of what looks like poverty. Yet a scorn for materialism, the measurement of wealth, is fundamental to Buddhism which is rooted in the national psychology. Because

Burma: Tea-break for monks at the Schwe Dagon Pagoda, Rangoon

A fortune-telling stupa at the Pagoda makes an unusual religious sideshow

Dominica: Once the childhood home of the writer Jean Rhys, now a 'sleazy guesthouse'

A very public convenience beside Freshwater Lake

life is an illusion, what is the significance of development? Why worry about efficiency? Of course the buildings decay, and so must everything!

This fatalism lends itself to the infamous Burmese bureaucracy, partly because bureaucracy looks like efficiency, partly because bureaucracy fits so neatly into the unchanging Buddhist worldview. And inevitably a static officialdom leads to corruption. Yet, as an ageing journalist in Rangoon explains, corruption is a Western value judgement. Bribery, familial influence, the black economy are endemic in Asia. Because Burma is not a rich country the potential for racketeering is limited, and shrugged off. For those Burmese who want one foot in the material world, at least so far as the occasional bottle of Scotch is concerned, the black market exists. At times in Rangoon it seems that the second economy is all pervasive, and gaps in conversation are filled by discreet requests to change money.

Rangoon airport is the first contact with the workings of the second economy. Guidebooks advise travellers to bring their fully duty-free quota, to offset the official rate of exchange. Moving through the customs shed, itself a film set from *Casablanca,* new arrivals encounter a pantomime. On one side of the desk officials leisurely scrutinise and catalogue every marketable item, and on the other, baggage handlers maintain a cacophony of stage whispers, demanding 'Johnny Walker'.

Yet even the black market in Burma has an ease unknown in the rest of Asia. Hustlers are polite and accept refusal amiably. Apart from a few pickpockets in Rangoon, street crime does not exist. It is a remarkably well-adjusted society where the alienation of adolescence, universal throughout Europe and Asia, is unheard of. The largest identifiable youth group are the monks.

Although Burma is an oil producer, national lassitude and the lack of a desire for 'development' ensure a leisurely extraction, and petrol is rationed. A lack of foreign exchange means that, apart from a few Toyotas, there are virtually no new cars in Rangoon. Overladen buses trundle about the city, and a taxi fleet pensioned off in colonial days still plies its trade like a permanent veteran car rally. What rush hour exists is merely a breeze of bicycles.

The Schwe Dagon Pagoda on the edge of Rangoon is a religious city. Armies of monks in blood-red robes hang around the place. They stand about chatting, smoking cigarettes and chasing dogs from the temple grounds. Some monks sweep the long expanses of the stone plateaux; some carry offerings of donated food; some undertake pagoda business, receiving visitors in drafty offices where money is handed over. For Burmese, the upkeep of religious centres is a way of acquiring merit for a future incarnation.

The main courtyard is a jumble of shrines and small temples. It is a mixture of the spiritual and the profane. Yet an unexpected feeling of fun and clutter pervades the complex. Children daubed with circles of yellow ochre offer tiny figurines and toys for sale. Old ladies peddle incense. Child monks play in the alcoves. There is even a sideshow where a large gilt *stupa* rotates on an electric motor. Punters throw coins, trying to score a hit in the tin trays. When they are successful a bell rings and a mechanical buddha lights up and makes a creaky obeisance. The prize is the motto printed next to the tray: 'Freedom from Five Enemies', 'May you be Well and Happy'.

A couple of English-speaking students explain the hold of religion on the populace. All young boys spend time in monasteries. They grin at the idea, crinkling their noses in mock distaste, suggesting that the monastic life holds no attraction for them. There is no dividing line between the pagoda and life outside. Recently when a gang stole some large buddha images from the temple complex at Pagan, the whole country was outraged. There were no 'safe' houses for the thieves, who were quickly apprehended, and the images were returned.

The students mention the seventy-year occupation of the Schwe Dagon by the British army, and the devastation they left behind. They relate the story in a hushed tone, watching carefully for a reaction. And then to dismiss any embarrassment they laugh. The history of Burma has been one of imperialism. The Burmese are descendants of the Mongols, and now they try to dominate the Shans, the Kochins and the Karens. The students shrug; that's life, they seem to say.

Pools of rainwater collect on the uneven pavement. Tiny gilt bells record the passage of the wind, and an amiable buddha expresses a worldly, less than tranquil smile on the bustle around his feet.

The Strand Hotel, near the waterfront, was the Imperial equivalent of the Schwe Dagon. Like Raffles in Singapore it holds in amber a record of the past. Yet, whilst the Burmese retain a grudging respect for the British, they exact a characteristic vengeance upon the sanctified edifice of their former masters.

The palm court, both vegetation and orchestra, has long since been repossessed. Only the clank, clank of the wrought iron lift cage provides a kind of background music, echoing through the empty building. Damp stains creep down the walls to join in sombre triumph the black fungi ascending from the floor. Cadillac cockroaches, friction-driven, ply the roadways of the corridors. Cigarette burns lacerate the teak furniture.

In a far-flung foyer three Burmese officials drink in silence, as though in respect for the spirits of the departed. There is no barman but the hotel receptionist, under duress, rummages a bottle of beer from a tin box and wanders away in search of a glass. Above, in the gloomy upper reaches of the hotel, a lavatory cistern clangs. Dust-wreathed propellers turn overhead, twisting and turning the grime of centuries into the crannies of the moulded ceiling.

Beside the reception desk there is a large glass cabinet, labelled 'Lost and Found'. It is one of the sights of the city. A time capsule containing the personal effects of a long dead civilisation: the pince-nez of an extinct dowager, a tarnished cigarette case, two withered clasp handbags, indeterminate items of jewellery, and the desiccated remains of insects. Each item is separately labelled and lies on perpetual display, reducing all the pomp and ceremony of Empire to a few mute and pathetic items. On the last silvered patches of a fading mirror, the ghost of Orwell smiles.

A Visit to Dominica

DOMINICA

A strange thing happened this year. A man I'd met only twice, a bit of a loner, invited me to go with him to the West Indies. I fancied him so I said yes.

I knew of Dominica only as the birthplace of Jean Rhys, a writer I deeply admire. Now when I read about the island I discovered that it is volcanic and mountainous and is the last refuge of the Carib Indians, the descendants of proud cannibals who starved to death rather than accept the fate of slavery. It is one of the wilder places on earth and contains rainforest, and boa constrictors.

The Caribbean is a vast sea, the islands so small. From the air they all look different. We flew over dry, brown Antigua with its ruined sugar mills standing solid as castle puddings; butterfly-shaped Guadeloupe with city boulevards; green Martinique and Marie Galante. Then sliding reluctantly over the ocean came a thunderous grey cloud, and under it was the crumpled, dark green lozenge of sulky Dominica.

There wasn't much of an airport: just a largish shed with a corrugated iron roof, open at the sides like a cattle shelter. Roseau, the capital, had primitive street lighting, no smart shops, and nowhere to post a letter. Concrete drains ran down the sides of the streets, with a bridge across to each house. In the botanical gardens a huge tree had fallen and crushed a bus. It looked startled and bedraggled, like a rat in a trap.

The town ended sharply, and we were driving along a bumpy lane through the jungle at reckless speed. It began to rain. In the porch of a wooden shack a small boy dangled a land crab on the end of a makeshift fishing rod; it clawed the air, defensive and gaudy.

When we arrived at Papillote, which had advertised itself as being 'in the rainforest', we found that its flimsy buildings were half engulfed by the surrounding forest. The owner of the guest-house, Mrs Anne Baptist, was a small, shy, American woman. She greeted us guardedly, smoothing her wispy hair. She urged us to order supper straight away from a painted board which said:

KINGFISH
FLYFISH
CRAYFISH
CHICKEN
MOUNTAIN CHICKEN

'Mountain chicken is not available,' she added, 'because the frogs are still in their breeding season.'

We sat in the open-sided restaurant and saw forest all around. There was a pressing, gently swaying wall of vegetation in a thousand shades of green. Beside the kitchen a communal bath, fed from a hot sulphur spring, was built into the wall. A whole family sat in this, nattering and chuckling in the brown steam. They had walked up the road from Roseau. With a tinkling sound, the spring emptied into a shower basin at the edge of the jungle. Fowls stalked out of the vegetation, looking incongruous: geese, peacocks, guineafowl. Mrs Baptist grumbled, 'The snakes are very unpopular here. Boa constrictors. However you build your henhouse they'll sneak through a crack. Then of course, when they've eaten they can't get out again.'

Our room was tiny and wooden. Through the slats of the shutters we saw the high, green sides of a ravine and a solitary tree fern growing luxuriantly, a living fossil from the coal forests of the Carboniferous.

'I'm sorry I don't love you,' my friend said.

'Don't be sorry.'

We heard a chorus slowly start up and deepen, far back into the forest night. Something high in a tree clinked sharply, over and over again like a coin thrown into a metal dish. Other voices mewed, rattled, croaked, quacked and barked. They were frogs. One of them was the mountain chicken, emitting a discreet 'woof'.

I lay in the cacophonous darkness thinking about magic. There was magic here. Even in our short journey the taxi driver had spoken of the *soukoyant,* the witch who takes off her skin at night and flies about like a bat. Magic: it lubricates the gap between what we can see and understand, and what unhappy feelings haunt our dreams.

Anne Baptist joined us as we explored her jungle garden before breakfast. She showed us trees with calabashes and wooden fruits, and a thicket of juicy ginger stalks which sheltered huge, pink plastic blossoms. She pointed out tiny, delicate orchids growing on trees, and the dammed ponds in the river where she planned to breed crayfish.

Some way below the garden a man stood quietly washing himself in the hot water from the spring; it was channelled down there in a home-made aqueduct of halved bamboo stalks resting on forked twigs. 'For every improvement to the guest-house, I make something for the local people,' Anne said. 'It's their island.'

I wanted to see the rainforest I'd read about, a place where vast trunks rise up like the pillars of a gloomy cathedral, where lianas hang down, where bright parrots chatter in the sunlight of the tree canopy.

'Before the hurricane we had rainforest everywhere,' Anne said. 'Now it's just jungle.' The hurricane struck in 1979 and blew the roof off Papillote. A wall fell across Anne and her Dominican husband and protected them. All over the island tall old trees crashed down, and less tall trees whipped about and were filleted of their leaves and branches. 'Trouble is,' Anne said, 'hundred-year-old trees take a hundred years to grow.'

We hired a truck and a driver and explored the island, jolting along rough wet roads through an endless banana plantation. Yard-high walls of bananas waited at road turnings for the Geest lorry to collect. We saw the pale brown, almond-eyed Caribs spiritlessly making baskets for tourists. We saw dead volcanic lakes, grey under the grey sky. We picnicked on beaches of jet black sand under windy coconut palms, where surf rolled in from Africa. We swam in the chilly river of the Titou Gorge where it winds through caverns underground.

On our last evening in Dominica the weather was clear, after days of rain. Anne's husband, Cuthbert, said there'd be fireflies tonight. He asked, with relish, 'Ever seen mushrooms that light up in the dark? Like to see them?'

He led the way up a path through the jungle. We saw the moon appear and disappear, veiled by clouds. Gradually we could make out the shaking fronds of the trees, the thick herbs at the side of the path.

'Fireflies!'

The small, brave lights wandered among the trees, keeping together for comfort. They were like tiny aircraft following a demented flight-path, having lost their way.

Something else was alight in the undergrowth. Cuthbert drew out a damp stick on which were two pale blue, phosphorescent toadstools with delicate gill clefts, glowing like the harsh strip lights in a modern kitchen.

By the time we reached the airfield next morning a tropical storm was raging. We waited in the shed while rain boomed and clattered on to the metal roof, and no aircraft took off or landed for hour after hour. When we realised that we'd missed our flight to London from Antigua, my friend said,

'Let's find where Jean Rhys lived. We could stay the night there.' Anne had told us it was in Cork Street, Roseau, and had been converted into a sleazy guest-house.

It was a two-storey building, rather flimsy-looking, not old. The courtyard behind was now a restaurant, and had a tree which Jean Rhys might have remembered. Inside, Vena's guest-house was certainly sleazy. The small lobby had a high plastic desk at which the manageress sat. She demanded payment in advance.

'It's like a brothel in a French film,' my friend muttered.

From somewhere *inside* the house came the loud, curlew-like cry of a tree frog. There was no character to the room we were shown into. It was impossible to tell what part of the house it had been. A pantry? A slice of a larger, more commodious room? Cheaply varnished, huge furniture leaned into it. The shutters were wedged shut behind a carelessly installed washbasin. When it came to sleeping on the horrid, plastic bed in the sultry room we had the choice of suffocating in the heat or enduring the groaning clatter of an electric fan, which sounded like the *soukoyant* flapping her leathery wings, rattling at the unopenable shutters and trying to get in.

It was a relief to get a flight the next morning, yet I felt I'd been dragged away from Dominica: I had not explored its dangerous magic as I ought to have done. The island had cheated and spared me, like a love affair where there has been no delusion, no passion and no remorse.

Since we returned, I've seen my friend twice. He is a bit of a loner.

GODFREY F. DUFFEY

BUSMAN'S HOLIDAY

I decided this year I would try a working holiday, and after a successful interview in London I was taken on as a courier by the travel company Astros. I perused an Astros brochure and found a description of myself.

'Our tour escorts are chosen from thousands for their linguistic ability, local knowledge, sense of humour and patience . . .'

I smile when I remember my training weekend in London. We were a motley crew: students, ex-students, the unemployed, the unemployable, the wise, the wise-crackers – all eager, and all potential couriers (so the company told us). My training tour began a week later in Ostend. I boarded with the rest of the passengers, and as far as they were concerned I was the mystery man who didn't seem to be enjoying his jaunt through Europe. But of course the courier knew my identity. She was French and the majority of passengers were Americans of the worst kind – loud and flashy with a wealth of ignorance. Monique proceeded to introduce herself in a thick, sexy French accent which sure impressed the all-American males. In her brand of English she informed the informless about the Belgian 'munachie' and how Rotterdam was the capital of Holland. The Americans began to cringe and smirk as this female Inspector Clouseau twisted well-known English words out of all recognition. Why, I thought, could they not have got an American or a Briton to conduct this tour? The irony was not lost on me when I began my own first tour, which began two days later when I received a phone call summoning me back to Ostend. What I had learned on my training tour was negligible; what I was about to learn was unforgettable.

'Come in Mr Duffey, sit down, sit down,' barked Mr Blujzec as I entered the Ostend office.

'OK Mr Duffey, you will be doing a ten-day tour of Germany and France,' he continued as he looked through his papers. I thought logically, as a Spanish speaker, I should be sent to Spain, but logic did not play a big part in the Astros organisation. In fact organisation did not play a big part in the Astros organisation. This I was to learn as my tour progressed. The training weekend had been a sham, a softener with a couple of the company's pretty boys; but now we were out in the field with the organisation's heavy mob. The boot was on the other foot and I was being booted all the way to Germany.

Inside an Astros coach at Ostend docks I sat with Giovanni, my driver, watching the torrential rain whiplashing the other eight Astros coaches. Giovanni frowned and pushed his chin skywards whilst muttering obscenities in Italian. I smiled and spoke to him in Spanish and he answered in Italian. Gestures took over. I was preoccupied thinking how I was to commentate on passing scenes without guidebooks. The night before, I had searched the bookshops of Ostend but could find no books in English, only one in French which I was translating. As for the other guides, if they were experienced they had their own books and considered my situation a *fait accompli,* or they were like me – new, on edge and clueless.

Suddenly they were there, trudging begrudgingly along the docks, avoiding the trolleys full of suitcases, soaked and jabbering like refugees from a forgotten war – the passengers. I braced myself to tell them that before they boarded the coach they must first identify their baggage. When that ordeal was over we were off, first stop Brussels. At this time I had only twenty passengers (Americans), but at the Brussels hotel another thirty-four would join us.

Mr Malgrotti made an immediate impression. I christened him 'the Suit' because of the blue satin one he wore for the Monte Carlo casino. His voice continually boomed from the back.

'I can buy anything,' he said. 'If I can buy it I will. When I was in London I bought a whore. Do you know what we used to call them in the war? Piccadilly Commandos; yea that's right.'

Outside the hotel entrance were four more Astros coaches, and when I went into the foyer there were four couriers with clipboards and about two hundred people. An irate manager was shouting *Impoziblay.* He was right, it *was* impossible; but somehow Astros had arranged for all the buses to arrive together at the same hotel with the maximum inconvenience to hotel staff, passengers and couriers. By the time my last passenger was booked in it was after midnight and I was exhausted with a head about to explode. A last check with reception revealed that out of the thirty-four passengers who were to join us only six were booked into the hotel. That suited me. With fewer passengers there would be fewer problems, and with that thought I went to bed and studied my 115-page Astros manual. Next morning I found my passengers locked out of the breakfast room arguing with the staff. (Who had arranged for everyone to eat at the same time?) After breakfast I went outside to find chaos had arrived; so had the missing passengers and, worse, they were French-speaking Canadians. Another forty minutes passed and they were on board and their luggage loaded. I gave Giovanni the green light; next stop Luxembourg.

'Excuse me, sir,' chirped up a middle-aged American spinster. 'We have a passenger without a seat.' On a 54-seater coach we had fifty-five passengers and the impossible had happened again.

When we stopped at a motorway service station I phoned Mr Blujzec in Ostend and told him of the extra passenger on the floor. He suggested I had made a mistake and so I read him the passenger list. 'That's it,' he said. 'Miss Armitage, she cancelled.'

If she cancelled, I argued, why is she here? No answer, and then Mr Blujzec told me to check her papers. If they were in order, I had to tell her we'd transfer her to a parallel tour at the next overnight stop. The next overnight stop was Lucerne. Could she hang on? We had volunteers ready to take her place and various ideas, especially from Mr Callow, alias 'Let Me Tell You'. Mr Callow was travelling with his wife, and they were not too happy. Already he had told me how 'crap' this tour was compared to others he'd been on. He usually began in his New York Jewish accent, 'Let me tell you something', and finished his gripe with 'and that's for nothing'. We were through Luxembourg before he'd finished his complaint. When we got to the Swiss border I got Miss Armitage to walk up and down the bus while the police checked the passports – and it worked; they thought we had fifty-four passengers.

By the time we were booking into the Lucerne hotel the 'Frenchies' were getting restless and wanted a commentary in French. Their spokesman, Monsieur 'the voice' Le Crec, frequently sprang to his feet and gave me a tirade of Rhubarb which I ignored. Yet from the French quarter I got some help from Françoise, their guide, who could speak English. From then on we did dual commentaries – but why she could not have told me earlier, I don't know. She also informed me that the French rooming lists were different from mine. I went through the checking procedure and their papers checked out, so this meant I had to telex all the coming hotels. There was no point in contacting Blujzec. The people had paid.

Mr 'Crusher' Williams was amused by all this. He was from somewhere west of Redneck county and delighted in shaking people's hands and trying to crush them. Mine was his favourite hand.

I often found the passengers' itinerary didn't correspond to my Astros itinerary, so although they thought they were staying in Nice with an excursion to Cannes we did in fact stay in Cannes, so I suggested an excursion to Nice. Just to clear it I went by the book and phoned Ostend. As often happened, there was no answer, so I phoned HQ Lugano and what I got was no permission. I informed the passengers and there was uproar with some walking off and the 'Frenchies' refusing to move. I made another phone call, and this time asked to speak to someone above the rank of Divisional Manager. I got through to Mr Poletti, Tour Controller for the whole of Europe and just below God. I got permission. The Grand Prix was a wash-out. The Yanks with tickets thought Giovanni would take them but Giovanni refused. 'No, no impoziblay, traffico too much.' The famous casino (Monte Carlo) was another flop with tourists watching clapped-out David Nivens and paying for the privilege. Mr Malgrotti lost money and Miss Armitage was still on the floor as the parallel bus had passed us and, anyway, there were no spare seats.

We passed swiftly through Grasse and stayed overnight in Lyon. It was there I sold my optional excursions for a Paris nightclub. If I had not sold the optional excursions I would have no money until I was paid at the end of the month. The float that Astros had given me was finished and I was paying for frontier crossings, tolls and telephone calls.

In the nightclub I met the Paris Area Manager and he quizzed me about odd reports he'd heard. I answered him with grunts and 'dunnos' as I was not in the mood for Gestapo interrogation and, besides, I had decided to resign. He continued acting as *Grüppenführer* and gave me *Odessa File* style instructions for coming to the Paris office. All of Astros's offices were hidden away to prevent passengers discovering their location and stringing up the *Grüppenführers*.

I found the office in an apartment block. As I entered, Mr Cadelli ordered me not to walk on his new carpet. He studied me and I studied him with his five rings, big cigar and oak desk. Finally he said:

'Ow deed dis wo-man efeel about she sheet ona de flora?'

'She was very happy about it,' I replied. He grimaced and handed me over to his second on another table and I wanted to resign then. The next day some passengers stayed on in Paris and the rest came on with me to our final stop, Calais. As my passengers trudged off in the rain for the boat I wanted to tell them I hated Astros and all it stood for. But what could I tell them? Their holiday was over and I had finished obeying orders. I resigned.

ELIZABETH A. McCORMICK

BIG GAME IN THE OKAVANGO SWAMPS

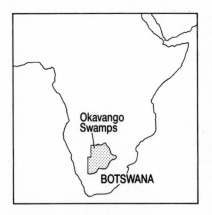

Stranded in the Kalahari desert we had no water and half a packet of Marie biscuits. The bus from Francistown had broken down again and the passengers disembarked, squatting in the cumbersome shade of a baobab tree. They, like us, were shifty-eyed; there had been no rain in Botswana for four years and the lions of the Kalahari were getting hungry. In Gaborone, a week before, we had watched the mauled body of a German girl carried into the hospital. Her death reminded us of the dangers of complacency in Africa. In the shadow of the bus, a vulture wheeling overhead, I kept my eyes fixed on the bush behind us.

The driver and friend tinkered with the engine which had burst into flames twice, and been push-started once by the passengers. Nobody seemed in any great hurry. Perched on the step of the bus, circa 1935, an old man in a military coat fished a handful of polished knucklebones out of his pocket. He rattled them between cupped hands and threw them into the dust. He stared hard at the pattern, gathered them up, threw them down again. He raised his eyes from the pattern and stared a long time at my friend and I – the only two white people on the journey. The wings of the vulture rustled over our heads. Feeling uneasy, we turned to our *Africa on a Shoestring* handbook, learning that the Kalahari consists of some of the most arid and remote land in the world. We realised that only two cars had passed us all morning. By midday we realised we had finished our water and were sweating profusely.

The driver whistled through his teeth. Nuts, bolts, a broken fan belt dropped from the engine. It was 40°C in the shade and so quiet that all we heard was dust settling, the rattle of bones and the rustle of wings. A spring fell out of the engine. But it coughed, wheezed, and shrieked into life. The driver cavorted round the bus, beaming – no less surprised and pleased than we were.

After 100 miraculous kilometres we met the other bus returning to Francistown. Discretion erring, our driver announced we would swap buses. There followed much confusion. Passengers were still climbing off while the second load of passengers were scrambling on. Rugs, clothing, mielies, were tossed on top of the buses while the first load of passengers were still trying to reach their luggage. Finally, each bus made a three-point turn in a cloud of dusty exhaust, and off we went; 300km to Maun, on the very edge of the Okavango Swamps.

I woke, cold and stiff, at 4am as the bus lurched into Maun. The heat of the day had been replaced by searing cold and the bus was nearly empty. I dimly remembered having watched the sun set, copper orange over a colourless world. Then I had slept and awoken as the bus stopped amongst a scatter of mud huts. Somebody told me we were halfway to Maun and gave me some water which I was too thirsty to sterilise.

Sitting up in the cold morning light we could have been sprayed by a fine grey snow as we slept – dust from the Kalahari which I can still smell in my clothes.

The Okavango river flows across the desert to form a huge swamp-land, a watery jungle where animals roam; a fascinating, dangerous place. With a friend we visited the local hospital and saw victims of crocodile, hippo, and lion attacks, and a man blinded by a spitting cobra. The patient with the hippo bite told me that hippos have become the most dangerous animals in Africa.

'Once they were shy,' he told me, 'but now they attack because the white man . . .' he pointed an imaginary rifle at the window and pulled the trigger. Using exceptionally sharp teeth, the hippos can crunch up both dugout canoes and their occupants. Indeed, the injured man did not even know he had been bitten until the water turned red as he swam to shore. I found this vaguely reassuring; a short, sharp death seemed preferable to a long, slow chewing underwater. However, as if this excitement were not enough, we were warned against malaria, bilharzia, and tsetse fly, all of which flourish in the swamps.

The following day we flew into the swamps in a six-seater plane. Dry desert gave way to blue lagoons full of water lilies, palm trees, islands and deep blue lakes. Herds of giraffe and waterbuck raced across the swamps in our shadow as we swooped on to the sandy airstrip.

A 15-foot canoe waited along with our poler for the week, Matata. As he pushed away from shore, the reeds of the swamp parting before us, I asked him what his name meant in Setswanan. 'Problem,' he translated with a very disarming smile. Did it mean he was a problem, or could he solve problems? We did not dwell on it.

We slid through the swamps while animals criss-crossed our path before and aft; kudu, zebra, buffalo, impala, and a herd of fifteen giraffe, splashing through the water with feet big as plates. Matata poled gracefully; he could have been punting down the Cam as his pole pushed blue and white water lilies aside. His ears were sharp as a jackal's and he could spot the tracks of a hippo from an extraordinary distance. The lilypad sized footprints, at least one foot across, sank deep into the mud – heavy, purposeful tracks.

We camped on an island of palm trees. Matata built a fire over which we cooked a supper of beans and rice while he caught a fish with a piece of string and what seemed very little else. The night air amplified the snort and splash of animals and I was very grateful for the orange glow of the fire through the canvas walls of the tent. Matata slept outside and promised to keep the fire burning; I hoped he was a light sleeper.

When I awoke it was very dark and the fire had gone out. I lay very still, the hair rising on the back of my neck as something nudged me through the canvas. There was a snuffle, a grunt, followed by the sound of chewing. It started to rain. The animal pushed against the floor of the tent. The German girl killed by a lion had been sleeping in a tent like ours. I screamed.

'Matata!'

My friend, slumbering fitfully by my side, awoke with a yell. Matata's voice said in my ear, 'Let me in, please. Quickly. It's raining.'

For an hour the three of us crouched inside the leaking tent. When the rain eventually stopped Matata crawled outside to relight the fire. I closed my eyes but seconds later there was a scream and the sound of crashing undergrowth; Matata had found a snake curled up in the warm ash of the fire. There was only one thing to do; light another fire to drive the snake away. We spent the rest of the night collecting wood, examining each piece by torchlight before touching it.

We soon learned to give animals the right of way in the swamps, sitting for hours at a time in the dugout, watching elephants plod by. Our unwound watches lay in our rucksacks and when they stopped we followed the pattern of night and day instead. Eating supper early, we were asleep by eight, before waking at five for the dawn.

In spite of Matata's shock-horror tactics, he was the most wonderful guide, in tune with the swamps by some atavistic sixth sense. After we woke, he would take us on to the bigger islands, known as the 'Big Bush'. Here he tracked animals, and we followed, wading waist-deep through swamp water, crawling on our stomachs to be as close as possible.

The brooding atmosphere of the swamps accentuated our smallness and vulnerability. Even sounds at night dominated us, as the firelight picked out bright eyes, blinking through the darkness. I was comforted when Matata showed me a Boer war rifle wrapped in rags in the bottom of the canoe. I doubt whether it could have found its target but the very shape of it in my hands was reassuring. A very small pocket penknife (with hoof-pick and corkscrew) hadn't been lending me much courage.

We told Matata we wanted to go further north still, into the Chobe and Moremi game parks. He missed a beat with his pole and muttered the word *'Caprivi'*, shaking his head. He told us his cousin was a game scout in Moremi, employed in order to prevent poaching. He was the only man for hundreds of miles, without radio or vehicle. He saw no more than four people a year, and was given three bullets a month with which to catch his food. Matata shook his head again, as if we were fools.

After a week in the swamps he left us in a camp at the north end of the Okavango. We drank from the crocodile-infested river, and lions visited the camp every night. I missed Matata's sixth sense and the Boer war rifle. I missed the wet, swampy jungle and the snort of the hippos. I found my penknife and kept it close as the shadow of a vulture wheeled over the tent. I remembered the old man in the military coat and knew I would have felt safer with a handful of dry knucklebones in my pocket.

A Second Shufti at Jordan

The Queen beat me to it – she got to Petra first! But I doubt if she had as much fun. There was she, a horse-loving woman, bumping through the Siq in a Land Rover, wearing a skirt and hat. Whereas touristy me – town-bred and with no more knowledge of nags than a few donkey-rides sixty years ago – I rode high and proud on Suzy, a two-year-old Arab who was full of wind and nervous at moving so slowly.

Holding my back straight and clutching the plaited strings that had once been reins, I felt as intrepid as Stark, as hardened as Lawrence, as much the explorer as Burckhardt. I was there – at last!

Petra to me had been listed with the Pyramids, Timbuktu, Venice, Hadrian's Wall and Troy as places that I had to visit before I died. Some of these have been 'ticked off' and none has failed me. But *Petra!* Petra surpassed anything that I had visualised in my kitchen fantasy-life. That 'rose-red' cliché rang true but Burton hadn't gone far enough in hyperbole.

Here were all the colours of the pink-side of the palette, from blush-veined ivory to the deepest purple. Layer upon layer of shot-silk sandstone soared skywards in the warmth of the sun.

However, not everyone sees Petra so romantically! Edward Lear's Albanian cook declared – 'O Master! We have come into a world where everything is made of chocolate, ham, curry-powder and salmon!'

Well, we can't all be poets; some of us get no further than alliteration!

I'd done my homework in advance. I knew I'd see the facades of Nabataean temples chiselled into the rock and that the cliff-walls would be riddled with empty tombs. But I hadn't realised that there were extensive Roman ruins as well, and that the wide valley waited for archaeologists to dig deeper.

At this *karavanserai* merchants had bartered Damascus brocades for Chinese spices; camels and goats for slaves; thin, brittle pottery for water or weapons. Only when Red Sea dhows replaced camel-trains

Matata mending his nets (*Big Game in the Okavango Swamps*)

The monastery at Petra in Jordan, cut into the rose-coloured sandstone cliffs

Turkey: Getting up a head of
steam on the way to Kaiseri

Bizarre landforms in Cappadocia;
pinnacles of rock pitted with deep
black holes

did Nabataean prosperity diminish.

Nor had I expected to see people living in this city of the dead. As we climbed up the crags of Petra, black goats eyed us warily from black holes. Donkeys saluted our passing with those howls of anguish that had made maiden ladies establish animal sanctuaries in Cairo between the wars. Tiny children, barefoot and dirty, tried to generate enough courage to touch us for a few '*fils*'.

The caves gave shelter to a new generation of troglodytes – European nomads, Australian girls ending their 'Grand Tours' by going native, those few English women who had felt the lure of the desert so intently that they now nursed fair-haired, olive-skinned babies and hung their washing-lines from one eroded pinnacle to another.

Another day I went into the Siq when the sun was setting and the air was already chill. Smoke from charcoal fires swirled from these windowless dwellings. Birds argued sleepily in the thornscrub. The older children were back from school in Wadi Musa, the village outside the Siq where water bubbles from the rock once struck by Moses. Here the nomads water their flocks and the horses drink their fill when the tourists have dismounted.

Wadi Musa has electricity, provisions, a mosque, teachers, police, a doctor and cultivated terraces of crops, the only green in that wilderness of tortured stone. Petra is parched and primitive. Those who choose to live there keep it undefiled. Perhaps they feel an affinity with its ghosts.

If this is so, time is *not* on their side. Soon simplicity must give way to sophistication. Petra's new hotel, built outside the Siq, is run by an Englishman who cut his catering teeth in the palaces of Saudi Arabia. He has the personal directive of the King to develop the tourist-appeal of the site and already talks of a helicopter pad and a VIP's 'cave' on one of the mountain summits.

So the Queen and I just made it before the deluge! If you have the same urge for desert places – go *now*. The pioneering days are all but over.

Jordan has no oil. It has very little that anyone covets, so the Hashemite Kingdom has no choice but to woo the traveller; to see that he has ice for his drinks, a soft bed, a flushing loo and a dash of Bedouin mystique to add zest to his package-deal.

Let's have a 'shufti' at this kingdom. Do you know this word? If you do, you give away your age. Shufti was Desert-Rat slang in the Forties. To 'take a shufti' was to explore a new posting. To find a girl was to 'shufti bint'. For me, this was a second shufti, for I had visited Jordan almost forty years before.

I was working then in Palestine, a territory torn apart by Arab and Jew, held together by the British Mandate. A boyfriend offered me a weekend in Amman, with no strings attached. A chance to buy presents in Amman's bazaar to take home to 'utility' Britain.

We left Jerusalem and breakfasted in Jericho! The Middle East is like that. Bible stories of Sunday-school days become reality. The 'Land of Milk and Honey' shimmers on the far side of the Dead Sea, when seen from Mount Nebo; from 'the Place of Sacrifice' in Petra, the white tomb of Aaron is a gazelle's leap away. Such sightings prove that those ancient wanderers actually lived. And what hardships they endured! For this is a land without water in the desert. Only around Jerash and Amman in the north is there the year-long green of vegetation. But when rain *does* fall, then the desert blooms and the parched earth sings, as the shepherd-boys sang in the Psalms.

On my first visit Amman was an overgrown, untidy Arab village, surrounded by seven hills. The palace of 'Black Ab', the grandfather of King Hussein, overlooked the mosque, the bazaar and the huddle of insanitary buildings that made up the capital. Only the musty Hotel Philadelphia was considered fit for Europeans. Opposite the Philadelphia was an almost perfect Roman amphitheatre; other Roman ruins lay scattered on the hills, barely investigated by the experts. Camels, goats, pye-dogs and donkeys scavenged the verges of the dusty, rough roads.

The British officers of the crack Arab Legion entertained us for our weekend. Off-duty, the subalterns took to their Jeeps and accelerated into the desert to shoot antelope. Their Arab legionnaires galloped behind, firing their rifles exuberantly into the sky like extras in a Beau Geste film.

Today, that 'sport' is banned. Conservation is 'in' and wildlife protected by order of the King. Oryx and ibex are scarce, but they are there. Rare blue lizards scurry among the rocks of Petra; clumps of black lilies grow beside the King's Highway; the few oases teem with birds.

Now the old Philadelphia is to become a Museum for Antiquities and Amman has superb hotels offering all the amenities of our TV culture – but, beware the muezzin at 4am. I flung open my double-glazed windows before I went to sleep and the first call to prayer of the Muslim day was a strident awakening.

The hills are built over with Royal Palaces, villas and apartment-blocks. The civic services work, the new trees and flowers are well tended, the Greek and Roman remains are catalogued and cared for. Jordan's airline is reliable, the medical services are efficient and the government rest-houses are clean. Within five years, it is claimed, every house in Jordan will have electricity. And the nomads are not overlooked – Jordanian army officers try to bring a smattering of schooling to the children who live in the goat-hair tents. Jordan is catching up with the Western world.

The Crusaders also left a legacy to the Arabs, as did those other invaders who came and went. Crusader castles cling to jagged crests or rise up from barren plains. The bones of Christian soldiers who did not return home lie beneath the stones of the desert, sometimes disturbed by the foraging goats.

T. E. Lawrence was a hero to my generation – a hero who is debunked today. A railway line, built by the Turks to link Muslim pilgrims with Mecca, parallels the asphalt of the Desert Highway. As the Turks cut down the oak-trees to fuel the trains, so Lawrence blew up the track. This line is to be reopened soon for tourists and again the steam-trains will chug to Aqaba on the coast.

Shanty-towns of refugee Palestinian Arabs keep the King's Army on the alert. 'Peace' is a fragile word, but the King has said – 'I want to hear the tracks of bulldozers, not tanks . . . the footsteps of travellers, not troops.'

He is a man of vision, whose Bedouin roots give him respect for tradition and the belief that the pursuit of peace must come through diplomacy.

His countrymen show a natural courtesy. Their hospitality is genuine. Their food is good, their coffee, spiced with cardamom, is delicious. And they laugh, so that you laugh too.

See for yourselves, and when you leave Jordan it will be with the words – 'Go in Peace, with God's protection' following after you. Jordanians mean it.

JACQUI STEARN

TURKISH DELIGHTS

We ignored the guidebooks and began our journey east to Turkey's central plateau by train. Haydarpasa Station, its name aptly redolent of the British Raj, is reached by passenger ferry across the Bosphorus, the minaretted outline of Istanbul's western shore receding, while ahead the station's grand stone frontage grows to fill the approaching quayside. As you step within the spaciously marbled ticket hall, feet echo on the tiled floor and voices vanish into the air. Dwarfed, and to the side, are wooden ticket booths complete with iron turnstiles, and as the smartly uniformed clerk writes out tickets in triplicate on a little pink pad, the station clocks could be telling the time fifty years ago.

Standing on the platform waiting for a train was reassuringly familiar amongst the strange language, faces, clothes and endless bundles of possessions. Our diesel pulled in, red and powerful, its nose chevron-striped. The bundles were hoisted on board, many hands exchanged farewells through the windows and Istanbul began to slip away. Neat suburbs of pastel-shaded flats were replaced by Turkish urban fringe. Half-finished houses, surrounded by a lattice-work of wooden scaffolding, the lower storeys already occupied, gave way to even more impromptu housing; the stiffened legs of a dead horse poked from a ditch, its head lolling in the filthy water.

But the train's leisurely pace gave us time to meet Jusuf, our carriage companion, as well as to stare. Our one-word conversations, aided by crude sketches in my notebook, established that he was an electronics engineer, had a family and a brother in West Germany. In the shop he owned they sold records and he loved pop music. We did not, which rather stunted a potentially limitless topic of conversation. But food intervened. His wife had made some *dolmades*; would we like some? Adding our cheese, smoked horsemeat, bread and state-produced red wine, we consumed our feast against the backdrop of a rapidly changing landscape.

One scene shift opened to a reed-fringed lake, the brilliant blue flashes of kingfishers bursting across the still water as we sped by. It changed again as we climbed through the mountains, their worn limestone peaks a slow panning backdrop to the foreground rush of fields around ochre-toned villages and the blur of trees that fused to woods on the distant slopes. When the light began to fade we all moved to the restaurant car, ordered supper and sat sipping *raki* as the sun sank behind golden, lion-paw hills.

Sleep on trains is a misnomer. The train's rhythms, the day's impressions crowded into fitful dreams, pierced by the alarm's shrill tone just as I'd convinced myself I was asleep. Two hours later at dawn we stood beside the track, our fellow travellers asleep on their bundles, all waiting for another engine to pull us the last few miles into Kaiseri. Then, unbelievably, we heard a spine-shivering sound, confirmed seconds later by a trail of smoke above the trees. Surely not? No, it's too good to be true.

Not only was it true, but we were invited on to the steam train's footplate as honoured guests of the driver and fireman. We said farewell to Jusuf and hands pulled us on board, excitement dispelling frustration and tiredness. We squeezed into a perch by the whistle, and watched as, with an easy elegant rhythm, the fireman shot coal into the beast's belly. It consumed flames and breathed steam all around us while we ate delicious engine-baked sweet potatoes. The pressure ready, the driver invited us to squeeze and pull the triggers and levers that turned steam into motion. She heaved herself forward, and with the gathering momentum our whistle-blowing to the boys playing chicken on the line grew increasingly frenetic. They nimbly leapt aside, turned and waved, smart in their white and black school uniforms.

We shuddered down the track passing people sitting amongst great piles of sunflower heads and picked seeds. Donkey carts jolted their way along the stony road running beside the track, the drivers sitting crossways on carts heaped high with bales of cotton. We sped past a tank factory surrounded by rusting examples of its products, guarded by tin-hatted soldiers and barbed wire. Then ahead, on the water tower, was KAISERI and we'd arrived at our point of change for Cappadocia.

Kaiseri, a thriving market town of modern buildings ranged around a centre of crumbling hovels, owes its existence to the silk route, being a camel's day away from towns in either direction. The *karavanserai,* now a covered market, was a place of shelter, and from outside vantage points it appears to be a series of grassy mounds. Inside, the shops and workshops beneath the domed ceilings spilled bales of cotton, wool and carpets from their doors. Cloth caps were being stretched with wooden blocks, steamed then sized by their maker fitting each to his own head for comparison. There was more to explore but, eager to reach Cappadocia and its famed landforms, we left.

Next morning, the muezzin's call to prayer long faded, we pulled back the curtains to reveal the most bizarre scene we'd ever set eyes on. 'Fantastic' assumed its true meaning as we gazed in one direction at the parched plateau, bisected repeatedly by snow-white gashes, and in the other at isolated pinnacles of rock, their surfaces pitted with deep black holes. Wolfing our breakfast of aubergine jam, olives, cheese, bread and tea, we began our ascent of the 'citadel', a pitted pinnacle dominating the village of Uchisar where we were staying. As the path wound through the village past stables and piles of fruit drying in the sun, children rushed to our side saying 'ingleesh, ingleesh' and offering handfuls of dried raisins and seeds. Winding higher we reached the tufa-carved caves that gave the pitted appearance. Many were still used for fruit drying, their sweet smells escaping through the heavy wooden doors. Others were reduced to gaping black holes hanging in space, their names of access lost to the wind.

At the citadel's peak the panoramic view revealed the landscape's formation. Close to, the pure white rock became buff and pink bands of grainy volcanic tufa, the gashes in the plains were wind-blasted, water-dissolved valleys whose sides were themselves incised, leaving cone-shaped rock forms protruding. Where the weather had gone to extremes these were then left as isolated pinnacles. The whole effect was Dali-esque yet reminiscent of the nursery image of the old lady who lived in a shoe.

More bizarre yet were the labyrinthine passages of Derinkyu, where Christians, seeking to escape persecution, had excavated a giant wasp's nest of interconnecting passages and rooms. Clutching at the crumbling walls, we slithered down slopes into a maze of chambers ten or more storeys deep below ground. We wandered from wine cellar to food store, stable to bedroom. At intervals a circular boulder had been cut from the rock with such ingenuity that only a stake through the central core was needed to roll it into position blocking the passageway. Air shafts linked the human warren to the surface and must have helped make the colony more bearably habitable.

That evening, walking through the pale, still village, we stumbled into a living cultural tradition when we followed the sounds of drums and discovered the men's half of a Muslim wedding. This was the third night of four and the groom and best man who stood up to greet us had to be in attendance night and day. They sat back down on the only chairs in a room packed tight with smiling faces, the guests ranged around the walls sitting crossed-legged in their voluminous trousers. Squeezed in one corner, the musicians, with a table-like drum, clarinet and lyre, began a new dance tune. The men leapt to their feet and, dancing in pairs, imitated the women's harem dance movements. Wishing to see if they were also dancing the night away, I asked where the women's house was. I was led through the alleys and yards to where they were gathered. They played no music, but the bright chatter and delight at my visit were compensation.

The women wore the same voluminous pants, but in many colours at variance with their tops and head coverings which they continually fiddled into place. The bride, though, also seated on a chair, had her bleached, permed hair piled high above her face in a fifties bouffant style. I stretched out my hand in greeting; she extended a tight-bound stump. I questioned the younger girls, but they were more eager for me to read their English primers than to explain this custom to me. Then one of the older women took hold of my wrist, held my hand flat in hers and coated my palm with a thick helping of henna. Curling my fingers into the muddy mess, she pasted my nails, then bound my hand with cloth. As she took the other, the girls explained that this was a good luck charm for marriage. Marriage or babies? Shaking my head vigorously I backed to the door. The women laughed and bade me sleep well.

Next morning, when I passed two of the women talking together, they came over and pulled my hand, eager to see the dark brown stains. Pointing in turn to us both and my darkened palm, they grinned mischievously.

RICHARD WARD

MANI

Five hundred drachmas for the room: the matter was soon settled. Just over £3 for a generous bed, a vine-clad balcony with a splash of bougainvillea, two lemon trees in the garden below, and a view over olives to the sea – not a bad deal. Then the old lady took me firmly by the arm and led me into the bathroom. She pointed to a large hole in the ceiling. The sight of it seemed to provoke in her a torrent of recrimination. She spoke fast, too fast for my rudimentary Greek. What was she trying to convey? 'You can't get a plumber these days, not for love nor money.' 'You simply can't trust the workmen any more, can you?' Together we contemplated a knotted cord dangling from the black hole. *'Ipárhi neró zestó?'* I persisted tiresomely, 'Is the water hot?' *'Zestó, zestó,'* she echoed shrilly, irritated by a fatuous question, and launched into another dramatic monologue with a wealth of expressive gestures. Then suddenly she was gone, leaving me to ponder along the unpredictable and intractable nature of language as a medium of communication.

Well, the water wasn't hot, then or at any time. And indeed, who cared? Outside were the mountains of southern Greece, and in the days that followed there were more important considerations than hot water.

I was in Kardamíli in the Mani. A year ago the name Mani meant nothing to me. Then I read Patrick Leigh Fermor's classic and felt an overriding desire to follow in his footsteps. *The Blue Guide* too was encouraging: 'The predominantly mountainous region south of Sparta is seldom visited by foreign tourists . . . superb scenery and unexpected traces of the past.' How much had the Mani changed since Leigh Fermor, that most distinguished of scholar gypsies, explored it in the late 1950s? I intended to find out.

Kardamíli seemed a good base, since the author himself writes of it with such affection. Arriving on a hot afternoon in October this year I found a pleasant but unremarkable village spread along a bay. What sets it apart is its situation, with the massive range of the Taygetus mountains towering above. It is reached by bus from Kalamata through scenery of Arcadian gentleness. Then, for the last twenty minutes, the road snakes down the mountainside. Mountain, plain, sea and sky – the scale has grown suddenly grander. Yet there is nothing gentle about these scorched mountains. The traveller is moving now through terra incognita. You enter Kardamíli full of expectation.

The first thing you hear on leaving the bus is German: *hochdeutsch, plattdeutsch, schwitzerdeutsch*. There are German speakers everywhere, of all ages, from strident young back-packers to the discreet elderly, all deeply tanned, moving with the assurance of long-standing expatriates. These German tourists pervade the Peloponnese and the islands. There seems to be a seasonal mass migration from the Rhineland and the Ruhr, extending well into October. No corner of southern Greece is immune – not even, alas, the Mani.

There is one escape: take to the hills. This never fails. During five weeks in Greece I met four other walkers, all British, two of them women.

The hills above Kardamíli are a good place in which to loosen up. I followed the main road up the mountain leading west, then struck off along an old mule track. The goat bells receded and I seemed to be moving through even deeper layers of peace. There was stillness, an immense blue sky and only the olive trees for company. These olives – their trunks warped, gouged, carbuncled, abrasive to the touch – seem indestructible, as if they could survive even a nuclear winter. The trees gave way to scrub and there was little shade. I was sorry I hadn't brought more water. Even in an October sun one can get quickly dehydrated on these exposed slopes. I headed for the white gleam of a village in the distance and was grateful to find that the one and only store sold iced drinks. The storekeeper asked if I was German. When I said 'English' he started on some obscure anecdote in which I could make out little except the name 'Margaret' and the repetition of *'kato, kato'*, 'down, down'. Days later I realised he was trying to tell me about the Brighton bombing; it had occurred the same morning.

Another memorable walk was the nine kilometres from Yeroliména to Vátheia. This is the deep Mani, almost as far south as one can go on mainland Greece. The road passes through a landscape dotted with crumbling towers, those 'brooding castellations' which are the most striking feature of the region. It was from their gaunt tower houses that the feuding Maniot families of the eighteenth century bombarded each other with musket, cannon and rock, while a cowed population of serfs crept from their semi-troglodyte hovels between the fusillades.

From a distance Vátheia looks like a stricken Camelot. The towers seem grey at first, but grow golden as you approach. Most of them are in a ruinous state with their upper storeys missing, shattered by earthquake, war, neglect. The Government is restoring several of them as

holiday flats, a slow process but tastefully done. An odd experience it
will be to sleep among these spooky and decapitated towers.

In fact, as I soon discovered, these ruins are inhabited. I met the old
lady as I was walking down a steep path out of the village. She was
struggling up, bent under a heavy sack. We greeted each other. The
skin of her face hung in purple folds and the old eyes were blurred with
cataract. When I offered to carry her sack she waved me aside. Who
was this impertinent stranger eyeing her baggage? We moved on up to
her tumbledown tower on the last crag of the village. At the base was a
terrace with one stool on it. Before us stretched an enormous view of
mountain, promontory and shimmering sea. From my pack I offered
her an apple, the only food I had. She dismissed it with a regal gesture.
Then I saw her toothless gums. I left her in peace with her bundle, her
stool and her majestic view.

Like so many villages in the Mani, Vátheia is a ghostly relic. Life
has receded from it. When Leigh Fermor passed this way and was
quizzed and befriended by the fair-haired girl Vasilio with the lamb
slung round her neck, it was still a living community. No longer. If re-
naissance comes it will be in a new form: foreign tourists in holiday
flats.

The road continues south, though not much further. The enterpris-
ing walker could reach Cape Matapan and look for the cave entrance to
Hades. For those like me who fail to make it to the banks of the Styx,
there is compensation at Vlykhada to the north, near Areopolis. Here
is one of the finest cave systems in Europe. It is in fact an underground
river so extensive that the trip in a flat-bottomed boat lasts twenty-five
minutes. You glide through endless caverns of gleaming stalactites
and stalagmites and all this time the boatman, dour Charon, speaks
only once: 'Mind your heads.' The passengers first whisper, then fall
silent. And still you glide. The Mani, which offers many curious experiences, has none more bizarre than this.

Yet the Mani is not for all tastes. It is a place apart, the last bastion. To
this bleak peninsula the Spartans came as refugees. The Maniots, who
trace descent from them, boast of never having been subdued by Slav
or Turk. The ruggedness of the terrain was its safeguard: an arid
mountain region peopled by warring clans in a perpetual state of
anarchy. No-one coveted it.

Where the Ottomans failed, the travel agencies are succeeding.
Coastal towns with beaches are succumbing to the fat profits of the
tourist trade, while the hill villages become ever more depopulated.
Greece has changed immeasurably in recent years. Many of these
changes are for the better: accommodation is much improved, the
roads now are good. Even Greek food – previously lumps of meat and
veg afloat in an oil slick – has acquired an unexpected finesse. But the
impact of six million tourists on small vulnerable communities has

been profound. The human landscape so lovingly evoked by Leigh Fermor, Lawrence Durrell and others is now a wistful memory.

But the hills remain, for these mountain ranges of southern Greece do not lend themselves to the blandishments of the travel brochure. The Mani above all is not cosy; this is no man's dream of Arcadia. It is harsh and scarred and full of ghosts. Yet as you walk these hills you feel that nothing has changed. Goat bells, the smell of thyme, a path winding among olive trees, and the hot sun on your back: this is the Greece that endures. It is enough.

NICK MANDER

Gypsy Serenade

By the time the train arrived in Madrid the Arabs had stolen my coat. I had not been long in the restaurant car: ten minutes, the length of a cognac. I was coming south from England; they were returning home from a factory in Germany.

On the way to the hotel I stopped the taxi to have a drink in a bar. Outside it was winter and raining. He was standing inside, an old brown overcoat and a white shirt buttoned without a tie, around forty. One of his sons was dancing in worn-out boots, the other singing for him, to the clapping of hands without a guitar. They looked about ten, with long hair, both so brown and handsome I could have hugged them; if I were a woman I would have made a date with them for ten years' time. The hair of the third son was cropped almost to the skin. He neither sang nor danced, but with his six or seven years could already dominate both the public and his brothers. When they had finished he ran round with a hat and allowed none of the audience to escape, saying:

'Gentlemen, for our art.'

Afterwards he brought the hat to his father, who counted the contents then placed it empty among the shrimp and peanut shells on the floor.

'And the rest,' he said.

His son swore there was no more.

'And the rest.'

The boy remained silent. After a moment he dropped some coins from his pocket into the hat and stepped back.

'Now the other pocket,' said his father.

He hesitated, then did the same and withdrew into a corner. The father looked stern for a while, but soon went to him and, whispering something into his ear in gypsy, gave him a kiss.

I too had put money into the hat. The father drew me aside and we exchanged names, Nicholas and Gonzalo. He discovered to his surprise that I was English, not American. Then he invited me to a gypsy baptism which was to be held that night in the suburb of Vallecas.

When I accepted he suggested I might like to give him a certain sum to help the wine flow. I hesitated. He turned to his sons demanding to know whether there was or was not to be a baptism party that night, and whether or not I would be the only white present. They told him. The sum changed hands, but underneath the table because it embarrassed him to receive money in public.

On our arrival the bar was full of hopeful faces, most of them gypsy ones. Gonzalo introduced me. When I inquired after the baptism he said he had been mistaken, it had been yesterday, but that there would be another in a few days and, anyway, who needed a baptism to enjoy themselves? We ordered Jerez wine and he presented me to his wife. She was the only woman there. She looked forty but must have been younger, and was dressed entirely in black – for her brother who had died three years ago, they said. She held a sleeping baby in her arms. When I asked how many there were in her family she said seven, but that the young ones were at home, and did not mention her pregnant abdomen. She was very polite and, like the rest of her people, never laughed if an outsider said something coarse. When her husband began to sing a little, snapping his fingers in rhythm, she smiled and for a moment looked like a young girl again; but the barman came immediately and reminded them that singing was not permitted. Then he said the father ought to be ashamed of himself, using children who should be in school to make money, and that one day the police would find him. So we moved to another bar, remarking how times had changed.

There in a tiled room in the basement the pleasure began: Gonzalo's daughter danced for us. She was fifteen, lithe, conscious of her own body and beautiful in her art, and all the while as the spectators' enthusiasm grew her father watched her, drinking Jerez, nodding his head and smiling.

Presently he drew me aside to suggest that if I would like to give him a certain sum his wife and daughter would go immediately and prepare a gypsy supper. He explained that their house down under the railway by the Bridge of Three Eyes had only one room, but his own eyes shone as he described the delights of a gypsy supper. When I said I did not have the sum he drew me even further into a corner. From somewhere upstairs came the sound of a group of people singing songs from their own province. He cleared his throat and laid his finger along his nose. It seemed as if the world had stopped to listen.

'You,' he said, '. . . that is, you . . . are my friend. I . . . that is I, my wife and my children . . . we, I, do not like to invite a friend to a party and not give him the best. Do you understand? Like this I can't treat you as I wish to.'

But I said it was impossible. I could not afford more of his hospitality.

We returned to the centre of the room. Gonzalo poured more Jerez, coughed and examined his throat in the mirror. Then he turned to his son and told him to sing *fandangos* in the way he had been shown. The guitarist began the familiar descending cascades and the boy entered. But after a while his father stopped him to say he was not singing what he had been taught. The boy looked at the ceiling. He had big eyes. His father told him to listen now to the way he himself was going to sing them. We all listened. Afterwards the boy tried again but was stopped once more. Suddenly a fat gypsy stood up. A few years ago he had been one of the best-paid dancers in Flamenco. There were several rings on his fingers and his shoes were still beautifully polished.

'Listen,' he said to the boy. 'I am only a dancer, and I'm too old now even for that. But I know more about singing than your father will ever know. You go on as you yourself are and one day you'll be good.'

'And you,' he said, turning to the father, 'should talk less. The kid isn't singing badly. He's just singing a style you don't know.'

The guitar was playing again, this time in slow rhythm, and after a while a voice broke in. It was an elderly gypsy who had been sitting silently all evening, and the voice was as rough as the open road but when it sang the room became quiet. The singer loosened the collar of his shirt and let his voice flow out as turbulently and tranquilly as he desired. That night he had reached a moment of feeling no-one else had, and his cigarette burned unnoticed in the fingers of his hands which stretched out parallel like mute ghosts. He did not sing for long because he was old, but it was enough.

After that we went up. As we passed out of the bar it was raining again and all Madrid's lights were swimming before my eyes, reflected on the street. Stepping carefully over the gutter, Gonzalo remarked that I ought to wear a coat like he did. When I explained what had happened on the train he shook his head and said one should never trust the Moors.

It was midnight. As we were giving our hands he looked up at me intently and told me that in two days there would be a gypsy wedding.

When I told him I could not come he turned up the collar of his coat and walked away, looking at the pavement beside the unlit shop windows, hands deep in his pockets, and passed into the night going towards the Bridge of Three Eyes.

By now the Arab with my coat would be in Malaga waiting for the boat across to Africa. Twenty-four hours earlier, we had both been in Paris.

GAY HODGSON

PEDALLING AROUND PAPUA

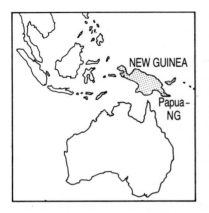

Shadows of brown and blue smoky light under the coconut palms, slow-burning waste fires where copra is being harvested, rows of sacks for collection, like milk churns in the old days in England, carefully covered to keep out flies or probing fingers. Knives of strong, bright hard light shine down the gap where the road is, dull and dusty. A college friend of Ian's, riding in a pick-up with many others, had a coconut fall on his head and died instantly. In the multitude of combined chances – the speed of the van, the point in time at which the coconut detached itself and fell, the area in which it might fall allowing for the wind swaying the palm – why did it fall on him amongst all those others? Actually they seem to be coming down all the time; they fall from a great height and they are very heavy and nobody who has been in the lowlands of Papua New Guinea for even a short time will not have been startled by one falling frighteningly near.

I was in Madang, at the end of the wet season. I had the day to my-self and the loan of a bicycle. Oh! gasped everyone, it's too hot to cycle, you won't get far. But I did. I'd set out early, with a bunch of bananas, a drink and a sketchbook, to spend the most independent hours of my stay in the country. The fruit bats, replete, had settled high upside down in the trees, like rotten fruit themselves; there was moisture on the grass and the air was still cool.

Mastering the art of this bicycle took some straight roads, a lot of patience and some bruising. It was heavy, had a pedal brake, a most unnatural device, and a child seat of inch-thick wood screwed to the crossbar, causing me to cycle in a bandy-legged, wobbly way. Rush-ing rather too fast down the grassy slope towards prickly coral rocks and the sea, I forgot the bicycle had no handlebar brakes and came to a shaky swerving sideways stop or fall, hitting my leg. A flash of blue and a glittering kingfisher, startled by my noise, flew away.

Weaving drunkenly, I set out again from beside the sea to find what I thought would be a brilliant short cut out of Madang. I found the short cut and I found downtown Madang too. This town, quite a pretty one, is bisected by inlets and salt water marshes, some drained, some not. The inlet I wanted to cross was the filthiest, most un-tide-washed one of all. The water lay grey and greasy, gas bubbles popping up from below, and my short cut was a suspension footbridge which reeled loopily to the other side. I walked, pushing the bicycle slightly ahead; the bridge was narrow and, at the middle, the whole thing was turning turtle. Nine inches or so above the surface, I hoped that even alligators would know better than to come to these dark waters; my stomach froze rigid and I toyed with the possibility of walking back-wards the way I had come. Mosquitoes danced around my face and nipped my ankles; the brackish water smelt horrid as the sun warmed up. I looked along the narrowing perspective of the bridge and pushed on, jaws clamped shut.

'*Gut Moning!*' Surprised nationals on the other side, dwellers in hardboard, iron and wooden shanties can seldom have seen an idiot white woman with a bicycle crossing their bridge. Bumping and skid-ding, but back in the saddle, I found the airport. Trying again, I soon ran out amongst the coconut plantations.

Badly cared-for palm groves have stags-horn ferns up the trunks, holding their own little world of ponds and land, plants and creatures. Badly cared-for palm groves have castinea borer, a beetle which drills the trunk, causing the tree canopies to tumble to the ground leaving rows of curved telegraph poles, useless and dead. Carefully-tended palms are injected with insecticide, causing nectar and pollen in the flowering palm to become toxic, poisoning honey and killing the bees.

Cocoa grows under the shade-giving palms, curious low trees with the ripening fruit green, yellow and orange, sprouting from the trunks and heavier branches. Brahma-Shorthorn cattle are run into the groves to keep the grass and weeds low; thus the fallen coconut is spot-ted before it germinates and can be collected. Contrary to popular view, the palms are not climbed and the nuts are not shaken down. Where the grass is long and the nuts missed, they come up rapidly, fat bud and roots from one of the circular depressions at the end; then up come the green paper fan leaves, two small ones and then longer and longer on their stiff, ochre-coloured, scale-wrapped stems.

Giant snails with sharply pointed shells, having crawled up and on to the road, were crushed by a passing lorry which covered me in yellow dust. A huge toad, steamrollered flat, dry and leathery, left a moist imprint when I kicked its carcass away. Its brothers croaked on in the weeds and ditches, almost syncopating with a guitar and kundu drum in a palm-thatched hut high on a rise accompanying the wailing, wordless song that the players sang. Palm leaves, huge and torn into segments by the wind, are the staple housing material here. The thatch criss-crosses under the shade of the criss-cross green palms overhead.

On a bridge crossing the Wagol River, endlessly shaken by huge timber lorries taking giant tree trunks to the Japanese woodchip fac-

(*left*) Gonzalo teaching his son to sing fandangos (*Gypsy Serenade*)
(*right*) Native of Papua-New Guinea, sketched by the author (*Pedalling Around Papua*)

The village of Vatheia in the Mani region of southern Greece

(*left*) Hi-tech confectionery: a chocolate calculator
(*right*) Sacred smoke: a sniff a day ensures long life and happiness

JAPAN

A typical breakfast includes pickled plums, mussel soup and seaweed

tory, I stopped to draw huts. They were slotted in between the palms, and all reflected leaf by leaf in the still water below until a nut plopped into the water and the upside-down palms waved and swayed in the widening rings. I was joined by a big girl who leaned up close to watch. Speaking to her in nervous Pidgin, I was answered in perfect English. I liked to be surrounded by people watching; when they moved away I felt lost and exposed. Cycling out into open country, I could peer up little paths through the grass to groups of huts tucked away privately. I turned off a main road on to an unpaved one, very unpaved, more pot-hole than track, and was glad of the chubby tyres on the bike.

'*Moning Missis*', from high up in a hut on a hill, the thud of a *garamut* drum, a hollowed log that is struck with a heavy stick, inside or out. I found a place I had hoped to find, a Sepik settlement, far from its original home, where carving was done and artefacts made for tourists – a genuine Sepik hut with carved and painted inside posts and open bottom with loose grass hanging, tied back to let in air, and a painted entrance. The small and portable gewgaws were dull but I yearned for the flutes with figures carved on the ends – big, far too big to either carry on a bicycle or take home safely – or the huge *garamut* drum, or the tapa cloth shields. I watched a cross-legged man carving with a steel blade bound to a wooden handle. He told me they once used sharpened pig tusk.

Inland and midday, the heat was like a wall. I sought the sea and, though heading the right way, I was going up and up. One day, I thought, this hill will be a mountain. On the north side of New Guinea the land is being heaved up by the ocean plate pushing underneath, hence the volcanoes and the earth tremors. At the top of the hill I saw the sea and islands, lots of them, each crowned with a fuzzy green hairpiece, and the breeze blowing off the sea was cool. Below me, inaccessible, was the village and beach I sought. By a devious and dangerous route, I pedalled, fell and walked to the sea, to a beach that felt so private I was afraid of trespassing. Two men mending a canoe waved and smiled. With my back to the warm wooden side of a palm-covered boat, I settled down to draw an outrigger canoe, at once graceful, sleek and utterly primitive. The body of the craft was a hollow log cut slim and tall. The paddler sits on the top, one leg tucked in front of the other. The single outrigger is attached by saplings tied with wiry vine and supports, well away from the water at the bow end, a sort of parcel shelf. On the sea, this light flexible craft can travel quickly and easily, even in the hands of tiny children.

School was out and hosts of betel-nut-chewing tots came to wait for parents to take them out to the islands. They settled in a group around me, watching and chattering until all had been whisked away over the waves.

Returning home, I was circled by a proud youngster on his BMX bike, wheelying in the dust and sending grit into his and my eyes. We ended with a race, which I lost. Men were shooting fruit bats, flying foxes, down from the tree – easy targets, but do they let go when dead? Two parrots, like any old sparrows, were courting on the telegraph wires, the cock sidling up to the hen with a brisk nodding of his head. Seeing me, they flew away to more private places and I went home to shower.

FABIAN ACKER

WOMEN AND SOCKS

Once Europeans had become accustomed to flip-flops, it wasn't all that difficult to get used to mitten-shaped socks, each holding the big toe in its own little pocket and letting the other four doss down together. But the very first visitors to Japan assumed, from the local socks, that the Japanese had only two toes. And the Japanese, on the basis of the visitors' socks, thought that Europeans had none.

Well, that's the essence of Japan: mystery and misunderstanding. You can't understand what people are saying, you can't read the street signs, and you can't find out where the buses are going to. Nor can you read the Tokyo tube map. Even if the trains are coloured according to the line they run on, the map itself is like an action painting by a hyperactive centipede.

But the compensations for being unable to read or carry on a casual conversation are overwhelming. The sight, for instance, of a fat wrestler dressed in a bright open kimono and what appears to be a black chastity belt sitting on the train reading a comic book. Or the children from primary school on an outing, dressed in sailor suits like Victorian children on their way to the seaside, snaking behind their teacher in twos, each round head and pair of button eyes topped by an identical pudding basin of black hair and blue sailor hat.

The cafés provide a nice easy introduction to the delights and puzzles of Japan. Avoid the hotel restaurants, and beware of Colonel Sanders. His larger-than-life statue with its slightly oriental cast of features serves as a warning that you are approaching the junk food area.

The most intriguing cafés have steamy windows filled with plastic replicas of the real food inside. It is certainly a better way of choosing food than trying to read the menu. The displays clearly represent food. The question is: what food? You can't go wrong with anything shaped like a noodle. It is almost certainly a noodle. But look out for those exquisite confections that look like liquorice allsorts. About the size of matchboxes, they are perfectly symmetrical – some tubular, some round, and some square, with black and white patterns relieved by little buttons of green or red. They are not liquorice allsorts. They are fish; that is, they are made from fish. There's nothing wrong with the taste, but it's a culinary shock if you order one or two for dessert under the impression that you are about to eat some oriental sweetmeat.

If you see something that tickles your fancy you'll have to force yourself to bring the waiter outside and use sign language. But it's less risky than pointing to totally unknown items on a menu.

Sign language is almost essential in shops too, but it's a little less embarrassing because you can be more discreet. A tiny gesture towards a desired item and a slight flick of the eyebrows is almost enough to complete most transactions. Not like dragging a waiter out of a warm café into a cold street while you point at plastic puddings.

Paying for your goods will lead to further mysteries. In this country of robots, minuscule calculators and pocket TV, they use little wooden abacuses to add up your bill. You can, for instance, buy a computer, a digital watch and a transistorised tennis game, and the shopkeeper will reach for his abacus (called a *soroban* in Japan) to calculate the cost. In the upmarket shops they'll use a calculator to start with and then check the answer with a *soroban*.

It's obvious that in their heart of hearts the Japanese don't really trust calculators.

The same uneasy juxtaposition of man and technology is evident if you take the lift in a department store. Two uniformed girls will bow you in and another two will bow you out. They will also say something to you. Could it be: 'Did you have a nice trip?', or: 'You're looking well today'? Whatever it is, they say it hundreds of times an hour with endless patience and cheerfulness. The lifts of course are automatic and run without attendants.

Another way to get the flavour of Japan, but requiring a little more courage than merely eating in a local café, is to stay in a Japanese-style hotel. There are five or six in Tokyo and many more throughout the country. You can get a list from the Japanese Tourist Board in London, which for some inscrutable reason gives only half of them. You can get a full list in Tokyo.

In this kind of hotel you will sleep on the floor, wear a kimono (provided by the management) instead of pyjamas and share a bath with strangers. You'll also be given a new toothbrush every evening. Of course, if you're more comfortable in a lounge suit or twin-set and pearls, prefer eggs and bacon for breakfast, insist on using the same boring toothbrush day and night, and like to take baths alone, then you can go to the Hilton. There's one in London too.

In the Japanese hotel your bed is a comfortable mattress on the floor. In the mornings the chambermaid will roll it up leaving the floor space free. This is covered in rush mats which is why they ask you to wear slippers, not shoes, when you go into your bedroom. The surface is quite delicate.

Whatever breakfast consists of, it is brought to your table arranged so exquisitely, and with each dish packaged so cunningly, that you cannot refrain from tasting. You'll discover mussel soup and pickled plums among other unknown delicacies, and you can find out what those liquorice allsorts taste like. You can always fall back on good old rice and tea if the aesthetic qualities of the food are not enough to overcome your apprehension. But persist! After a while you'll find yourself beginning to enjoy breakfast.

As for the communal bath: it's not really for washing. This is Japan after all; part of the mystery, and so on. If you want to wash yourself you can go to the real bathroom, usually en suite. In there you'll find a sink on the floor, just large enough to stand in, and you can have a good long soak up to your knees. You'll have to wash the rest in air, as it were. Then, when your're really clean, put on your kimono, drape a bathtowel over your shoulders and join the other guests in the big bath.

There are Western-style concerts in Tokyo; if you're brave about food and hotels, I reckon you can treat yourself to a bit of Bach or Mozart, usually played with maturity and feeling by six- or seven-year-olds. Don't forget: this is where Suzuki started. At a recital I attended, when an elderly twenty-one-year-old was performing, the first two rows were taken up by tiny children watching the performer's every move like little sparrows watching their mothers bring in the worms. And God help the little sparrow that dares to close its eyes or shuffle its tiny feet during a performance. Mums and dads in the rows behind will soon give a practised twist to its ear.

I saw so many of these earnest young hopefuls that one day, I'm sure, we will be invaded by battalions of these *wunderkinder* descending by parachutes above the Royal Festival Hall, violins strapped to their backs.

The nice thing is that, at least in music, the girls are on par with the boys. Not anywhere else. The Japanese male seems to think that women have only recently developed skills and abilities they never had before.

'Women and socks,' the men say, 'have greatly improved since the war.'

MARGARET GILLIES

AN EDUCATIONAL EXCURSION TO PARIS

The school assembly hall buzzed with conversation. The long-awaited educational excursion to Paris was about to begin. Parents were tearfully hugging their adored eleven-year-olds, most of whom displayed apathy in a desperate attempt to convey to their demonstrative parents that they were simply an embarrassment to maturing scholars who were about to embark on an exciting and enlightening adventure.

As one of the five intrepid teachers who had actually volunteered to care for the forty-six assembled innocents abroad, I surveyed the situation not dispassionately and made a supreme effort to concentrate on organising the assortment of travel sickness tablets I had accumulated from my charges. I tried to reassure myself that I had made the right decision in offering to escort those trusting young people around Paris, and that I was mentally prepared to cope with the ensuing events, whatever they might be.

After a relatively uneventful, sleepless overnight bus journey interspersed with the usual convenience stops, and a bracing ferry trip to Boulogne, we faced yet another tedious five hours aboard the bus before we finally arrived at the Maurice Ravel Centre, where we were to be in residence for the next three nights.

We were ravenous, and thoroughly exhausted, and most certainly in no mood for the frosty-faced Evil Edna who presided over the dining-room. She was, during our entire stay, intolerant, unpleasant and rude, and we just loved to hate her. We disarmed her with politeness and encouraged the children to do likewise; and occasionally that dour façade would crumble ever so slightly to reveal just a tiny trace of bewilderment, or could it be amusement, or might it even be pleasure? We shall never know.

She complained with wild gestures in her raucous French that the children had no speed, no memory, no manners and no French. They knew, to quote her, *rien*. Anyhow, we all endeavoured to remember to put everything we needed on our food trays *aussi vite que possible,* and to greet the old bag with *bonjour,* but we continued determinedly to drink our coffee from the bowls in true British fashion, rather than dunk *à la française*.

We found more than 'dunking' a trifle unusual. We were horrified to discover that the shower compartments, although partially separated by a tiled wall, were in fact unisex. Bespotted French teenage youths peeked at our innocent *jeunes filles* while they lathered their budding bosoms, and scantily-clad teenage girls chased, caught and kissed our impressionable *garçons*. After the fiasco on our first night at the Centre we decided it might be advisable to shower at the nearby swimming pool, where at least segregation of the sexes was still in vogue. Washing à la Maurice Ravel was limited to a douche at the wash-basins, not one of which was fitted with a stopper.

During the night the teenagers had parties. They smoked. They drank. They sang. The following day they were ill. The following day we were tired. The management had introduced a somewhat ineffectual deterrent. A fine of five francs was imposed each time there was a disturbance. By this time the teenagers had no money, and were dead drunk anyway.

On the night we organised a disco for the children we were the ones to make a noise, and we were the ones to drink; but I doubt if anybody could object to Fanta orange being consumed till 11.30pm. Maurice Ravel provided us with a room and hi-fi equipment, and we played our own tapes. An otherwise perfect evening was marred when some of our girls paid a call to the toilet. En route they were accosted by a group of inebriated black basketball players who created great consternation by 'flashing' themselves.

Our nights were certainly eventful, even alarming, not at all restful but nonetheless educational in the light of experience. Our days spent sightseeing were absolutely delightful. The French guide, Natalie, charmed the children with her amusing anecdotes about the French aristocracy, and Robbie, our good-humoured bus driver, had the children eating out of the palm of his Glaswegian hand and knew Paris like the back of it. Surrounded by the beauty of Paris and chaperoned by Natalie and Robbie, we soon forgot about the unpleasant nocturnal incidents.

Bateaux Mouches was the first excursion. Once aboard *L'Hirondelle* the children couldn't wait to spend their francs on hot dogs and cans of juice. The gastronomic delights over, they concentrated on counting the thirty-two bridges over the River Seine, while (when we weren't reprimanding someone for not using the litter bin) we marvelled at the architecture.

We visited Notre Dame on Ile-de-la-Cité, counted as we climbed the several hundred steps, only to be disappointed that Quasimodo wasn't there after all. We went to the magnificent Place de la Concorde, where the children showed predictable sadistic pleasure when told that this was one of the spots where a guillotine stood during the French Revolution. To them the Egyptian obelisk which now stands there in its place, although admittedly quite majestic, was of secondary importance.

We explored the Conciergerie, and heard in lurid detail about the many tragedies which took place there. We visited the Palace at Versailles where the Hall of Mirrors greatly interested the children, as did the tales Natalie told. How could such powerful kings and beautiful ladies have had such deplorable habits? We decided that the Maurice Ravel Centre wasn't so bad after all.

The view from the top of the Eiffel Tower is breathtaking – if you don't suffer from vertigo and if you've any breath left after climbing to the top. I shall take the lift next time. What I remember most clearly from up there in the dizzy heights is the Arc de Triomphe, and the avenues and boulevards radiating from it. Even from the top of the Eiffel Tower you can see that the French drive like maniacs. Robbie must have had nerves of steel.

No visit to Paris would be complete without a visit to the Louvre. Our visit there was rather shorter than we had hoped, as we had to hurry back to Madame Edna for the evening meal. We did ensure that everyone saw the Venus de Milo, but of course not many of the children were impressed. At any rate, she wasn't their highest ideal of feminine beauty. She had a flat chest and no arms. Leonardo da Vinci's Mona Lisa gazed enigmatically at everyone from behind her protective glass case, and the children were hysterical when they read a sign saying NO FLASHES. After the baseball players, the message conveyed a somewhat different meaning to the one intended.

Our sightseeing culminated in an illuminated tour of the city on our last night, with Robbie as driver-cum-guide. Paris is truly beautiful. We all gasped in wonder. *La ville lumière* impressed everyone. The romantic atmosphere of Paris surrounded us, and the promise of excitement lingered everywhere. I made myself a promise there and then, that I'd return one day to this beautiful metropolis of pleasure, and I shall. But can you guess? It won't be on a school excursion.

GWYNNETH BRANFOOT

THURBER COUNTRY

Taking care not to fall off my sandals, because I was free-standing rather than strapped in and buckled down (the straps rubbed, the metal buckles burned, and the heat of the sand could take the soles right off your English feet), I kept nodding my head as I balanced on one foot and riffled my other through the unfamiliar sand, and listened to the man with the small beard. Everything about him was boring, beginning with his accent and including his two pushy children, who kept biffing each other about and almost toppling me off my sandal into the hot stuff. I don't burn *that* easy, but we were used to those wet little ridges you stride over, manfully, on your way to a grey sea whipped up by a killer of an east wind, at Whitby – so I wasn't complaining. Apart from the children. As your own grow up, you can kiss goodbye to a certain kind of sticky-fingered shuffling, although I suppose they were behaving fairly reasonably, considering their father had been talking for twenty minutes. He had the perfect job. That's what he told me. His kids fought like small wolves over shells in the sand; his vowels sounded like pancakes someone had tossed in the air, missed, and trodden on. He was about my age, and I envied him with something physically approaching heartache. He not only had the perfect job. He had the perfect life.

It was something I'd wanted since the age of twelve, this trip we were making now; this country. The man at the Embassy was amused because I'd written under Purpose of Visit . . . 'I'd like to see the country that produced Thurber'. Maybe it made a change from dream-seekers. They must get tired of being everybody's rainbow's end.

There was an unforgettable, unforgotten smell in Customs and the first words we heard came downwind from an official, holding his nose as he rooted through about sixteen suitcases, saying 'Oh, my Gard, the baby wenna the baythroom'. He had, too – he was quiet, but he smelled right over to where we were standing. You can always tell when a baby's been eating bananas.

We bought the cheapest VW bus we could find, which took most of our cash and broke down within a week; but the guarantee said 'First month or thousand miles' so we were in on both counts, which meant three days waiting in Charlottesville, West Virginia, in a hotel with ceiling fans and porch rockers and a man who adopted us and drove us everywhere singing 'I'm a ramblin' wreck from the Georgia Tech, and a helluvan engineer'. They understood us, though. 'Say it again,' said the salesman in hardware, dangling a bath plug at me. 'Ploog,' I repeated obediently. 'Do you sell ploogs, please?' They understood us right the way to the West Coast, although some people thought Yorkshire was a part of Scotland and some others thought we were Germans. Germans, with not a blond hair between us! But people do make mistakes.

One night we drove through a secret base in Tennessee and were stopped only on our way out by MPs who accepted that we thought it some kind of holiday village – rows of wooden shacks – but found it hard to believe that we had driven unarrested right down from New York through Florida on sidelights instead of the compulsory dipped beams. Then, in our headlights, we saw snakes, and I would not wee in the grass any more. Because many gas stations prefer you to buy their petrol when you use their rest room, we became stuck with the Ten Dollar Pee. My husband was all right, he could just stand there (and they wonder what we mean about penis envy).

We ate off-highway food when we could, and we liked it – okra, hush puppies, catfish. The deep South drew us, perhaps because coming from the North of England we felt the bond of being thought second-best, with voices the butt of other people's jokes. But friends in Manhattan had warned us of small towns, and of drivers arbitrarily arrested for speeding. 'But officer, I was only doing twenny!' 'Okay, so you were loitering. Overnight, or fifty bucks.' It wasn't true, though.

We saw roadside posters showing drunken pin-men lying flat on their backs with their toes turned up, beneath a headline saying 'Moonshine can kill'; and we hated the chiggers, little flies that filled our bus and bit us. I remembered a neighbour who had visited Australia and told us 'Nobody ever tells you about the flies'. Nobody ever told us about the heat, and they should; it can fell you. Our Manhattanite friend who left London twenty years ago wore a pith helmet as he soared along the turnpikes in his MG. (Porsche is more popular. They send about a dozen sports cars over for a hundred waiting customers, who grow tired of waiting and go next door and buy a Spyder.) But remember that in Las Vegas the midnight temperature is over ninety. We crossed the desert with me wrapped in wet blankets in the back, and gave Death Valley a miss altogether.

By the time we got to Tucson we were running out of money and living on fruit, and running . . . water melons are worse than bananas in that respect. Crouched in a Nevada toilet I saw carved on the wooden door 'F . . . Reagan, he was a lousy sheriff'.

On the beaches we looked white and weedy, as though we had grown up eating bread and marge. One day, after a landslide near Pacific Palisades, we gazed up and saw a man peering down without anxiety, still holding his highball and conferring with his wife. They went back inside, and I imagined he was saying 'Hell, Ethel, when did we last use the patio anyway?' and I remembered Thurber. They call junkies hopheads in California and we knew we'd arrived when, eating breakfast in a diner, the man behind us ordered his eggs 'sunnyside up and basted with coke'. A hophead chased us all over LA one night, banging our back bumper with his front fender, until I swerved off the road and my husband hit his head on the windscreen.

We discovered why Americans say New Orleans is the only city they really love besides that other city, by the sea, which we also visited and wondered if they should re-write the song, 'I left my wallet in San Francisco'. We came back through the Mid-West, where everyone has cheekbones like Red Indian chieftains; and we could not sell our VW and lived on Colorado omelettes (onion, bacon, green pepper) all that last week, and I know when I die my soul will dither forever between Ilkley Moor and the Grand Canyon. They eat three pork chops at a meal instead of one and they still buy oranges for juicing, the way they did in the last war when Steinbeck wrote of a troopship dumping sacks of squeezed orange skins, and watched English children fighting over them. Women carry guns; cars really need the refrigerated air-conditioning we thought they were just boasting about; and perfectly normal citizens fly the Stars and Stripes right on their front lawns . . .

The man on the beach with the beard was a film producer who said he lived six months in London and six months in Beverly Hills. Wouldn't you have tasted bile and green gall too? His children were searching for coral, he told me. They looked all the time they visited the ocean, all of them, but they never found any.

Just then my toes that were sieving the sand hit something hard and I bent down and picked up a huge, enormous piece of coral that looked like the inside of a cathedral. Everyone stared. 'Two years,' said the man, thickly. 'Never saw one little bitty piece.'

Now, I am fond of children, even noisy ones, even my own; and even though a man who went to Oxford speaks in a way that makes someone from Leeds feel like a person who eats stoats and bites beer bottles in two, and this guy had all that plus mid-Atlantic twang, and was a twice-yearly-commuting successful movie-maker my own age or *less* . . . that wasn't the reason I kept the coral and would not – could not – give it to him.

I swear that wasn't the reason, even though it took all my will to say

'Luck of the draw, I expect', and slop off on my sandals like snow shoes, holding tight to the coral as though it were my own soul he might try to take from me. It stands on the bookshelf now, and I look at it almost every day and think of what a time we had. Oh, we had the time of our lives!

HIGH IN BOLIVIA

We had come to Bolivia to explore the high mountains of the Cordillera Real, and one early morning, ourselves and backpacks stowed in Ramiro's Land Rover, we set off from La Paz heading for Ulla Ulla, a remote region near the Peruvian border north east of Lake Titicaca. Adobe houses scattered over the altiplano glowed golden in the early sun; the lake perfectly mirrored every cloud, reed boat and eucalyptus tree, and the snowy peaks of the distant Andes made the toes tingle with anticipation. Campesinos herded cows along the roadside, men in ponchos and *chuyos,* those woolly hats with ear flaps, women in bright bulky skirts and bowlers perched above glossy black plaits, carrying babies in striped back bundles. We bought a cooking pot and our last petrol in Escoma, a village which was to figure more than once in our lives over the next week. Then, heading away from the lake, we climbed through a wild landscape of stony track and sparse yellow grass, stalked by high mountains smoking with dense cloud. At a puncture-cum-picnic stop a flock of ravenous sheep galloped up to devour our banana skins. On our way again and suddenly, after nine hours, we were on a vast plateau ringed by snow-capped summits and grazed by herds of llama and alpaca as far as the eye could see. And, in this vastness, the minuscule dot of Ulla Ulla village.

In some disbelief we approached over a marshy causeway. There was no sign of life in the square, but then out came the mayor, a tiny stocky Indian with bright eyes in a leathery face. Yes, we could sleep in the new school and use the pump for water. A snowstorm, which had been lurking darkly, broke over us and we retired indoors to light candles and warm our pot of soup on an unwilling primus stove. The cold was penetrating and the village poncho pedlar did a brisk trade that night.

At 14,000ft the morning was sharp and sparkling, and alpaca, gathered round the school since nightfall, were lurching to their feet under loads of snow as we set off on the trail of the rare ojojo bird. And then we discovered the hot springs of Ulla Ulla. There they steamed

and bubbled, in the absolute middle of nowhere. Stripping off, we lay
up to our chins in the most improbable hot bath ever, vicuña grazing
in the distance, hot sun melting the snow and the Andes glistening in a
great circle all around.

Back at base that evening we waited eagerly for the hot stew we had
arranged to have cooked for us, but discovered that the entire village
had gone to bury an old shepherd and, having run the corpse round the
cemetery boundary 'so the soul won't lose its way', were rounding off
proceedings at the graveside with home-brewed alcohol. So we sang
carols round a candle, which seemed appropriate in the circumstances,
and then, fully clothed, gloved and hatted, crept supperless into our
sleeping bags.

Our road next morning took us above the clouds at 17,000ft before
zig-zagging steeply down into a spectacular narrow valley, soaring
black rock faces on either side and craggy slopes thick with Andean
winter flowers, yellow, orange and blue. Llamas looked down their
noses at us from high places, and a village schoolroomful of white-
coated scholars sprang to their feet as we jolted past. But our goal was
Curva, at the far end of the valley, the traditional centre of the
Kalawayas, itinerant medicine men, where we were to drop off two
researchers. The village perched high on the precipitous valley wall,
spindly trees waving over thatched roofs. Our entry into the square
drew the men warily into the open but the women, wearing pancake
hats and heavy silver ornaments, stayed in doorways. One of our
party produced photographs of his previous visit there and silent delight lit the assembled faces. Handshakes all round, sweets and bal-
loons offered to shyly-smiling children, and an impressively stamped
document was produced, declaring us to be the *padrinos,* or god-
fathers, of the new benches for the village square. A hasty peso collection among ourselves to match this honour, more handshakes and
group photographs, and we were heading back along the valleys on
our way to Aucapata, another isolated mountain village where we
thought we might find lodgings.

The valley we now entered was perhaps even more breathtaking in
its wildness than the last. We ricocheted off boulders, stream beds and
scree slopes, plunged alternately into thick cloud and bright sun. It
seemed as though we would never again see a living soul. Suddenly
there was a flock of sheep and a shepherd with a long cane flute over
his shoulder. Would he play for us? A few shy notes from him, a present of oranges from us and he vanished into the clouds. On we
bounced and slalomed, over a mud landslide, straining up to the highest section of the road. At this point Ramiro announced that he hadn't
enough petrol to get us to Aucapata and back to La Paz, nor was there
enough to get us straight back to Escoma and the nearest supply. We
decided to continue and that Ramiro would leave us in Aucapata. So

we crawled on downwards into the gathering gloom, stopping frequently to douse an over-heating front bearing with the remains of our drinking water. We heaved the rocks aside and drove into a pitch-black village. A silent line of figures approached, ponchos flapping like bats' wings. The road led nowhere: we should have forked right. On the final run down the twenty-two hairpin bends into Aucapata we startled a cow bedded down in the roadway. Then dark shapes of houses, a narrow lane and into the village square where, miraculously, Doña Blanca stood on the corner as if expecting us. Yes, she could house and feed us and would we like coffee? Would we! Up stone steps from the courtyard to a creaking wooden-balconied room where shadows danced. We had arrived.

Aucapata clings 9,000ft up on a valley side. Many of the villagers are fair-skinned and blue-eyed, possibly descendants of Spanish gold-diggers. Others are Indian and wear the woven full-sleeved shirts, double trousers, striped ponchos and tasselled *chuyos* of their Inca ancestors. The plaza is wide, empty and silent. A hedge of white rose and periwinkle surrounds a central garden, where a stone idol clutches his mysterious pre-Inca origins close to his chest. A duo of lean black pigs trot round, hoovering all before them – and that isn't much. The ramshackle church and belfry stand beside the thatched museum, opened recently with the discovery, 3,000ft below, of Iskanwaya, a ruined pre-Inca city. 'But nobody comes here,' Constantino, the curator, told us mournfully. The road to the ruins was impassable but he could provide horses and take us down.

Next morning the horses had disappeared in the mist, so we settled for one elderly mule. The path took a near vertical course down the mountain, passing cactus, bamboo and banana palm, with humming birds and bright butterflies flashing by. A green shriek of parakeets caused a momentary disturbance in the warm, drowsy midday as we gazed out through trapezoidal windows into the void below, speculating on life in the Cordillera Real 600 years ago. Our climb back was slow, too slow for the fleet-footed Constantino, who left us to the mule. That evening, as we ate supper in Doña Blanca's shop, the town band of panpipes, drum, guitars and *charango* serenaded us, inspired by a bottle or two of alcoholic orange to ever greater heights of exuberant cacophony.

Transport out of Aucapata is a gamble. You either wait and see if the fortnightly lorry will arrive, or you walk up to the mine and hope to hitch a ride in a petrol lorry. Three of us decided on the latter course and set off, armed with a rudimentary sketch map and a hard-boiled egg apiece. The path led inexorably upwards through thick cloud. Once we passed a sow and eight piglets; once two mule drivers who assured us that yes, we had a long way to go. Dusk was falling as, eight hours later and 5,000ft higher into the Andes, we staggered under our backpacks into Wanku village. Pedro at the store sold us lemonade and pilchards and said there was a school we could sleep in 'just down the road'. This proved to be another few kilometres and it was by the light of a thousand stars in the wide night sky that we spotted our refuge, a small hut by a still black lake, and drank a mug of coffee with the teacher before crashing out on the concrete schoolroom floor.

First light saw us on our way again, climbing to a rocky pass. There below us lay the mine, a desolate shanty town with cemetery. We scrambled down a knee-shaking scree slope as a lorry revved up in the distance, but it wasn't going to La Paz. Nor, it transpired, were we, for the next two days. A Bolivian tin mine at 14,500ft is not perhaps the stuff of holiday brochures, but it has its moments, like when we discovered the hot shower, when an Indian miner asked us if England was in the jungle and when, in search of candles, we found ourselves in a tiny mud dwelling, miming 'light' to an Aymara-speaking lady, while her miner husband snored in the bed surmounted by a row of bowler hats in plastic bags.

The journey back to La Paz was finally accomplished in a petrol lorry lacking all electricals and with vestigial brakes. We set off from the mine in a snowstorm up a series of hairpins requiring three-point turns, and while one of us hung on to the handbrake, another of us passed the detached wiper to the driver, who hung out of the cab to clear the windscreen. Having no lights, he made all haste to reach Escoma before dark, and it was a bruised and battered trio who eventually fell out of the lorry and into a loft full of snoring campesinos for the night.

We woke to the sound of cowhorn and drum in the snowy market place, but an hour later our lorry was trundling under blue skies across the altiplano and our adventure in the high mountains of Bolivia was over.

Bolivia: The high mountains of the Cordillera Real

The village of Aucapata, 9,000 ft up

DIANA PHILLIPS

IN NORTH BIHAR

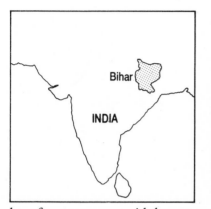

We knew the train would take at least four hours to cover the sixty kilometres from Raxaul to Dhang. The journey was meant to last three hours, but the train always left at least an hour late. We knew it would be late but we still hurried through the waking village, across the fields, past the hospital and along the railway track to Raxaul station. One morning, after heavy rain, the field by the hospital was full of giant yellow frogs; no-one paid them any attention.

Although it was one of the train's first stops and there were never many passengers on board, the people waiting at Raxaul always crammed around the doors, clambering up and forcing themselves in. Why didn't they wait for the passengers to get off first, instead of squeezing themselves, their sacks of wheat and bicycles on at the same time that others were dragging their possessions off? They pushed and shoved, reaching through the carriage windows to reserve places by laying their scarves along the bench.

At stations all was noise: bells ringing; people clamouring to get on and off; men walking up and down beside the train shouting mysterious cries, selling food and cigarettes from trays around their necks or from baskets on their heads.

As we prepared to get off, our fellow passengers tried to tell us we were making a mistake. There was nothing for white people in Dhang: just a cluster of shops and shacks; stalls at the side of the road leading from the station; a bicycle repair shop; little wooden shops on stilts which sold biscuits, cigarettes and sweets. And lots of lean-to teashops with their sticky mud floors, mud walls with greasy pictures of gods and film stars; the hole in the ground at the back where plates and glasses were washed and mouths swilled out; grimy tables with uneven legs; ants and wasps crawling around on the food displayed in front of the shop. Hardly a tourist trap.

It takes forty minutes to walk from Dhang station to the farm along

(*Opposite*) The railway at Raxaul, North Bihar

a road which starts as a stony track then turns to mud. There is a short cut across the fields, zigzagging along the boundary banks. There are always people on this land: a boy sitting on a grazing buffalo, a girl cutting short, dusty grass with a sharp hand–held hoe, filling a basket to take home for the oxen. They are there; they have been there for years. For hundreds of years it has all been exactly the same. Walking along the tracks and paths between the fields, it feels as if thousands have walked there before you. A security.in the ground felt through bare feet: warm, hard ground, smooth and dusty. Guidebooks say the Bihar plain is barren. For them it is: there are no temples or museums, only people living by and for the land. Every scrap is owned, small banks separating each field. On the map it is divided up into feet. Every inch looks well used, whether by a girl foraging grass for oxen or by people resting at the side of the road.

The farm has nine acres of land, including the ruins of an old British indigo factory – a long redbrick wall with trees and bushes growing on the old factory floor, weeds climbing along the bricks. Children played there instead of minding their animals which would then wander out on to planted fields. A road runs in front of the farm, its tracks worn deep into the ground. Three crops a year are grown and the earth looks pale and tired in the hot sun. Buffalo dung is the only thing put back into the soil.

We started at five and worked until eight when we had breakfast, saved from the previous evening's meal. After breakfast we continued working until eleven, then returned to the long hut. Each of the men had his own lunchtime routine. Some washed under the pump before cooking rice and vegetables, while others seated by the heat of the cooking fire then washed before eating.

When there was water in the pond behind the hut, Goshai used to go fishing, damming the pond in the middle and scooping the water over to one side, leaving little fishes panting on their sides in the mud. He liked fish.

Work started again at three; we rested until then. At one time the big tree was where we all lay on our scarves and mats. Then the men took to lying under the mango tree, away across the fields at the crossroads of several paths. There must have been a better breeze there.

The sun should have paled slightly by three. But, carrying baskets of buffalo dung from the pit by the cattle shed, along the road and down towards the mango tree to put it on the furthest field, my nose was burnt before I'd walked twenty yards.

I remember the hottest day. One of the fields had been ploughed and our job was to weed out the wiry roots and tufts of grass that the wooden ploughshare had failed to dislodge so that the field could be smoothed out ready for flooding. That morning it was hot by six. After breakfast one of the men returned with an umbrella; everyone else worked with scarves draped over heads and necks against the sun. It grew hotter all the time. At eleven the earth was dry and thirsty, the field baking: it was like being fired in a kiln. At three it was no cooler. Moving from the shade to the middle of the field seemed sheer madness. The weeds that we'd uprooted in the morning were shrivelled and brown; the earth looked as if nothing had ever lived in it. It was still too hot so we all left the field for the shade of the big tree.

This tree is holy. There is a platform around it, natural on one side, made from the tree's roots, and built round by brick on the other. Where the roots stick out the bank gives way to a hollow where the buffaloes are tethered during the day.

At the time of weddings, a group of women and children came across the fields with baskets and scarves full of sweets and rice which they touched down under the holy tree to be blessed, before going back the same way they'd come. The men didn't like us to sit on the platform.

Evenings were beautiful when work was finished and the sun had gone. The land became active at dusk: oxen appeared in their fields, and buffaloes having their last feed before being led home after the day's grazing. All day long, boys and girls sat on the buffaloes' backs, lounging in expertly comfortable positions.

I remember one evening when we were returning home from Sitanarhi in the bullock cart. At dusk, passing through the countryside, everything was slowing down for the night. Everywhere there were children, crouching by the roadside, minding goats in the fields, cutting a last shaving of grass. In the dimming light the men were sitting together outside their hut, small children playing between the crouching forms. Away across the fields was the train, steam drifting out from the engine, people spilling out from inside and on top.

The bullock carts were empty, the oxen eating from huge shallow dishes raised up from the ground on stands made of branches. The threshing floors lay bare, pale, trodden and packed down in a circle around the post where the oxen had circled. As the cart passed, frogs jumped into pools made under pumps, women with bundles of twigs and leaves on their heads stepped to the side. Oncoming carts appeared in the gloom, the drivers calling to each other, one moving over for the other. The bamboo leaves bending low over the road whisked us as we passed and birds called in the mango groves.

When we got back, some of the men were asleep and some were finishing their supper. Each slept in a special place: one group in the shed where the chaff for the cattle was stored, some in the main room of the hut beside the cooking fires and others outside under the porch.

The nightwatchman sat on the bamboo bench at the side of the road as everyone else went to bed. He made rounds throughout the night, checking on the oxen and buffaloes tethered in the field. After the wheat harvest, there were two nightwatchmen. The men told us that the area was dangerous, that robbers used to hide in the mango tree at the crossroads and jump down on people returning home to their villages.

After the wheat had been harvested and the rice transplanted we were no longer needed, and took the same train back to Raxaul, leaving the buffalo grazing, Goshai fishing and villagers making their offerings under the holy tree.

MARTIN HOWARD

IT'S A LONG WAY TO O'MARA'S

'Oh, you'd not be staying at O'Mara's,' he exclaimed after we had talked for a while. 'No sanitation! No electricity! Jeez, you'd need a Rolls-Royce or a helicopter to get me out there.'

We were in O'Toole's shop-cum-bar in the village of Tourmakeady in the west of Ireland, in the Gaeltarra, or Irish-speaking, area of County Mayo. We were there to collect the key for our rented holiday cottage and to buy some food for our stay.

As Mr O'Toole took down the provisions from the shelves (where custard powder lay next to 'liquid for the treatment of sheep scab' and the foot-rot powder just above the biscuits) he kept muttering 'no sanitation' under his breath and shook his head in disbelief.

We had got this far without recourse to the comfortable and quick forms of locomotion the man had mentioned, relying mainly on public transport. We'd left the Dublin Busarus at eight o'clock in the morning following a night-crossing of the Irish Sea. Before dropping off to sleep as we motored along the N4 towards Galway, I glimpsed the unusual sight of a street or, perhaps more correctly, a pavement, market. It was unusual because it had no stalls. Apparently the vendors simply brought along their few spare possessions – old irons, trinket boxes, shoes, record players, cardboard suitcases filled with dingy old clothes – and arranged them at the base of the railings that ran along one edge of the pavement. Even at that early hour there were quite a few potential customers rooting through the piles. It was a pity we could not stop, but the coach swept on and we were away and gone before I could have a closer look.

I awoke to hear the driver announce a break. Looking at a map, I discovered this was Kinnegard, on the border of Meath and West Meath. The stop was at a modern bar that served refreshments and the women's lavatory contained a novel vending machine. It carried the slogan, 'For those who care'. Could it contain contraceptives? No, after all, we were in the heart of Ireland. What it housed were disposable toilet-seat covers. If you had a few coppers to spare, you could place one on the seat and go about your business feeling completely safe. Safe from what? You may well ask. It could be that in these parts people aren't quite so quick to condemn or deny the rumours about what can be caught from toilet seats. Perhaps they're hiding the truth – it wasn't immaculate conception that caused all the trouble in the first place, just an unprotected toilet seat.

Ablutions over, we joined the N6 and continued through the Midlands of Ireland. The countryside was flat and largely pastoral but the villages and towns were more interesting: Rochfortbridge, Kilbeggan (where an old water-powered distillery was being restored), Moate, and Athlone. The latter – pronounced Atlone as the Irish seldom take notice of the 'h', preferring to sound the 't' alone; hence 'tatched' cottages and 'Tursday' – was larger than the others. A sprawling town, it was spotted with light industry, camps of travelling people and what appeared to be run-down council estates. In these, the streets were alive with scruffy Dickensian urchins, kicking stones, running from pavement to pavement, chased by dogs and carrying those animals' fluffy offspring. Their clothes were ill-fitting; one moth-eaten jumper on top of another, and yet white skin still showed through. Braces held up trousers too big, and rubbed even more holes in the shoulders of the pullovers. They took little notice of the coach and seemed happy with their puppies and games.

When, five hours after leaving Dublin, we were at the outskirts of Galway, memories of our last visit to the city came floating, smiling back, particularly of the welcome we received. The greeting this time was typically Irish – a heavy shower and a friendly chat. A man at the bus station asked where the coach was from and was amazed and impressed that we could travel so far so fast.

'All the way from London in less than a day,' he said, bemused.

His naivety seemed incongruous for we found Galway more cosmopolitan than before – there were now shops selling Italian clothes and health-foods – but we had only an hour there before catching another bus, this time north to Mayo.

Thankfully, our country bus was not as old as some still in service and the ride along the T40 towards Westport was initially smooth. The landscape here is very rural, the fields interrupted only by the ruins of cottages, churches and castles, and a few working farms. When we were close to Shrule, the bus stopped at a farm entrance to let off an old farmer. To our surprise he was followed by the conductor and then the driver. The two short, roundish men crossed the road and climbed over a wall into a field. Then, producing white plastic bags from their pockets, they began to pick mushrooms. For the next five minutes or so the two blue uniforms crossed and recrossed the field at a trot. It was like an old silent film – the roly-poly figures scampering from mushroom to mushroom.

We were dropped off sixteen miles further on at the Tourmakeady 'cross', a road junction in what appeared to be the middle of nowhere. To the east lay the plains of the county of Galway, and to the west the broad expanse of Lough Mask (we could hear herons calling). In the distance, just visible through the damp mist to the north-west, were the Partry Mountains where our cottage lay.

We started to walk towards the hills, glad to be on our feet again if slightly disheartened by the twelve miles still to go, cheered and re-freshed by the well-laden blackberry bushes but a little perturbed by the light drizzle that was falling. Along we trudged, too tired to talk much, stopping only to pick berries or to raise our thumbs to the rare motorists. Despite our large rucksacks we were picked up after about three miles and driven as far as O'Toole's. We were grateful for this ride, albeit short, for we knew we would have to walk from there.

O'Mara's cottage is at the western end of the Glensaul valley, the southernmost valley in the Partry Mountains. The tarmac road from Tourmakeady, five miles away, terminates just a few yards past the white gate, and it seemed about twice that distance as we staggered and stumbled along that evening.

The lane turned and twisted down the valley floor between lush green hedges spotted black and red with berries and fuchsia. As we passed small enclosures, I noticed how the farmers made use of the abundant brambles. Once dead, the thickest, thorniest branches are em-bedded into the tops of the dry-stone walls in much the same way that barbed wire is used. The thorns are much longer than the spikes on wire and so this method is probably more effective, not to mention cheaper, for keeping sheep in place. Brambles are not the only thing used to supplement the walls and hedges. One hedge in the lane is sup-ported by a rusting bicycle frame and a common substitute for fence-posts is an axle from a car or tractor.

We finally reached our destination – a white-painted cottage oppo-site a barn with a red tin roof – about 6 o'clock. It was one of about eight buildings in the valley and there was only one, a small croft nestling in fields near to the head of the valley, beyond it. On arrival, we met our first problem – the gate, which opened neither inwards nor out. I managed to squeeze through, strode up the slope to the door, unlocked the padlock and entered.

'It's lovely,' I shouted to Janine, who was still wedged in the gate. She appeared shortly afterwards and joined my stare of delight at the eighteenth-century cottage interior. Our holiday had begun.

In case you're wondering about the electricity; it's true, there was none. And the sanitation? Well, it's an easy mistake to make since the tin-roofed outside toilet masquerades as a sheepfold and the water is supplied via a syphon from a small stream close by.

FLYING HORSES

Whenever I've been asked to take a sponsored parachute jump I've declined, giving the excuse 'fear of flying'. Of free will I chose to fly to India, taking as my travelling companions a stallion and two mares, in the back of a decrepit Boeing 707 on its third time round the clock. The interior was like a dingier station on the Northern Line, complete with peeling, dripping walls. Outside, the Flying Carrot, as this airline's cargo planes are affectionately known to the handlers at Heathrow, has peeling orange and green livery. She'll be all right when she's finished, said one. Finished what?

The first leg of the first occasion I had flown horses from Heathrow was made bearable by a bottle of whisky and a regular itinerant groom. His responsibilities were for a single grey pony bound for a Kuwaiti Sheikh. They said *au revoir* at Beirut, the first port of call, having given me a crash course in survival.

We were jammed unceremoniously among sinister-looking unmarked packing cases, obviously best left alone. Compared with our own disembarkation, when the all-change was announced at Beirut they were unloaded with a certain amount of deference. Beirut! What could they do with more weapons that hadn't already been done? Rising columns of smoke from the ruined city, shell craters and baggage handlers with machine guns gave the airport the appearance of M6 Bank Holiday roadworks. After five hours (feeling a bit over-exposed) parked on the tarmac, flying off towards the Gulf was an appealing prospect.

The experience of travelling with horses need not be unpleasant. Horses won't be airsick all over your lap; they don't drone on about overbooked hotels, or insist on playing Scrabble to pass the time. Ideally a canopy should separate the beasts, and ideally a stallion should not accompany two mares on a pallet the size of a diving board. They should be let down properly before the flight and not, as in the case of one of the mares, introduced to racing a week previously in a Windsor selling hurdle. No-one accompanying thoroughbreds expects to glide along aisles adjusting headphones, providing pillows and dispensing drinks, other than the odd bucket of water. Then again the most beleaguered hostess would not swap a cantankerous granny on a Poundstretcher for a panicking mare trying to lie down in her stall at 30,000 feet.

The mare alongside the stallion rubbed her hip to the bone attempting to do just that, while we took turns swinging from her head and tail as a preventive measure as turbulence upset the flight across Europe. A hay net can be improvised as a seat belt, especially if there is nothing else (no seats either). Meanwhile the stallion's attentions were diverted by his own terror, and mine. The other mare obligingly took little interest in the proceedings – until the Beirut–Sharjah leg. By this time the new cargo of contraband televisions for India was tumbling about our ears. This threat posed less of a distraction to the horses than I would have hoped. When both mares began aiding and abetting one another to increase the confusion and alarm, somewhere high over the Gulf I made for the cabin to solicit help.

There I found an Australian pilot, German co-pilot and Lebanese navigator arguing above the noise of the engines, which sounded as if their exhausts had blown. These cargo planes are the modern equivalents of the tramp steamer. They flip from one airport to another collecting and dumping in remote corners, removed from passenger terminals. The aviators who fly them, while not (generally) sporting eye-patches, are particularly hard-baked salts. The exchange which I began, 'Could one of you give me a hand with these lunatics?' went as follows:

'Sorry sport, international regulations; can't leave the flight deck.'

'If you don't leave the flight deck at least one of these horses is going to be joining you on it.'

'You know what to do – shoot the buggers.'

'Where's the humane killer then?'

'Under the coffee pot.'

'There's only an old fire extinguisher here.'

'Use that then.'

When I got back to England, someone commented on my bravery in the crisis. What else could I do, I replied – bale out on the Iraqi trenches? Fire the extinguisher? Pray? Well, as I explained to the Almighty, at 30,000 feet I was much nearer to him than ever before and, shouting to make myself heard above those damned engines, perhaps there was an even money chance of being heard. I was certainly sincere.

When we landed at Bombay (for the story has a happy ending) I asked to be shown the piece of tarmac pasteurised for the Pope to kiss on his recent visit, so I could bless it too (*poojahs* is the Hindi word) and give thanks for deliverance. That's when I noticed oil dripping from the fuselage.

Whether or not horses understand landing procedure (they don't smoke or have to cope with seat-belts), it occurred to me that we had taken a couple of bites at the cherry on our approach – I could only guess how near we came to dismantling the gateway to India, for there are no windows in those vehicles.

There is a sweet old chestnut about the JAL jumbo mistakenly landing on a tiny nearby private airfield in smog. On that occasion three miles of slums were levelled as a pathway along which the stranded plane could be dragged back to the International Airport runway. Only from here could it be reasonably expected to take off.

Our problem had been landing at all. The hydraulic lines had burst and the wheels had to be lowered manually. The crew hadn't been able to knock in ('locate', for the purposes of the Captain's log) the nose-wheel pin. They took near-disaster as an everyday occurrence, which it probably is. In fact, the Captain, miffed that there was no hotel taxi waiting, was preparing to return to Abu Dhabi with his leaking plane when I left. I'm sure he did.

Deposited on the runway, horribly close to the fast lane, we must have been an unusual sight for incoming international passengers, gazing at a three-horse traffic island. The horses oggled back, equally bemused – especially the stallion, who would have failed dope tests for the next six months. At Heathrow I'd been asked specifically not to tranquillise him in case of the possibility of side-effects which could have seriously affected his future stud career. As he reared and kicked all those miles above the earth, the decision narrowed down to him or me. He had three syringes administered to him. The last one I saved, just in case, for myself.

To be brave, or blasé, was not my ambition. Having worked in racing stables for a number of years, I went to India with every prospect of enjoying racing despite the absence of luxuries like *The Sporting Life*. When we landed, the problems weren't nearly over. All the paperwork seemed correct, except that most important paperwork of all – the baksheesh. There weren't enough rupees to oil the wheels for those 'whose hands are greased not from honest toil', as an Indian newspaper euphemistically described sticky palms.

Two pretexts were given for the failure to release us from the airport: that one of the mares wore a head-collar with an obviously masculine name embossed, and that one of the fillies' passports was stamped GONE TO STUD. India has a number of diseases all her own, but if there is any suggestion that a foreign filly has been on the loose in a British stud she is rejected as unclean. So my first act on Indian soil was to telex a friend at Weatherbys, the British racing bureaucrats, to get them to explain the facts of life to the Bombay Turf Club.

After three days – as Indian delays go, lightning – the caravan moved to one of the best-run studs in India, in the grounds of the Maharajah of Mysore's Palace in Bangalore. Here I encountered some of the problems indefatigable Indian breeders deal with. In the middle of Bangalore, as you thread through a jungle of exotic trees and over-grown ornamental gardens, cross long neglected croquet lawns, tennis courts and disused summer houses, you are confronted with Windsor Castle, or at least a very passable facsimile locked up and in pawn to the Government to pay Royal debts. This is the Palace. There was no water, though, for an artificial Thames; and the whole relic, presently used as a backdrop for the film of *A Passage to India,* is patrolled by a pensioner who served the last war in South Shields.

The stud occupies the old cavalry stables and, imaginatively, the elephant houses. Nowadays it is run by an Englishman who arrived in India forty years ago with his billiard cue and eight shillings. He went on to become leading trainer in Madras for eighteen years and is set to retire to his property in Cheshire, which is fenced by the running rail from Castle Irwell, Manchester's racecourse.

The traditions of the British Turf, like the last Englishman, are safely enshrined in Indian racing centres like Bangalore, where scribes still describe jockeys as 'knights of the pigskin'. Horses with names meaningful to English ears have passed this way: Lance Corporal, Red Indian, King Midas and now the stallion I had delivered, Pink Tank. An effort was made to set up the stud in a more favoured, not to say more conventional, site in the foothills of the Nilgiris. This was de-feated by panthers who ate the foals, and by wild elephants on whose walk the buildings were sited. Now the Palace Stud lives on borrowed time as Indian racing moves up a gear. Apart from delivering Pink Tank and the two mares, and six foals in the stud season, my contribu-tion to the future of Indian breeding was almost certainly sacrilegious. Snakes abounded in the palace grounds, as did ants. They, and all of life in India in its own way, are sacred, but the holes bored by the former and the mounds erected by the latter in the paddocks were a threat to the horses. Occidental logic demanded that the one could best be filled by the deposition of the other. This was achieved but the worst was feared.

In my book, more danger would come from the vet, whose tetanus syringes were kept in his bicycle puncture outfit. But he meant well, and the place and his practice thrived in the way that life tends to in India. Fecundity and infinity make happy bedfellows: there are proba-bly 1,000 million Indians and – who knows? – the only impossibilities in this country are finding a size-three horseshoe nail and a bath plug that fits.

Given the chance, I suppose I'd take the Flying Carrot to Bombay again, though by that time I'd have taken parachute lessons.

CAREL TOMS
_____

TO THE MIDDLE OF NOWHERE

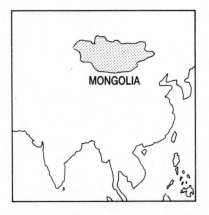

MONGOLIA

The train from the Back of Beyond is about to arrive at the Middle of Nowhere. A week out of Moscow across Siberia and five time zones later you somehow land up in land-locked Mongolia.

Galloping horses, endless deserts and grassland steppes. People with faces like unworked mahogany stand around in their tunic-like costume and ill-fitting boots with turned up toes. All are heavily wrapped against searing Siberian winds which bear the ghosts of Genghis Khan, Marco Polo and 'living' Buddhas.

A flat-faced, slit-eyed courier smiles from her yellow moon face and says the baggage will follow on a lorry. It did and was dumped outside Hotel B, one of only two in Ulan Bator, capital of this People's Republic. Built just a few years ago it looks battle-scarred by usage and needs a good smartening up. The bedroom lock is insecure and only one hot tap on a swivel trickles into both bath and basin. Mongolia is remote, not easy to reach and feels like it.

Everyone is out to please and eager to show off their millions of desert acres. They have not long entered the twentieth century and in many ways still live in the past. Remnants of their old ways still abound. When you have shown your disguised appreciation of the country's monuments to the 1921 revolution and to the Great Patriotic War against Fascism and seen the palace where the last king lived, you will be taken to a Buddhist lamasery. There you are advised to hold your nose as you egg your way through groups of shuffling, shaven-headed and saffron-robed monks amid a stifling mixture of stale incense and body odour.

This is the country's one remaining lamasery and its last vestige of Buddhist splendour. There are sounds of tinkling bells and subdued, mumbling voices as the monks, sitting in the lotus position on wooden benches, turn the pages of their scripture books. Outside they prostrate themselves on wooden prayer beds. They call this enlightenment.

Sixty miles east of the capital is Terelj. It's a village of felt and canvas tents called yurts. There are also some wooden huts and everything is fenced in to keep out the wolves and curious locals. It's a kind of health farm and you go there to sample a simple lifestyle which Mongolians have been enduring for about 3,000 years and you are going to put up with for twenty-four hours.

To reach this desolate spot you set off at sun-up and head toward mountain ranges which scarcely ever get closer. The coach driver weaves his way through washed-out bits of road. The countryside is deserted but for groups of distant yurts which resemble pickable mushrooms. The rows of white tents are numbered like a council estate. A gravel path wanders between them. Here and there a duckboard keeps your feet off the mud. If yurt accommodation runs out, then there are the chalets. In the compound centre stands a model of a Buddhist temple and a prayer bed. It's fun but utterly phoney.

They say 40 per cent of the population of about one-and-a-quarter million Mongolians still live in yurts. None has any sanitation. They are designed to be portable and enable herdsmen and hunters to move around the countryside in search of new pastures for their camels, sheep and yak.

A rickety building called a 'hotel' is where you eat on the site. The washroom is outside, where there is a smell of scented Russian soap and bad drains. Mongolians, of course, use the steppe.

We share our yurt with an Australian couple. He snores and she complains about the lack of a good cup of tea. Because of our 'unexpected' arrival the restaurant can summon up only tinned salami, half cold packet soup and some dry cake. Americans in the group flee for their vitamin pills and demand hot water to make coffee.

A yurt is comfortable and a wooden floor raises it from the ground. Lino and thick carpets cover the floor. Exposed woodwork of the roof struts and main pole are beautifully decorated. It's all rather like an old-fashioned gypsy caravan. But six-foot Aussies and Englishmen have to jack-knife their bodies at the four-foot door which leaks substantial amounts of air – as does the roof where the stovepipe pokes through.

A 'chambermaid' who looks about eighty goes from tent to tent with a wheelbarrow full of logs and lays all the fires in the dustbin-like metal stoves. We put a match to ours and it goes up with a rocket-like roar, heating the yurt in a flash. The reconditioned air attracts the flies so we wander round like lost nomads thinking about the next meal. There is not even a postcard to buy, let alone a stamp.

If you follow the electricity poles over the steppe to the next village, the people there are partially settled inside bricks and mortar. Down by the river the boys fish with rods cut straight from the surrounding forest and grill their catches on an open fire.

No-one asks for a re-run of this one night stand. 'Scenery great, food awful' is the consensus. The traditional beverage here is *kumiss,* a thick curdly drink made from mare's milk which has been allowed to ferment. They say it contains eight per cent alcohol, and the locals down it by the gallon. You need an iron stomach as it tastes like some awful medicine.

We return to civilisation after a wash in cold water, a breakfast of buns and sour cream and a ride through knife-sharp mountain air. This is the stuff of travel.

PEGGY TABOR

JOINING THE LADIES

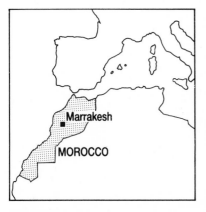

The colours were flat brown and blue outside the train windows as we pulled across the first plains of North Africa. Inside went the dealers hissing 'hashish' and then kindly translating their sales cant into a handful of viable languages. The only women I'd seen since I'd left Paris on the train bound for Algeciras were part of the backdrop outside. Now they were dressed in *djellabas,* only dark eyes showing from the cloth that shrouded them. They carried babies in bundles on their backs and they remained silent and out of reach. The men in the carriage chattered and smoked. The last russet glint of a breathtaking sunset died behind a scorched hill before the train slowed for Rabat. A quiet boy who had been my companion since Bordeaux dissolved into a crowd of exuberant relatives on the platform and I was alone in this strange, dark country.

Two days later I was wedged on a banquette amongst a host of brightly made-up ladies. In the shadowy side room of a large Moroccan house, the air swam with clashing perfume, face powders and rouge. Here were the women then. Townsfolk on a fête day, squashed against the four walls as if they had just been thrown there. Like cushions, they were trimmed with gold brocade and sequins, exploiting their kaftans as we once exploited our school uniforms.

I had come to this house with a girl I'd met as I wandered through the streets of the kasbah, looking at the scissor-shaped doorknockers. They were a fairly wealthy family, friends of hers, celebrating a birthday, and would have been furious if they knew she had met a foreigner and not invited her. She explained this to me as we dodged hawkers and stepped over baskets of eggs in the medina. Tailors were bent over pedal machines and men in dark corners smoked *kif* pipes. We passed stalls selling cassettes, underwear, pots of kohl and acorns. Outside the mosque blind men called out for alms in the name of Allah. The air smelled strongly of coriander. It seemed in this labyrinth of passages and arches impossible that there could be any space left to live. Yet when we stepped through a child-sized studded doorway into a brightly lit spacious courtyard beyond it was like entering a palace through a magic door in the Thousand and One Nights.

Here were entrances to shady rooms whose backs were turned on the din outside. Here were silver teapots filled with mint tea, cloyingly sweet and smelling of rare English summers. Small children ran back and forth in headscarves and aprons, oblivious to the meaning of the word 'play'. They were the poor relations, adopted by the family to run errands, to clean and serve, in return for food and clothing.

Now in the crowded room a young girl stood up and, tying a long scarf around her hips, began to dance. Her smaller, younger aunt went to fetch an armful of drums, the room of soft cushions shifted, the girl sang, the women chorused, beat the drums, whooped and relaxed into torrents of raucous laughter. Just as the courtyard had come as a surprise, so did these vivacious women without their veils.

I was soon to meet an old lady who cleaned the apartments in the French quarter. 'I wouldn't cover my face if I was young and pretty,' she said. 'But who would want to see it now?' Her eyes sparkled. She would act out stories, waving her henna'd hands in the air to illustrate the crowds who had once filled the room of a *Monsieur* she had worked for. She had found him unconscious in his own bathroom, knocked out by gas from a leaky cylinder, and had given the alarm. It seemed the whole medina must have gone up to see the spectacle.

'But I'd covered him up,' she said. 'For he was stark naked, his little thing *comme ça.*' She crooked her little finger graphically. Then, chuckling, she pulled her hood down over her eyebrows and went to get on a bus crowded with other women, their smiles hidden behind their veils.

Hyat, who had taken me to the fête, insisted we travelled together to see her cousins in Marrakesh. It worked well. Her family would never have allowed her, a single girl, to travel alone, and I had the benefit of her company and ability to translate from Arabic into French, which she seemed to do without thinking. Her cousins, two girls, lived a protected life in Marrakesh. They worked at home making embroidery on hand machines, and rarely stepped outside the rose-coloured walls of their house. We drank mint tea together on the flat roof from which we could see the tall date palms marking this ancient trading point, and the peaks of the Atlas mountains beyond. They commented on my colouring and rolled with laughter when I attempted a little Arabic. Their mother was sitting on a pile of cushions when I met her, wrapped in a stripey Berber blanket and watching an Egyptian soap opera on television.

Above her hung a print of the Mona Lisa. At one end of the room was a large kettle on a stand, used for washing guests' hands before they tucked into *couscous* with their fingers. She pointed at it and roared at me, trying to penetrate my incomprehension. I nodded, and she rocked back and forth slapping her thigh and wheezing with

Mongolia: Buddhist temple in
the capital, Ulan Bator

Mongolian women queuing to
spin prayer wheels at the
lamasery in Ulan Bator

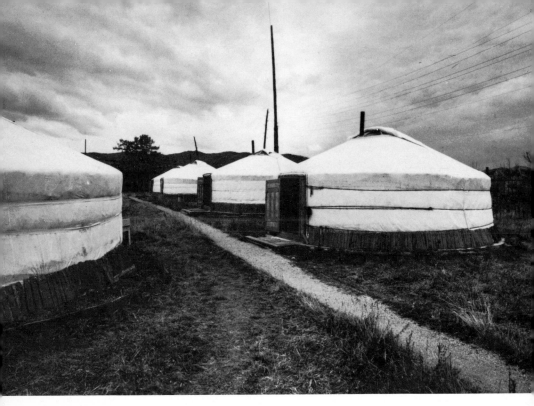

Mongolia: Yurts to let in the village of Terelj

Inside a yurt: the accommodation is basic but comfortable

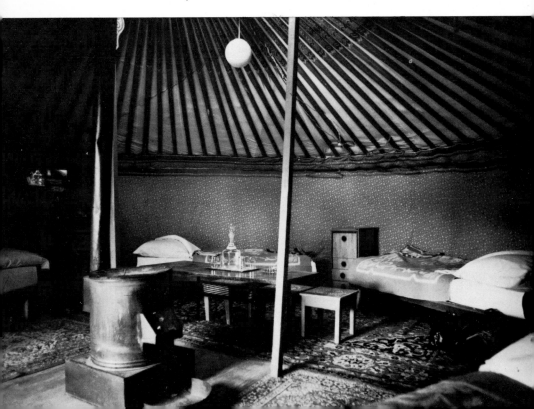

laughter. 'She says that is what Moroccans use as a bathroom,' Hyat told me. The old woman had worked as a maid in Europe many years ago and must have decided that our ignorance about everyday habits would one day be fine fuel for a practical joke of two.

At night we all slept together along the banquettes that ran along the four walls of the room. The large motherly woman would tuck us in three or four times, waking us long after we had fallen asleep to throw more heavy Berber blankets over us, for the nights at this time were cold.

I would sometimes be woken at three or four in the morning when she came in coughing and muttering from the chilly courtyard to curl up under her covers. The fact was that her husband, who worked as a baker and neither ate nor slept with his wife, came home at this time. On my last night in the house I was woken at 5am and asked to go and say goodbye to the man I'd never met. He was sitting in an enormous bed upstairs. In one hand he held a steaming glass of mint tea, in the other a honey and cinnamon cake. He seemed very small and precious on the high bed that looked as if it should have a pea tucked into it, to test his heritage. If there was, he certainly hadn't noticed it, so cosily ensconced was he. He shook my hand ceremoniously, and as the priest called out for morning prayers from the mosque I crept shivering back downstairs with his wife. Having been a maid in all the vague corners of Europe, she was little more than just that in her own house. Yet, when we were tucked into our beds again, the laughter tumbled out of her, while her husband sat alone in his bed above us, perhaps dreaming of train journeys into far off lands.

JONATHAN RICHARDS

MINOS BY MOTORCYCLE

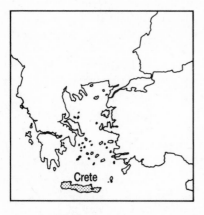

I prayed hard that the brakes of the motorcycle would hold up as I swooped down to a dog-leg in the road. A steep ravine bringing a dried-up riverbed of tumbled rocks fell below the bridge I was crossing, and away to my left to the sea and boulders several hundred feet below. The warm air scented with pine, wild marjoram and salt rushed past me; it was the coolest place to be in the midday Cretan sun. Yesterday I had flown over the great mass of Europe and down the Yugoslav coast, over northern Greece and southwards over the Aegean. From the plane I had looked down over islands that seemed to have been dropped casually like brown and green piles of dung by some monstrous legendary creature into the dark blue sea. Icarus, in attempting to escape these shores, had flown too close to the sun which had melted the wax that held together the wings constructed for him by his father Daedalus. I hoped that the motorcycle I had chosen from the collection at Hercules' Motor Scooters in Heraklion would live up to the proprietor's promise that his machines were serviced after every trip.

From the land on which I was travelling had been unearthed the remains of the five great cultures, layered like a gigantic historical sandwich upon one another – Minoan, Greek, Roman, Venetian and Turkish. In one day it is possible to visit with ease a Minoan palace from 1500BC, the site of a Classical Greek city state from 300BC, a Roman villa from the time of Christ, a Venetian fortress from the fourteenth century and a Turkish mosque built a hundred years ago. As an escape from the humdrum, Crete is hard to beat.

I was alone, several thousand miles from anyone I knew, unable to speak the language and not sure if I could remember which hole was for oil and which for petrol; but the Cretan landscape was having the desired effect. The contrast of the austere grey-brown mountains with lush plains sheltered in hollows in-between, and all of this surrounded by the deep blue sea, sharpened senses long dulled by urban monotony. 'Like good prose,' Nikos Kazantzakis has written, the Cretan landscape is 'well-fashioned, economical, shorn of excessive riches, powerful and controlled.' In the face of the majesty of the scenery, the richness of the history, one's own life and its difficulties become reduced to a quieter size.

From Palaikastro on the eastern end of the island the road winds continually and gently upwards through a community of small farming villages. Men returning from the fields leading donkeys laden with hay greeted me with a wave and I felt I had managed to escape the crush of mid-summer tourists perching like migratory birds along the narrow northern coastline. At Zakros the metalled road ends in a small square and I splashed my face with the fresh spring water that fell into a trough in one corner. From behind me a voice addressed me in German, *'Zimmer?'*. I was not as far off the beaten track as I had hoped. A short tubby man with a limp introduced himself as Maestro and explained he had 'rent room'. I accepted the offer and followed Maestro to his café at the edge of the square. He brought me a glass of *raki,* an unflavoured spirit made from the crushed mash after the wine juice has been pressed from the grapes, and a plate of peeled slivers of cucumber. Later that evening I followed his pick-up truck down a rough stony road to a small white cottage where I slept a sound sleep.

In the morning I woke and looked out of the window onto the edge of a huge olive grove that stretched to the mountains beyond. Maestro was pumping water into channels that fed his plantation of banana trees growing under a vast canopy of plastic greenhouse tenting. The wind had picked up since last night and the sound of the plastic sheeting flapping in the breeze brought to mind a dream I had woken from of a sailboat journey across the Aegean.

Below the town and built around a small bay, the remains of the Minoan palace of Kato Zakros were excavated by Nicholas Platon in the 1960s. Like the companion palaces of Knossos, Phaestos and Mallia elsewhere on the island, Kato Zakros was suddenly and inexplicably deserted by its occupants at around 1500BC. Whether from the lava of a violent explosion on the island of Santorini, or from one of the earthquakes that regularly rocked the island in the past, the frightened inhabitants seem literally to have dropped everything and run. They left behind them in each of the palaces an astonishingly beautiful collection of frescoes, finely-worked jewellery, painted vases and seal stones depicting their environment, lifestyle and legends, all of which are now displayed in the Heraklion Archaeological museum.

From Zakros I travelled a spectacular route, passable only by jeep or motorcycle, high up into the surrounding mountains, the dusty, rocky road changing its colour from brown to green to mauve and then white with the colour of the rocks it crossed. Further on, between the villages of Karidi and Handras, I came across one of the dramatic changes of terrain so typical of Crete. There, nestling between the arid, grey mountains was an unexpected area of tenderness, a region of wheatfields and small olive groves, apple orchards and almond trees all irrigated by a system of water channels pumped by short spinning windmills. Near the road was a huddle of wooden beehive boxes. No wonder the successive waves of invaders had prized this land.

Back down on the main road in the valley, a sudden bend revealed the Libyan sea and the south coast of Crete stretching away to the right. A further twenty-five kilometres and I arrived at Ierepetra, a sleepy seaside town where it is said Napoleon spent a night during his Egyptian campaign of 1798. It also boasts a minimum of 300 sunny days per year and, though rather despised by the guide books, provides a pleasant beach and fishing harbour to rest by. That evening I came across Adonis, an old man blind since birth, playing his mandolin-like lyre at a café at the water's edge. As he sang the customers would push banknotes past the strings of the instrument and into the sound box behind. Another evening at the same café a priest with his hair tied in a bun at the back of his head and dressed in dark green robes was brought an ice-cream sundae topped with a miniature parasol and ignited sparkler, compliments of the house. It was his birthday. Walking back to my room I heard a radio playing a Greek rendition of Ralph McTell's song *The Streets of London*. The cultural mix was becoming distinctly heady.

From Ierepetra I followed the road westwards up into the mountains again, passing through villages that cling to the edge of steep escarpments, a seemingly vertical line at times between sea and mountaintop above. Beyond, at Messi, a rough track leads away from the main road and down to the plain of Messara, the farming heartland of Crete. In the town of Timbaki, a base for visiting the nearby sites of Phaestos and Hagia Triada, the dust was swirled into every nook and cranny by the traffic in the main street. It was the time of the festival celebrating the Assumption of Our Lady, and that night in the square of the village of Klimi I found a huge charcoal brazier loaded with chickens roasting on spits. Small boys carried trays laden with beer bottles and plastic mugs for the villagers seated around the square at trestle tables. An amplified *bouzoukia* band played in one corner and an old man, dressed in knee-high black leather boots, black jodhpurs and shirt got up from his seat and moved in a slow dance to the music. Another threw a plate which broke at the old man's feet, providing a challenge to his movements which now had to avoid the shattered pieces.

Here perhaps was one unbroken link between the past and the present. Ritual dance was a centrepiece of Minoan religion and is depicted in tiny sculptures and painted on frescoes and vases from more than three-and-a-half thousand years ago. Theseus is said to have seen Cretan maidens dancing the crane dance in imitation of the circuits and exits of the labyrinth at Knossos from which he escaped with

Ariadne's help. Likewise I wondered whether the icons and crosses I had seen pilgrims kissing in a Byzantine church that morning were derivatives of the phallic stalagmites worn smooth by the touch of their ancestors in the cave at Amnisos and believed also to possess miraculous powers. Like the commune of French hippies I discovered living without clothes on a deserted beach between Loutro and Chora Sfakion further along the coast, I realised I too was on a pilgrimage to discover and honour the ways and spirit of easily forgotten ancestors who in this island crucible forged the origins of Western civilisation.

ANNA KIRWAN

COSTA DEL PEPE

A gang of louts at Manchester airport, all wearing Union Jack caps on their turnips, trailed 'music' after them like a bad smell. My heart sank. I needn't have worried, as it turned out; they weren't travelling with me to Southern Spain, their target was Greece.

I was fortunate in getting a window seat, so my first view of Spain was that of a condor in flight. As I swooped over the crumpled brown Sierras I felt the tingle that a returning exile must get on seeing those mountains – so vast, so ungreen, and already I was in love with Spain. Then when, far below, I saw the toy beach with its miniature blue waves, complete in every detail, I could have leapt out of that window there and then without waiting for the plane to land at all.

There was a revolution or something at Malaga Airport; loud speakers bawled urgent and incomprehensible messages at us. Aeroplanes screamed the sky; angry men bashed trolleys about and roared at each other. And from somewhere the voice of a broken-hearted woman wailed a flamenco lament. My God, what had happened, another Guernica? No, I was reassured, this was quite normal behaviour in Andalucia.

Imprisoned in a circle of luggage, I seized the arm of a passing priest, mistaking him for a porter:

'Are you engaged?'

He shook his head.

'Then take me . . .' I began.

He turned a long, God-fearing face on me and fled.

My destination was Rincon de la Victoria, east of Malaga; at heart it's still a fishing village. Rincon is not exactly unspoilt, but it's the Spanish themselves who spoil it and not the Chip Butty Brigade. The beach isn't pretty like the one I saw from the sky; it's dirty, lived in and worked in, for it's the workshop of the fishing community and if the tourists don't like it then they must lump it or go to Torremolinos. I liked it. A little squalor is a small price to pay to keep it typically Spanish. And anyway, their litter is more picturesque than ours.

The fishermen still haul in their nets pretty much as they did at the time of Christ, though their catches are not as good. They fish for *Boquerones* (Big Mouths), sardines and *chanquetes,* tiny white fish like little seahorses with enormous reproachful eyes. There's a ban on fishing for *chanquetes* this year, not because of their eyes but because they've been overfished for years. Knowing their fishermen, the Guardia Civil in their patent leather hats (for leaning against the wall) and uniforms of reptile green, carry out spot checks on the catches. After much waving of arms and shrugging of shoulders, the police accept a handful of fish – a bribe, I suppose, and leave the scene of the crime.

Sadly, that's not the only crime along this coast. In Rincon itself, I saw a youth being chased by a police car which caught up with him outside the Parish Church, Our Lady of Victory. Two be-rifled guards dragged him out of his stolen car and, handcuffing his arms behind his back, marched him off. He was no more than seventeen or eighteen, with great innocent eyes raised heavenwards and a beard; the dead spit of the crucified Christ. *'Era para mi madre,'* he told his captors, and I wondered what his mother wanted with a stolen car.

This being the Costa del Sol, I had to get up early enough to see that Sol rise and, for my money, it's the best tourist attraction of the lot. A big blood orange comes out of the sea, slowly turns to gold as it gets higher until it becomes a sizzling silver with rays sprouting from it like we see in the holiday brochures. It was as hot as hell in September.

It was while I waited for the sun that I first saw the four nuns walking barefoot at the edge of the sea. They wore pale blue dresses and white veils. One of them, after a quick glance round her, gathered up her skirts and ran deeper into the waves. She was a doll, pretty enough to sell in a souvenir shop. It wasn't long before I joined them in their early morning walks and learned that her name was Antonia.

They were from a convent in Madrid, on holiday for a month. They were like birds out of a cage. They sang hymns to welcome the sun and raised their arms to greet him; and I saw something I won't forget in a hurry. A fish shot straight out of the sea to add his greeting, or maybe to get a closer look at Antonia, and then disappeared. I had heard that fish did this sort of thing, but had never seen it for myself.

Everybody in Andalucia is called Pepe. There's Pepe the Postman, Pepe the Gardener and Pepe the Hairdresser, to name just a few.

Pepe the Hairdresser is the son of a local fisherman, also called Pepe; his 'salon' is his little cottage on the beach. From there he dresses the heads of the rich and famous; they come from as far as fashionable Marbella, for they've heard of his miracles. He runs his 'establishment' like a sultan in his harem, surrounded by beautiful women who lie in wait for his beckoning finger: 'Come please'. I had a hair-do there and nobody recognised me when I came out.

They have a new mayor in Rincon, who wears jeans, colourful shirts and a huge Viva Zapata moustache. He is much in evidence, usually carrying a spade to show he's one of them and can be seen drinking in all the local bars, it would appear, simultaneously.

I asked one of the Pepe's what he thought of his new mayor. *'Pues,'* the shoulders went up, as a sort of disclaimer.

'He's got a lot of personality, a lot of vitality,' I proffered, having done my homework.

'Si, si,' agreed the old boy. 'And a lota moustache.'

Though the mayor's conversation consists mainly in knocking the clergy, he and the parish priest did get together to organise a flamenco evening to provide homes for gypsies. From what I saw of the gypsies, they'd rather have the money and lie on the beach, but no matter.

Famous names were on the Cartel advertising the function which was to start at 7pm. I got there at a quarter to seven. And waited, and waited. The performers started to show up at ten o'clock, and the evening got under way at 10.30. That's pretty tardy, even for Andalucia, the land of no clocks.

It was held in an open-air theatre, so I needn't have bothered to book a seat at all; the singers could be heard in the next village. Flamenco is an art that only real gypsies are good at. The singing was very moving and those long-held low notes really hit me where it hurt, in the heart.

The applause would have raised the roof if there'd been one on. They applauded and cheered not only the singer himself, but the mother who bore him. Probably long since dead. When the Spanish like a performer, they love him; but if they don't then God help his mother and his grandmother, for they go back not one but two generations to get at him. He is the son of a bitch, and his bitch of a mother is the daughter of a whore. Not on this occasion, of course, the performers were all *estupendo,* and so were their mothers.

Surprising the number of people who don't know that Picasso was born in Andalucia, in Malaga. Even the Malaguenos don't know. But in a square called Plaza Merced there is a plaque on one of the buildings which, though barely legible, lets us know that Pablo Ruiz Picasso was born there.

'Oh,' said my guide in surprise: 'They've put another nail in. For years it's been hanging on one.'

That's Malaga. A last look on my way to the airport.

'Giz a kiss,' I heard the spiky-haired youth say to the girl clerk at the GPO, as he claimed his child allowance, and I knew I was back home in Liverpool.

(left) Medical certificate Russian-style (*Not on the Itinerary*)
(right) Pepe the hairdresser (*Costa del Pepe*)

A familiar fresco in the palace of Knossos, Crete

(*far left*) His Holiness the Dalai Lama, 'The Living Buddha'
(*left*) Kangra in the Himalayas
(*below left*) Riding the subway in New York

(*right*) Dog meat on sale illegally in Canton
(*below*) Fishing with the aid of a cormorant along the river towards Yanghou – a neck ring prevents the bird from swallowing the fish

Contrasting landmarks in Berlin: (*above*) Charlottenburg Schloss, now a museum

(*below*) The Brandenburg Gate, on the wrong side of the wall

ACHTUNG
Sie verlassen jetzt
West-Berlin

J. W. ACTON

Not on the Itinerary

Although my churchgoing is confined usually to weddings and funerals, there are times when I am certain that one guardian angel at least has been detailed to watch over my welfare.

Such an occasion occurred halfway through my holiday in Russia. I had taken a package tour to Moscow and Leningrad primarily for the White Nights Festival of the Arts in June – an annual event of Soviet cultural life when the sun hardly sets for a fortnight and old men sit in the public gardens for half the night playing speed-chess.

One normally expects to see all the best opera, ballet and musical talent on this tour, but our group had arrived at the tail-end of a meeting of Comecon heads of state, the National Gymnastics Championships were in full swing and quite unexpectedly, a British delegation led by Sir Geoffrey Howe had arrived for peace talks. The net result of having so many favoured people around was that tickets for the Kirov and Bolshoi ballets were obviously rationed, and we had to be content with second league fixtures of circus and puppet shows to fill any gaps in the programme.

Five days of sightseeing in and around Moscow passed quickly enough. One marvelled at the two-mile-long queue for Lenin's tomb, and the loving care with which the Russians have restored the winter and summer palaces of the Czars after the destruction of World War Two.

But Leningrad is far more artistic in every way, and there is the strange experience of emerging from a theatre at eleven o'clock at night to find the sun still shining brightly. Now, on the Tuesday evening, I had obtained a ticket to the small Philharmonia Hall, where two of Russia's most distinguished musicians were to give a recital of classical favourites for violin and piano.

I left the hotel early and in pleasant sunshine, wearing a light jacket and bow tie, but alas did not bargain for a sudden change in the weather. After fifteen minutes on the Metro to Nevski Prospect I was met by a teeming downpour, heavy enough to keep me holed up under cover until ten minutes before the performance was due to start, and with the hall some hundreds of yards away along a back-street. At five to eight, the deadline, I decided to make a run for it, and was within sight of the doors when, without any warning at all, my stomach muscles suddenly began to roll up like a shop blind and I was violently and horribly sick. Doubled up with pain, I found support between two Lada cars (what else?) and emptied my insides with great gasping spouts. I was carrying a good supply of handkerchiefs and managed to keep myself clean, but it was ten past eight before I had recovered sufficiently to move, with attendance at the concert now out of the question.

My next problem was how to get back to the hotel before my stomach gave a repeat performance. Public transport was definitely out. In Leningrad's crowded streets a tram or bus ride is a virtual eyeball-to-eyeball body massage with the natives, while on the Metro, with the escalators descending at breakneck speed, there is little chance of a retreat and no toilets.

Bleary-eyed, I staggered back to Nevski Prospect, and there I spotted a dejected-looking husband sitting in his car outside a supermarket, obviously waiting for his wife to emerge with the shopping. It's the same the whole world over. Taking a one rouble note from my wallet, I tapped on his window. He looked me over before winding it down.

'Taxi?' I enquired, hopefully.

'You wish to ride?' he countered.

'Hotel Moskva,' I said. 'And quick!'

He snapped up the rouble and with a few deft movements had me seated, safety-belted and away. The drive would have done credit to a New York Yellow cab, and in no time at all I was being dumped at my hotel – on the blind side but within reach of my room and some assistance.

A young white-coated medico was called in, with an even younger sidekick to carry his bag, and a lady interpreter. Between them they took my pulse rate, temperature, and a decision that I was not, nor had been, blind drunk on vodka. There were other suspicions, though.

'You must come to hospital for correct medicines,' announced the lady. 'What have you eatings today?'

'Nothing but hotel food, nothing,' I replied most emphatically.

'Der best fodder iss domestic fodder,' said the medico darkly, as we descended in the lift. There was a red-crossed Land Rover waiting, and nothing more was said until we reached the hospital. On the outside it looked like something left over from the siege of Leningrad in 1944, but inside everything was in immaculate white, including a large wrinkled matron who proceeded to give the medico a verbal roasting, followed by expulsion from the premises. I learned later that, in the presence of a superior officer, he had wrongly suggested that I might be returned to the hotel after treatment.

'You cannot return,' said this matriarch. 'The 'otel has got thousands people. I must find what is your illness first, yes?'

The cross-examination which followed was alarming, and interspersed with words sounding like hepatitis and malaria as she filled in a long questionnaire with a series of *Niets* and *Das*.

By this time I was sorely in need of a toilet, and it was her turn to be alarmed when she suddenly grasped the meaning of my frantic gestures. We rushed along the corridor to a small private room with a bathroom en suite, and as the door slammed shut behind me a virtual volcanic eruption shook the other end of my torso . . .

Now I felt well under par. Lying on the bed, which was very old-fashioned but deliciously comfortable, I thought of my home, my Queen and my country. The time was now about nine-thirty, and I must have looked ghastly, for a young nurse who popped in with a set of pyjamas sized up the situation in a second and popped out again, running down the corridor calling for help.

Alarm bells rang. A kindly looking lady doctor arrived, followed by a porter towing a saline drip apparatus. After listening to my heart and extracting a syringe-full of blood from an artery, they connected my right arm to the drip-feed. A bustling staff-nurse washed my face and hands. A little ward-maid appeared at the bedside with an enormous vacuum flask of Georgian tea, refusing to leave until I had downed every drop.

They fussed around until the doctor left, when everything went deathly quiet, and I slept like a log until morning. I had come from the hotel expecting to return, and was quite unprepared. I had no razor or toiletries, but made the most of the bathroom shower and hot water and began to feel better. As I was about to get dressed, however, the doctor reappeared and began to administer the most thorough medical check-up I have ever experienced.

Apart from being pressed, prodded, tapped and manipulated whilst lying on the bed, I was cardiographed, x-rayed, blood-tested and biologically examined in a series of walkabouts and strip consultations. I was to be incarcerated for another two days and nights on a diet of three assorted pills and a curious fizzy powder in a paper wrapper, presented every few hours with instructions in mime.

The room was spartan and the furniture basic, but to my surprise there was a large colour television in perfect working order. So, as my whiskers grew, I settled down to watch France beat Brazil in an exciting football match, and enjoy one channel entirely devoted to children, where understanding was universal despite the language.

But I was to discover another facet of Soviet hospital life when, after the last meal of the day at six o'clock, I became aware of a plaintive female voice outside my window.

'Andrea! Andrea!' she called. I crept behind the curtains and looked out. The woman was middle-aged and handsome. She was scanning the windows of the ward above, and holding up a plastic shopping bag, through which I could discern two bottles of wine and several cartons of cakes and other goodies. Presently, her worried look changed to a broad smile as a hook on the end of a fishing line was lowered past my window. She attached the bag and it was swiftly hoisted aloft. After a brief conversation she said goodbye, blowing kisses, and immediately her place was taken by another hard-working housewife calling 'Victor! Victor!'

I began to think that I was in an isolation hospital, until I realised that nothing at all happens after six o'clock until breakfast next morning – not even a hot drink except in emergencies. And with hospital food also being the same the whole world over, I could have done with my own wife appearing outside with a food parcel. But she was not on the tour, so I had to grin and bear it.

As a final gesture of international goodwill, I was given a massive injection into my rump, before being released on Friday morning. Vitamins, they said it was, to build me up for the flight home on Saturday.

Those kindly people also provided a full written report on my state of health, with a diagnosis of gastro-enteritis, the tests and the treatment.

'You will present this to your doctor in England, please,' said the Matron at the door. 'It is something unfortunate on the table, goodbye.'

'*Do svidaniya,*' I answered, and kissed her on the cheek. She was built like a javelin thrower, but she blushed and I knew I had been in good hands. The medical report is written in Russian, with even my name translated into Cyrillic, so I've had it framed to save my local GP from having a brainstorm.

Yet my fate could have been infinitely worse. Much, much worse. For had it not been raining so hard on that Tuesday evening I would have arrived at the Philharmonia Hall in good time. Seated in the midst of an elegant and well-informed audience, my stomach would have erupted during the opening bars of Dvorak's *Humoresque* . . .

LEILA MARY STEVENSON

WITH THE LIVING BUDDHA

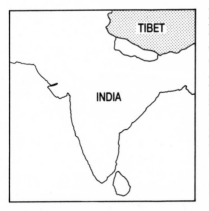

I lay on the bunk of my VW caravan huddled inside the *rosier* (Indian quilt) listening to heavy boots tip-toeing round my campsite as four protective Tibetans prowled on guard all night in the snow. They had come from His Holiness the Dalai Lama to escort me to his hideaway beyond Dharmsala on the Tibetan border.

Only last night I had gasped in the heat of the Indian plains listening to the whine of hungry mosquitoes and watching the antics of peach-pink lizards as they hung upside down on my windscreen. Yesterday the drive through hot, noisy, crowded, dust-filled villages with their yellow sand walls supporting dung pats drying for fuel had slowly given way to mountain tracks struggling through red-blossoming rhododendron bushes. Higher up, the paths spread over rickety bridges spanning rushing rivers hurtling headlong towards the arid plains far below, bringing life in their train.

Now the Himalayan tree-line was far behind and my Kombi could no longer cope with boulders, snow and gradient. Tomorrow the Tibetans would help me continue the journey by jeep – after that it would mean foot-slogging the rest of the way.

Sleepily I wondered how the Dalai Lama would react to my visiting him and his defeated but undaunted people, and what help could I offer to seek for them. The coming days would reveal their plight and their requirements. Judging from the Tibetan Refugee Camps at Mysore (South India) where I had visited, the basic needs themselves would be in very short supply. I was awakened at dawn by fingers scraping the ice from my windows and four pairs of smiling almond eyes encouraged me to rise and greet the day.

Dragging one's tired, middle-aged, body into action at daybreak is not stimulated by the mirrored reflection of puffy eyes, red nose, malarial skin and tousled hair, but a wash and mug of hot coffee work wonders and within minutes we were all jolting our way up the stony track, jeep engine screaming, en route for the borders of Tibet.

The crisp Himalayan air made my nose tingle and eyes water, but who can resist the glories of a sunrise on sparkling snow-covered peaks, clouds rolling below and blue-grey skies above – the tree-line a dark smudge far behind us.

The jeep coughed to a standstill in an icy clearing and, collecting my camera (and white stole as the required cultural offering for the Dalai Lama), we five prepared for the mountain climb to the sanctuary of the Living Buddha. This was situated on an overhanging bluff – remote, almost inaccessible, well guarded by heavily armed Indian troops.

Malaria and dysentery had rather spoiled my legs for mountaineering but with a tall, muscular Tibetan grasping each elbow and the other two guides assisting at the rear I was pulled, pushed, hoisted and coaxed over boulders, narrow, slippery wind-whipped paths, waist-deep in snow at times, grateful for strong shoulders even under my knees!

Hours later my weary but thankful gaze fell – uncomprehendingly – upon an archway of wood and greenery spanning the widening track. The Tibetan refugees had hauled wood, branches and leaves all the way up from the tree-line to produce a typical welcome for a visitor from overseas. Boulders had been scraped free of ice and snow, painted and decorated as shrines – lotus edged – to the Buddha. Tibetans are very adaptable and beauty-loving. In Mysore – despite their ignorance of heat and humidity – they had carved shrines from sandy mud using makeshift tools.

Our arrival was heralded by small, dark-eyed children scuffing through the snow with outstretched hands calling a greeting. All around were sheep and llama-skin tents, simple camping equipment and a strong odour of damp woollens. These were the homes of those who dwelt in the shadow of the Living Buddha, those loyal souls who would remain at his feet wherever he lived.

The guides were Ministers who had learned their English from Heinrich Harrer who had written *Seven Years in Tibet*; they had also learned the habits of Europeans from him. Courteously I was escorted to the Residence of Government-in-exile, shown where to clean up, then offered a delicious lunch of green, yellow, black, orange and white fungi. A young man – tongue protruding and panting heavily to indicate his haste to reach and welcome me – was seated at my feet as interpreter. The eagerness for up-to-date news was insatiable, and the fact I had met their people in Mysore an added bonus. Conversation was, perhaps, stilted but goodwill was evident. After the meal it was suggested – in deference to my age – that I might care to rest, but I preferred to visit the children whose cheeping voices had not ceased to make themselves heard ever since our arrival.

Down in the valley a storm was raging, and through breaks in the clouds below we could see the flashes of lightning and hear the rolling rumbles of thunder; but up near the mighty peaks only the creaking of green ice and the whistling of the wind broke nature's silence. My breath wheezed a little noisily from lungs unaccustomed to the rarified atmosphere, and thankfully I followed the doctor (from Geneva) to her hospital hut. Inside were home-made wooden bunks, two-tiered, about 7ft long and 3ft wide. Lying crosswise on these bunks, upon newspapers and covered in old sacking, seven to each bunk, were the tiny Tibetan patients. All together in one unheated room, suffering from malnutrition, exposure, measles, whooping cough, wounds, fevers and bronchitis, these young, uncomplaining little refugees waited for health to return. One small boy sat on my knee for nearly two hours while a needle was being sterilised in a tin mug over a minute fire: pressure is so low at that height. The gash in his head required six stitches but he remained stoically silent. Outside, young singing voices challenged the thunderstorms still raging below as the junior children provided entertainment for me: songs of Tibet and home.

Then it was time for my audience with His Holiness the Dalai Lama. Surrounded by his Buddhist Priests and Ministers of State the 'Living Buddha' greeted me courteously as I presented the required white stole on outstretched arms, head bent humbly. This was accepted with a charming smile and the stole passed to a Minister (*and* returned most graciously when I left!)

We talked for an hour, discussing future plans and present urgent requirements. These last were simple – a few sheep, farming equipment, medical supplies, looms and wool for rug-making. The questions were perceptive, topical and highly intelligent, delivered with gentle penetrating glances and great charisma. Their knowledge of the outside world was surprisingly extensive and accurate.

Two days later I was escorted on the long trek down the slopes to where my caravan waited, frozen into the ground. Our combined efforts released the wheels – hot cloths aided the firing of the engine but disaster followed. After a mug of hot coffee all round the Tibetans took up position at the rear to help push-start the VW. The back wheels spun furiously, churning the semi-frozen mud and completely bespattering my new friends from head to feet. As I gasped in dismay, the four Tibetans scraped mud from their laughing eyes and with typical cheerfulness waved me on, urging 'Don't stop, keep going, take care!' I wondered how they would ever get those long, black cassock-like garments clean again.

The visit was over for them, but my memories would last a lifetime. Notes to be typed, reports to be sent, help requested, and the world informed of man's continued injustice to man, amongst the inhospitable climate of the Himalayan peaks, where the 'Living Buddha' and his followers awaited their destiny.

EMMA BROOKER

A SLICE OF THE BIG APPLE

Six gritty months of fumbling with biros and over-read text books in A level tedium were wiped out. Wiped out by a five-hour flight to a city where riding the subway is an act of hedonism, and where the pollution on the streets works on the brain like speed, driving people scrambling to the summits of New York City's towers of granite and power.

'The movies are true,' screamed my eyes from the back of the yellow can which I took from the airport. I rattled in the corner of the great plastic sofa of a back seat. Monster cars sharked past, the cluster of Wall Street skyscrapers loomed; an elite of big names at a very mixed party.

Freeway became mapled streets, buildings flattened into the four-storeyed Victorian Brownstones of Brooklyn. The cab driver dumped me outside my home for the next three months. I dragged a bloated suitcase into the basement flat. Fans were purring; it smelt of moulder-ing heat on city rain.

So, I was going to be living in a district with a Wholeperson's Clinic, and a Funeral Home up the street. Around the corner was a Hardware Store selling Croak-a-Roach and Roach Motels. Next door to that I could buy carrot cake ice-cream. Compliments took the form of,

'Hello Mommy, I've got hurting in my bollocks,' yelled from a pas-sing Oldsmobile as I trod the sidewalk.

TV told me about the victim of child molestation who claimed, 'I owe my analyst my life'.

It showed sport in Super Slo-Mo, and got 'Close Up and Personal' with the stars. I was mesmerised by the prime-time show, *Lifestyles of the Rich and Famous*. One episode of this told the story of the bus boy from Ohio who bought an Italian baronetcy, owns three islands in the Canaries and is now the world underwater backgammon champion.

Equipped with such information, I decided it was time to hit the streets. First I went under. Dark, damp, noisy and stifling, the subway is an assault on each of the senses. It has an all-pervading stench of goat and rotting peaches. Even for the natives it is a point of pride to under-stand the system. Seeing me in a state of bewildered angst, they would come up and intone directions in a rhythmical and mysterious language.

> 'You take a D train down to De Kalb,
> Switch to a Double R, QB, or four . . .'

Surfacing from this Kafkaesque dungeon you can be sure only of confronting the unexpected. Nothing specific epitomises New York; its essence is extremity, and diversity, packed into the highest possible density.

My first shot of Manhattan was on emerging from the subway on to Fifth Avenue. I looked up at a sheer sheet of glass and steel, one of the 1930s Rockerfeller buildings. Indifferently magnificent, it sneered back at my eager camera lens, which could only fit in a pitiful few floors. The scale was intoxicating. Everything big. Fifth Avenue, sliced right down the centre of the island, felt liberatingly airy because of the gigantic proportions of every shape and space. Brash and confident as an arrogant all-American jowl. Looking down one of the Avenues is like looking at the inversion of a sunset. The outsized buildings march into infinity in shades of grey to mauve, blurred by a haze of fumes.

Pick a different subway stop. Washington Square; Greenwich Village, the part of New York which stays up all night and starts waking up around midday. A couple of middle-aged men with bluish legs were roller skating along the middle of the road. In the square a Quaker choir was performing, and old men in heavy overcoats were in uproar over a game of chess. Some man came up to me and asked,

'You wanna smoke?'

He proceeded to roll a joint, smoke it, produce juggling equipment and give a dazzling, impromptu performance.

I walked East to Astor Place, where the streets are paved with people sitting next to, and selling, their household rubbish. Perfectly safe, until I strayed a few blocks in the wrong direction and found myself, the only female, in a street lined with male prostitutes.

'Sexss lady?' hissed one through a gold tooth. The nearest subway entrance was blocked with trash. The place stank of violence.

Take an Uptown train to Columbus Circle; Central Park. I dodged herds of joggers, cyclists, people playing croquet, baseball, and walked into the theatrical bustle of an operatic cast preparing for an open air performance of Madam Butterfly.

Back Downtown, to Canal Street, where I found Chinatown, with the second largest Chinese community in the West, 30,000. I wandered into dusty, pungent shops selling live chickens, and dried snakes for rubbing into bruises. Pagoda-topped callboxes melted into the Mafioso restaurants of Little Italy, and the warehouses-turned-art-galleries of Soho.

Carry on down to the tip of the island; Wall Street. I bounced off fat people in double-breasted pinstriped suits, and strode beside young execs and briefcase-bearing, silked women, into the World Trade Centre. From floor 110, the highest point on the island, I gazed back at the midtown outbreak of skyscrapers, the Chrysler and the Empire State in their midst. With the edge of the island visible on either side, Manhattan sits in murky river, an absurd chunk of metropolis looking like a Gothic spaceship working up to an explosive departure from the planet.

New York is criss-crossed all over with fine dividing lines. As well as the grid system of streets, there is a territorial grid which is equally apparent. Starting exactly two blocks down from where I was living, there is a Hispanic neighbourhood, run down and emptying out. Ten years ago it was full of Italians, who, when the Hispanics moved in, drove through and shot from car windows. It was obvious when I missed my local subway stop. The line went on into a big Jamaican area, and I was the only white left in a full carriage. Feeling ridiculous, I took the next train straight back.

'This is a city full of alienated people,' my landlord told me. The blacks and Hispanics who live on the poverty line, in slum ghettos, feel alienated; so do the predominantly white middle classes in their 'good' districts, he explained. Not surprisingly, one common feature New Yorkers share is paranoia. I soon developed their reflexive habit of checking behind whenever someone walked towards me in a fairly empty street. Some people carry a ten dollar bill, to keep the potential mugger happy and stave off an angry attack.

Rent is high, accommodation scarce, and the chances of getting a knife in the stomach far from slim. The rats in this race bite back harder, and hungrier. Compensating for its disadvantages, New Yorkers live the city for all it's worth. The energy gets to you like a wire spring inside, being wound tighter and tighter the longer you're there. Once revved up to the standard, frenetic pitch of activity, one day becomes a limitless bank account with which you can do everything . . . and anything.

I met a boy in his mid-twenties, from Kentucky, who had come to New York to set up as a dentist. Down in Kentucky they call NY the nation's brain drain. He gave me two good reasons for moving to the city. He told me,

'I like to party.'

And then later, 'I like nice things.'

This is the reason why he chose to do dentistry rather than Art Restoration, despite the fact that,

'I lurv Russian icons.'

Doing it his way, he can make lots of money as a New York dentist, and buy a few nice icon things for himself. Such candid consumerism made a refreshing change after the squeamish English double stand over money. Money is the law of life there, which has to be lived by. No use in nobly pretending it doesn't happen. Rather than remarking on seasonal changes in the surrounding foliage, the majority of New Yorkers whom I met would relish a detailed discussion about the subtle fluctuations in Real Estate Value.

New York is a city of dreams. The dreams rely in part on the dreamer sustaining a faith in the American 'ethos' of freedom and liberty. Liberty, that is, to be like the bus boy from Ohio, liberty to realise any dream, be it at the expense of others, which, in this land-of-the-free, it inevitably has to be. Lack of adequate welfare services – health, housing, education – demonstrates the lack of sympathy for casualties. After all, they started out from the same nest of opportunities as the rats who are now fatter.

At the mouth of New York city harbour stands Liberty. She has welcomed the oppressed and disowned of the world to this paranoiac dreamscape for nearly a hundred years. This summer she was torchless, covered in scaffolding and swathed in white canvas. At night, lit from within, she looked like a stricken ghost, fleeing the city of glittering towers.

IAN LEWIS

A Sri Lankan Bus Ride

SRI LANKA

Shattering the stillness of another sleepy Sri Lankan day, the bus rattles to a halt and is immediately overhauled by a vast cloud of dust that dampens the sound and dries the air. The dust that doesn't manage to board the bus after its blind breathless pursuit slowly settles to the road to await the resumption of the race, quietly confident that the bus will never shake it off.

The softly settling dust is your cue to leap into action: pushing and shoving your way through the crowd you look for the conductor to ask where the bus is going. You locate the plain-clothes conductor by his surroundings rather than his dress: he can always be found at the centre of a seething mass of passengers, hemmed in on all sides like a Queen Bee. A waggle of his head and a smile sends you plunging back against the human tide to collect your bag, which you bundle aboard and dump at the back amongst the other passengers' paraphernalia. It falls amongst sacks of coconuts, green baskets of woven palm, pots, pans, brooms, buckets, a live chicken or two, and countless peculiar packages, each, in its own small way, an affront to Euclidean geometry.

At first, along with most of the passengers, you stand, crushed together in the intense humidity like sticky dates in a box. From the windows strangely scented moisture-laden air washes over you, causing trickles of sweat to tickle their way down your chest, your back, your arms, your legs, and your clothes to cling to you like wet wrinkled wallpaper. Suddenly, without warning, you're thrown off balance, all thoughts of discomfort forgotten as you lurch about trying desperately to keep upright: your journey has begun. As you fight for stability it becomes clear that even the privileged few occupying seats are liable to find themselves floored from time to time: Sri Lankan buses are, in every sense, a great leveller.

As the only white face on board you're the object of much curiosity: most of it surreptitious, some of it blatant. The youngest children stare, open-mouthed; the older ones suspiciously, if alone, but with smiles and shoves if with friends. The schoolgirls, a bewitching blend of angelic features and devilish grins, are interested too. Uniformly pretty in their immaculately white dresses and shockingly bright monochrome ties they giggle and nudge one another. Later, when they get off, they'll succumb to each other's dares and wave to you, but for now secret glances have to suffice.

Your rucksack comes under much scrutiny too. In their eyes you are a mythically wealthy creature quite literally a race apart and the contents of the sack a lifetime's aspirations, gift-wrapped: all the trappings of Western civilisation bending someone else's back double, weighing them down as they wander through life. One or two dubious individuals seem to scowl from you to the sack, and you nervously wonder if dark looks and light fingers go hand in hand. For the rest of the journey your eyes return to your bag every few seconds, just in case.

Looking around you, you note how slender everyone is: bamboo legs, sugar-cane arms – placid brown stick-people without a bark much less a bite. If you see a fat belly it's because there's another passenger inside. In a land where food literally grows on trees, the reasons are genetic not economic: Sri Lankans are built for marathons not sprints.

As the bus weaves along you study the tapestry of clothes that hems you in. Like their owners, the trousers, dresses, sarongs and saris have a faded worn-out look. There are holes covered by patches, holes not covered by patches and patches covered in holes; there are split seams and loose threads, threadbare elbows and knees, shiny seats and tattered hems. On close inspection, the chunky wristwatches much in evidence offer an insight into the Sri Lankan way of life: they're all broken, worn only as status symbols to proclaim: 'I'm a thoroughly Westernised modern man to whom hours and minutes mean something'. Timeless timepieces for a timeless place.

Nearly all those around you are barefoot which, on the wildly swaying bus, stands their owners in good stead. Their toes, tough strong-willed individuals, spread out and grip the dusty floorboards, exuding confidence and stability whilst yours, shy and secretive, institutionalised through years of confinement, huddle together, even sitting one on top of the other: unbalanced individuals who delegate the task of balance to wheeling arms and clutching hands.

People say little: talking is tiring in the heat, and besides, the bus itself tirelessly rattles off a deafening running commentary on the trip. Everything rattles: the cooking pots in the luggage, the cast iron framed seats, the loose panels, mudguards and headlamps, your teeth and, most of all the loosely fitting sliding windows. Then there's the horn. The driver, sitting with his bare feet propped on a few housing bricks, sounds the horn constantly. He sounds it when overtaking, or when being overtaken; when stopping and when not stopping; in anger, in joy; in greeting, in farewell; in impatience, in triumph; in irritation, in boredom; in fact, incessantly. No horn solo this, though, with every other road user joining in the medley. So everyone sits or stands quietly, impassively, some fanning themselves, most far too hot to bother. Occasionally a child cries, but mostly they sleep: hotch-potch piles of bodies so entangled that it seems impossible that they'll get off the bus with the same arms and legs they got on with. Here and there women unselfconsciously de-louse their children: an everyday, lifelong chore that goes unnoticed.

Signs of religion can be seen everywhere. Outside, Buddhist temples litter the landscape like giant whitewashed handbells; and inside, above the driver's head, there will be some objects of deep religious significance: perhaps an image of the Buddha or, more frequently, a pair of hollow plastic parrots which light up each time the driver brakes. Once in a while the bus stops at a roadside shrine (large Buddhas abound; large plastic parrots do not), the conductor dashes out, puts some of the takings into the awaiting slot, utters a very quick prayer and leaps back on board. When using the roads here it's well worth a few rupees and a few seconds to appease the gods: Sri Lankan driving makes stock car racing seem safe and uneventful.

At long last the bus rattles loudly to a halt at your destination. You've arrived safely and, if not entirely soundly, then at least noisily. Nodding your farewells you stumble off the bus and stagger along the road. For only a very few rupees you've travelled tens of miles, lost a few pounds and gained a whole new perspective. You're sweaty, filthy and completely exhausted. Every part of you is either aching, sore or numb.

As you walk beneath the iridescent kingfishers which dot the telegraph wires like quivering quavers on a stave, the bus ploughs past you; smiling to yourself you begin to whistle contentedly. After all, there's another bus to catch tomorrow.

CANTON AND BEYOND

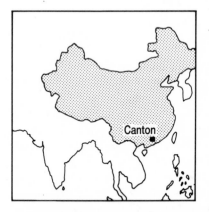

Had I walked unknowingly into a zoo? On each side of the street there were cages and water tanks full of extraordinary creatures. Reptiles, with corrugated skin and splayed gills, lay motionless. There were soft-shelled tortoises, and mongooses and snakes.

The place was Canton. The street, a market where every conceivable animal could be bought for culinary delight. It was evening, and dust filled the air in a yellow haze. I walked, and watched, a head taller than men and women alike as they moved agilely and with purpose from one stool to the next.

Each person bought just enough for a meal that night: a handful of vegetables, a chicken, or a fish hanging gutted from a length of string. Some chose exotic delicacies. The first glimpse of dog, hanging pathetically, naked; and my stomach reeled. 'This is their culture,' I said. 'A dog is no different from a pig or a neatly plucked turkey.' But simple reasoning offered little comfort. I turned my eyes. Only later I learned that it is illegal to eat dog in China. Canton is one of the few areas it is still commonplace.

The narrow street market opened on to a vast square. Everything was suddenly grey, except for a flash of scarlet lettering bannered across a central monument.

There were thousands of people – all dressed in their issued drill uniforms. The pavements overflowed, and the streets were packed with bicycles and dated 1950s trucks. My impression was they should be driving on the right, but I was never sure.

I sat on the pavement with my companion and watched. 'Can I help?' A smiling face looked down at us from his bicycle. We asked him where we could stay. 'I learn English from the BBC,' he said. He was delighted to be able to practise his vocabulary. Soon there was a small gathering of curious lookers-on. They perched on their bicycles. The late arrivals abandoned their wheels and moved in closer to our crouched figures. We looked up and could not help but laugh at their amused expressions. They laughed. 'Overseas Chinese Hotel,' they sang.

The hotel, or hostel should I say, proved to be cheap and clean. The standards were set by the government with a clear intention of providing every Western comfort a visitor could want. They had overlooked a few curiosities, though, which made one thankful they had failed. One such case was some headed writing paper in the room. Next to it was a small pot. Thinking it might be ink, I opened it. I found some glue and a tiny brush to stick down the envelopes.

Hungry and excited, we ventured on to the streets to be over-whelmed with a choice of dried fruits and roasted nuts, and woks of sizzling fish and spiced rice and noodles. The smells, so exquisite, made it impossible to walk past a single wok without at least a mouth-ful of whatever was on offer.

Before we knew it, it was eleven o'clock and the only light was from small piles of burning kindling wood on the pavement. 'The idea is to keep away the hungry spirit,' we were told. There were still countless bicycles zig-zagging the streets, and the stalls were still open to sell their odds and ends. Not a minute of the day was wasted. Did no-one sleep in China? It was a clear display of how the self-enterprised have responded to the freedom since Mao's death. They could advertise now, and clearly did so; and traded for themselves any hours they wished.

The brisk business manner of the city people is in sharp and alarming contrast to the quiet determination and composure of the rural dwel-lers. We had travelled through the night, by train, four hundred miles west of Canton to Gwailin, and well away from any influence seeping across the water from Hong Kong. For very little effort and money we picked up two regulation China bikes and cycled, quietly and steadily, along the straight dusty roads which divided the fields.

A good many of the fields were flooded, using finely engineered waterways which ensured each crop could be irrigated in turn. Some had just been ploughed; while others were almost ready to harvest fine crops of lettuce, or choysam or sugar cane. Seen together, they flowed like a river between the steep uncultivated hillsides.

Slender labourers worked the fields with oxen as the only means of power; but the techniques were modern. In one area we passed acres of polythene stretched over the land to hold in the warmth and moisture for the young crops beneath. Young girls and old men patiently hoed between every row. One woman smiled for a picture as she methodi-cally spread human excreta over the land. She smiled with pride – not shame.

That evening, in an eating house open to the street, a young man walked in and introduced himself as Yu. 'Are you married?' he said. 'No.' I turned the question to him. 'I gave up loving,' he answered. 'I had a girlfriend but she left and now I'm too old.' I was curious. He could not have been over thirty. 'I am thirty-two,' he said. 'Here the government say you cannot marry until you are twenty-five but at thirty no girl wants you as a husband.'

It seemed strange, yet unquestionable, that this delightful man was so tied to tradition. 'But I like being alone,' he said. 'There are many, many people without work in China. The government think I am out of work, but I am a "freedom person".' We had come across this term before. It meant that he did not have a state-issued job. It also meant he did not have the protection of guaranteed housing, medical care and education for his children. He chose instead to earn a living his own way. Yu was a local guide.

He proved his worth. A local guide obviously can get local rates, and the next day he accompanied us on an extraordinary venture from Gwailin, eastwards to Yanti and along the river to Yanghou. In places the river was so wide it swelled into seas and lakes; then it would funnel into a fast-moving passage with vertical cliffs on either side. Mountains projected like fingers from the water; and, for the first time, I understood how the Chinese artist can be inspired by the spirits of the land to paint so beautifully. One turn, and the water blackened in shadow. Another turn and it reflected a blinding glare.

'Look!' Yu pointed towards a small boy standing on a raft. A second later and a cormorant, ring around neck, broke the surface of the water with a fish held in its beak. The boy took the fish and added it to his pile. The same happened again, and again; and then finally the boy loosened the neck ring and the cormorant gulped down his hard-earned prize.

We left Yu, sadly, that evening. We had one more trip to make – back to Canton and then on to Hong Kong. Yu suggested we took the night ferry along the Li river.

Soon we were being hustled aboard the boat. Numbered cards were thrust into our hands which we could only assume were the numbers of our beds. We walked up and down. There were two floors, each with a row of bunks top and bottom along each side. This was it? One huge dormitory! Each bed had a quilt, a pillow and a window. The other passengers tucked up their children, and then themselves, until the whole dormitory looked ready for lights out – except for a singing chatter and an obvious expectancy of something to come. We followed suit, and waited.

Minutes later a jolly round Chinaman trotted up the stairs carrying a tray of soup bowls and chopsticks. Each of us sat up at the foot of our bunks and happily took the bowls and a ladle of broth with dumplings.

I lay down in my bunk that night and thought, sadly, that in the morning we would arrive in Canton, only to catch a fast and functional hovercraft back to Hong Kong.

A TALE OF TWO CITIES

'Hi there! How ya feeling t'day? The sun is up and the birds are singing. It's 8.30am and a heady 22 degrees here in downtown Berlin – and you're tuned to AFN radio . . . tell it like it is, Tom.' An incongruous mixture – Mr Waits sings in praise of owning an ol' 55 Chevvy and I gaze down Spandauerstrasse at the graffitti on the Wall. *'Keine Mauer, Anarchie für der DDR'* and 'Liverpool FC' hang side by side in red spray paint. Behind me, Frau Reinecke bustles about with the coffee cups and tells me of the delights to be found on the Kurfürstendamn and in the Europa Center, while her husband, Günter, hums tunelessly into his newspaper and their daughter, Kerstin, sleeps off a long night at the bars and discos. A more conventional family picture would be hard to find on the television screen – but barely two hundred metres away are the minefields, concrete and barbed wire that surround the land-locked island of West Berlin.

It is 9am on a balmy spring morning. Just two hours earlier, I was clattering through the mist-laden meadows of East Germany on the North-West Europe Express. A riot of tongues fought against the hum of the air conditioning – Dutch and German, Pole and Czech, two old Russians and myself. A solitary Englishman on a four-day trip from the Netherlands; a trip that came about after a five-year study of Len Deighton and John Le Carré. Stepping off the train at Berlin Zoo brought the visions of espionage rolling back with the morning sun; I half expected – half hoped – to find Harry Palmer and George Smiley taking *Kaffee mit Bratwürst* at the platform kiosk. Instead I saw portly businessmen, clerks, tourists and the inevitable drug addict, comatose in a sea of beer.

'No,' they said at the Berlin Tourist Office. 'Most dreadfully sorry, no hotels, everything booked I'm afraid – end of May is always such a busy time. Maybe you would like to stay with a family?' It seemed I had little choice; it was either that or a bench in the U-Bahn, and the financial position was very attractive too. For only £6 the Family Reinecke were offering B&B plus shower. No contest, Mein Herr, tell me how I get there. 'Small problem,' he said. 'It's near the edge of the city.' The Edge? The Wall? In the East? 'No,' he smiled patiently. 'It's in Spandau.'

The Zimmer was a split-level, wood-covered villa in a smart suburb of old Spandau city. It was a good hour from the centre by bus and train – but travel in Berlin is so effortless and cheap that I saw more of the city than most of the locals ever do. Nine pounds gave me the right to travel anywhere for four days – within the obvious limits, of course. My hosts were very friendly and filled my rumbling stomach with coffee and rolls, while the questions flew thick and fast in that nasal pseudo-American slang that only the Germans can master. Presently I was shown to a large, bright room with a picture window overlooking a fruit farm and the Wall. 'If you don't like it you may have Kerstin's room,' said Frau Reinecke. 'She won't mind.' There I was, a complete stranger, and she was practically offering me the house. Despite lack of sleep and the desire to take a shower, I left at once to see if the city could live up to my hostess.

Once inside the mêlée one could be anywhere – in London, Paris or Amsterdam. Wide boulevards and modern architecture stand side by side with cobbled alleyways and old buildings, still blighted from the war. But there is something more, a tension, a feeling that 'We have life now, so let's live it – but I can't help worrying about our neighbours'. West Berliners are normal schizophrenics, just like the rest of us. It's uncanny the way they can block off the dim, but not too distant, future.

Eager to be the Cold War tourist, I marched along the pavements of the Avenue des 17 Juni, so named after the battles of 1945 when Soviet tanks cut down soldiers and civilians under the summer sun. It's quieter now, except for the whirr of cine cameras, but the tanks are still there – at watch on concrete pedestals astride the Soviet Victory monument. From across the road in the cool woods of the Tiergarten you can spy on two khaki-clad Russian guards, who keep their rifles pointed up but their eyes point at you. To the right is the Brandenburg Tor, a huge pillared gate which stands just on the wrong side of the wall, barring the way down Unter den Linden. It must be tough if you're a *Volkspolitzei* or VOPO – they stand in watchtowers and minefields and endure the catcalls and fatuous gestures of coach parties from Basingstoke, Bologna and Baltimore. Holiday snaps are an occupational hazard; they hide their faces beneath forage caps and scowl like monsters. You might think that they were trying to erase your film by sheer willpower.

See through the uniform! Forget the Wall! Fifteen minutes by foot found me in the peace and tranquillity of the Zoo gardens. I have to admit that it's the first time I've ever enjoyed a zoo – the animals were perky and alive, not slabs of expensive meat rotting with boredom and pilfered ice-cream cones. Exhaustion caught up with me in the end and I spent three hours stretched out on a bench beside the leopard cage.

Night falls slowly on the Ku-damn, the glare of neon keeps the darkness at bay, so the night creatures can swan around in their cool shades and still avoid getting run over. The bright young spirits can be found on the Brietschiedplatz, break-dancing, body-popping and pulling stunts on their bicycles à la ET. While across the street a string quartet from the Conservatoria played popular classics for the smooching couples. Very bohemian. As a nightclub the Balhaus Resi is hard on the wallet, but as a still from *Cabaret* it is almost authentic. Elegant telephones linked the tables, but I was too shy to ask Table 7 if her name was Sally Bowles. I peered through the murk in an effort to spot the Aryan nose with the Swastika armband. Fortunately no luck: Berlin has shut the past in the bottom drawer and is concerned only with the clean shirts of today – no matter what the colour may be.

Saturday morning – the big day. The sun beckoned from above the trees – 'Come East, Young Man, leave the arrogance and elegance of bourgeois decadence' – as I moved towards Checkpoint Charlie, the Friedrichstrasse border gate for foreign visitors. A rash of adolescent MPs gazed longingly at yesterday's *Daily Mirror* as I wandered through the electric barriers. The VOPO took my crisp West German marks and handed back some tattered Monopoly money, all of which is ultimately accountable to them should you decide not to spend it all. He stamped my visas, made pleasant remarks about the weather and pointed me towards Unter den Linden. 'Bye,' he said. Oh, is that it? No frisks, no baggage checks, no remarks about Western Imperialist Piggery, Comrade? On the contrary, you have to earn treatment like that.

Into a time warp; it is 1949 again. The Wartburgs, Skodas and Moskvitches putter about like Dinky Toys and people wear grey, grey or black. Spot the tourist by the colour of his jeans! Even the English look loudly dressed for a change. I suffered the pangs of guilt and embarrassment. I hid my camera and I tried not to smile, but the East Berliners are totally bored by the trappings of Western life and look at you with a slight smirk of contempt. The thing that struck me most was the post-war architecture: despite the lack of holes and gaps left by the war, these buildings lacked grace, style, design and, dare I say, taste. Chrome and glass are obviously in vogue behind the curtain, or maybe they are just cheap. I spent the remainder of my day 'beyond' just eating and drinking – a pastime which I would not recommend to those who value their intestines. But I had a chance to watch another world go by – and that is exactly what it is. I limped back through the checkpoint with my surplus currency hidden in the bottom of my shoes. A souvenir, Herr Major, honestly.

Saturday night was party night and Kerstin took me out in her car to see all that I had missed on foot. All points West to Charlottenburg Schloss, Spandau Citadel and the Prison, the 1936 Olympic Stadium (a very eerie place) and the lakes and forests of the Grünewald. Whilst driving through the countryside I noticed runway lights and conning towers. It seems a shame that we should ruin the only bit of meadow-land they have with military airports. Later we sat together in the Far Out disco: no stares, no fights, no killjoys – they even apologise when they step on your foot.

I was sorry to leave Berlin, especially after making friends and seeing so much of the place. My parting comment can only be 'see it for yourself, it may not be there much longer'. Then perhaps you will understand what makes it so unusual.

JOHN WILKINSON

THE ROAD OUT OF PINJARRA

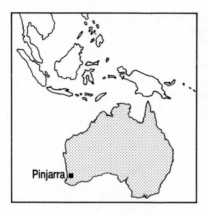

I am sitting in the shade of a gum tree, by the side of a dusty road in Pinjarra, Western Australia. It has taken me fifty lifts to reach Pinjarra; a name on the map you do not notice until fate holds you there.

After three months' travelling in Australia, hitch-hiking has become an addiction; the stimulation of a new acquaintance, a frank exchange of views, and then back on to the roadside – a self-contained experience without any repercussions.

I have been waiting for a lift for four hours. I seem to be a permanent figure in this small town, loitering under the shade of a eucalyptus, with my blue sunhat pulled over my eyes.

On the other side of the road, two old aboriginal women, one with a grey beard, stumble away from the local park after their afternoon drinking session. The road back towards the shops and bars melts into water, thanks to the oppressive dry heat. The beardless aboriginal, who is wearing a black polka-dot dress, collapses on the pavement. Her friend squats by her side, looking into the sun. I notice that she is squatting in the shade cast by a telegraph pole.

I have visited Sydney, Melbourne, Adelaide, Kalgoorlie and Perth thanks to the goodwill of timber-workers, fruit-pickers, farmers, sheep-shearers, pensioners, housewives, drunks, fishermen, truckies, a postman, a policeman, a ferryman and an inebriated, middle-aged Englishman who looked suspiciously like Ronnie Biggs. My duty was to supply conversation to break up the monotony of the heat-haze on the straight roads through the bush.

What will I discuss with my next host? How many snakes and kangaroos he has killed in his car, English as opposed to Australian beer, a possible Test successor to fast bowler Dennis Lillee, or Conservation. The latter can be a dangerous word for hitch-hikers in Australia, particularly with farmers and timber-workers. Most farmers I travelled with regarded National Parks as scrub full of snakes. One farmer was livid that he could not go into his local National Park and chop wood for his barbecue. Unless you like being marooned in out-of-the-way places with a half-empty water bottle, it is not a subject a hitch-hiker should get drawn into.

I fell into the conservation trap again with a Sydney chiropractor concerning native, and non-native, birds in Australia. After tea, if he was in the mood, the chiropractor would go out and shoot starlings in his garden, because they had been introduced from Europe. I suggested that starlings had probably been in Australia longer than his family, and if his argument was translated into human terms then an aboriginal would have a justifiable right in hoisting a spear into his chest.

'Do you mind being called a Pommie Bastard?' inquired the chiropractor. 'I hear that England is in a bad way. A lot of people out of work. Most of our trade union problems are caused by infiltrating Poms.' Only a foolish hitch-hiker makes this mistake twice.

It is not only individuals who get ravelled up in this native/non-native business. In Western Australia it is an offence to cultivate blackberries in your garden, and it is also your duty as a citizen to report to the authorities any sightings of sparrows or starlings. The information board outside the Freemantle Police Station displayed a poster which offered a reward for information leading to the conviction of a person who had murdered a High Court Judge. Next to it was a picture of a rogue starling with the caption, 'Have you seen this bird?'

Back in Pinjarra the old, semi-conscious aboriginal groans, and then lapses back into sleep; another fringe dweller out for the count. A white Australian boy appears, and proceeds to do 'wheelies' around the two old women on his racing bike. Could this scene be acted out every day at 4.45pm on the road out of Pinjarra?

Sweat pours from beneath my hat, and my shorts are going raggy at the hem. My peeling, sunburnt nose resembles a small bundle of rags. Australian flies must be the most persistent in the world. I wonder if the British introduced them? The heat is getting to me. I drink the last few drops of water from my flask.

'Want a tinny, son?' inquires a voice from behind me.

I turn around and see a small, fat man leaning on his garden fence. He is wearing white shorts, and laughter lines run in deep creases by the sides of his eyes.

'Oh, thanks very much.'

He delves into his portable coolbox and fishes out an ice cool can of lager. The beer slips down my throat. No sooner have I got excited about the cool sensation in my throat than the can is empty.

'Those two old abos look like they've had a skinful,' observed my benefactor. 'My son works for the housing dept around here. You know that when a black fella dies the whole family moves out of the house and goes walkabout. They'll not return for love nor money, because of the bad spirits. Now where's the logic in that?'

'I suppose it's tribal superstition,' I reply. 'They were more nomadic before the whites colonised the country, and their tribal huts would be more temporary structures than council housing. I wonder if they would sooner live in a tribal hut than the white man's three-bed-roomed house with fully-fitted kitchen?'

'I'd like to see them get the plans through the government housing regulations. Besides, what sort of life would that be?'

'What sort of life is hitch-hiking?'

'Your choice, son.'

'Exactly.'

'I see your angle. The whites repress the aborigines. Don't forget, son, that a lot of Australian people's ancestors did not ask to be deported from Jolly Old England! You know we were the Poms, not you lot. We were the Prisoners of Mother England.'

'Fair dinkum,' I replied.

'Honours about even, son.'

We both laughed.

At that moment the blue flash of an estate car passes my field of vision. The brakes are applied and the passenger door opens. I turn to say cheerio to the old man, but he is digging under a pair of stringy barks, with his back turned towards me.

Vince and Fred are part of an Italian rock band called Casablanca. They are going as far as Collie.

'Where are you from?' asked Vince.

'England,' I replied.

'Someday I would like to travel abroad. Travel broadens the mind,' confirmed Vince.

It certainly does when it is hot in Pinjarra and you cannot get a lift.